Everybody Else

EVERYBODY ELSE

*Adoption and the Politics of Domestic
Diversity in Postwar America*

SARAH POTTER

The University of Georgia Press   *Athens and London*

© 2014 by the University of Georgia Press
Athens, Georgia 30602
www.ugapress.org
All rights reserved
Set in Minion Pro by Graphic Composition, Inc., Bogart, Georgia
Printed and bound by Thomson-Shore

The paper in this book meets the guidelines for
permanence and durability of the Committee on
Production Guidelines for Book Longevity of the
Council on Library Resources.
Most University of Georgia Press titles are available from popular e-book vendors.

Printed in the United States of America

18 17 16 15 14 P 5 4 3 2 1

Library of Congress Cataloging-in-Publication Data

Potter, Sarah.
    Everybody else : adoption and the politics of domestic
diversity in postwar America / Sarah Potter.
        pages cm
    Based on the author's dissertation at the University of Chicago.
    Includes bibliographical references and index.
    ISBN 978-0-8203-4415-7 (hardcover : alk. paper) —
ISBN 0-8203-4415-X (hardcover : alk. paper) —
ISBN 978-0-8203-4416-4 (pbk. : alk. paper) —
ISBN 0-8203-4416-8 (pbk. : alk. paper)
    1. Adoption—United States—20th century. 2. Adoptive parents—
United States—20th century. 3. Families—United States—20th
century. I. Title.
    HV875.55.P684 2014
    362.7340973'09045—dc23

                                        2013032125

British Library Cataloging-in-Publication Data available

CONTENTS

ACKNOWLEDGMENTS

This book would not have been possible without the generosity of Children's Home + Aid. I am deeply indebted to them for so graciously allowing me to use their records in my research, in the midst of all the important work they do for children and families in Illinois. Hilary Freeman, vice president of agency performance and quality, along with Nicole Johns and the staff at the organization's main offices, were unfailingly helpful and supportive in my research process. Likewise, when this book began as a class paper in 2002, Dr. Les Inch and his staff at the Evanston office, particularly Barbara Acker and Sue Puffpaff, made me feel right at home. From patiently helping me to track down papers and files that almost no one had looked at in forty years, to making space for me in their busy offices to do my work, to contacting colleagues to answer my questions about social work practice in the 1940s and 1950s, everyone at Children's Home + Aid made my research not just possible, but a pleasure. Working with these records has been a joy and a privilege, and I hope that my book appropriately honors and respects the people whose lives are recounted in it.

I also relied on the enthusiasm and vast knowledge of many archivists to complete my research. Mary Diaz and the staff at the Richard J. Daley Library Special Collections and Archives at the University of Illinois–Chicago were incredibly helpful in terms of assisting me in locating and photocopying materials, even when I was in Memphis. Similarly, the archivists at the Special Collections Research Center at the University of Chicago assisted me several times. Most notably, Ashley Locke went above and beyond the call of duty when she helped me locate and use materials in a collection that she was in the middle of reprocessing. The archivists at the Vivian G. Harsh Research Collection of Afro-American History & Literature at the Chicago Public Library's Woodson Regional Library were similarly helpful. I also received a generous research fellowship from the Black Metropolis Research Consortium (BMRC), which put me in touch with a number of archivists and scholars I would have otherwise never met. I thank Adam Green and Vera Davis for their hard work on the

BMRC's fellowship program, and all of the other fellows and archivists who participated, for their help with my work.

This book was also made possible by a number of individuals and institutions whose support has been pivotal to both its beginning and its completion. My wonderful colleagues at the University of Memphis have workshopped several chapters, and their insights have been incredibly helpful. I especially appreciate the support of outgoing history department chair Jannan Sherman, who has been a fantastic colleague and friend. In addition, support from the University of Memphis in the form of a Faculty Research Grant and a semester of leave provided me the time and resources to complete my research and revise the manuscript.

I have also received invaluable feedback on this work at conferences and through other channels. I would like to thank the following in particular for reading my work and providing such constructive comments: Eileen Boris, Aram Goudsoudzian, Moira Hinderer, Allyson Hobbs, Louis Hyman, Emily LaBarbera-Twarog, Matthew Lassiter, Alison Lefkovitz, Scott Marler, Paige Meltzer, Laura McEnany, Betsy More, Christopher Neidt, Arissa Oh, Timothy Thurber, and Jessica Weiss. Although all errors remain my own, their suggestions have made me a better thinker and writer, and this a much better book thanks to them.

This project began as a paper and then dissertation at the University of Chicago. I am deeply indebted to my dissertation committee, George Chauncey, Amy Dru Stanley, and Jim Sparrow, as well as the many other faculty members who challenged and supported me while I was in graduate school. My colleagues, friends, and classmates at the University of Chicago are too numerous to name here, but they have made a lasting impact on this project through their willingness to critically engage with my work. I am especially grateful for the collegiality and intellectual rigor of the Social History Workshop, the Gender and Sexuality Studies Workshop, and the Political History Workshop. I also owe a debt of gratitude to the University of Chicago's Center for Gender Studies (now the Center for the Study of Gender and Sexuality), which provided me a crucial dissertation-year fellowship and a number of wonderful teaching opportunities. The intellectual community I found at CSGS, along with the friendship and support of CSGS staff and faculty members Gina Olson, Stuart Michaels, and Debbie Nelson, made my life immeasurably better at the U of C. I am also grateful for generous fellowships from the University of Chicago and the Woodrow Wilson National Fellowship Foundation to support my graduate studies.

I would also like to thank everyone at the University of Georgia Press for making this book a reality. Derek Krissoff, Beth Snead, Nancy Grayson, Jon Davies, Mick Gusinde-Duffy, and their colleagues (including freelance copy editor Chris Dodge) have shepherded this manuscript into production with care and dedication. I could not have asked for a better group of people to work on a project about which I care so deeply, and I am proud and grateful to be working with them. I would also like to thank my cartographer, Bill Rankin, for being as invested in the book's maps as I am. They turned out perfectly.

While spending years of my life writing a book all about family, I could not help but reflect on and feel grateful for my own. Members of my family have made this project possible in too many ways for me to ever be able to fully express my gratitude. My brother, Chris Potter, and his wife, Ildiko Nagy, and their daughter, Anna, have been friends and confidants throughout. My parents, Ellen and David Potter, have been tireless supporters. They have shared my worries, cheered my successes, and always been there to give me whatever I have needed. I had the good fortune to meet Ryan Sellers as I was in the throes of trying to finally get this book published and out into the world. He has become my closest friend and my partner, and I'm delighted that we are now family. His patience, wisdom, smiles, and kind words (along with a number of home-cooked meals) have made this book far better and me far happier than I ever dreamed possible.

⌣

Portions of chapter 6 appeared previously as "Family Ideals: The Diverse Meanings of Residential Space in Chicago during the Post–World War II Baby Boom" in the *Journal of Urban History* 39 (January 2013).

Adoption, Diversity, and the Politics of the Postwar Family

In March 1955, Ralph and Alice Kramden, on the television show *The Honey-mooners*, adopted a child. The episode began with Alice receiving a phone call from an adoption agency where the couple had submitted an application months before. Ralph and Alice had been waiting anxiously to be considered but were worried when they learned that a social worker would visit their apartment to evaluate it. Believing their shoddy furniture and rundown living quarters would cause their application to be denied, the staunchly working-class Kramdens borrowed better furniture and new appliances for the worker's call. Their scheme was foiled, however, when a deliveryman showed up during the worker's visit with a block of ice for their icebox, which had been temporarily replaced with an electric Frigidaire. Ralph and Alice came clean with the social worker, describing their actions as the result of their overwhelming longing for a child. The worker explained that although the agency cared about a couple's ability to provide for a child and took note of the quality of their home's furnishings, the most important factor for a successful application was a loving relationship between the parents and their strong desire for a child. She noted that the Kramdens' plot evidenced both of these qualities, and she approved their home. A baby girl was soon placed in their care.

Ralph and Alice adored their daughter, but their stint as parents was short lived. A week after the baby's placement, the child's birth mother had a change of heart and said she wished to raise the girl herself. Even though the child was now legally the Kramdens', Ralph and Alice conceded that if they loved her so much after being with her a week, then surely her birth mother loved her even more. The episode closed with the Kramdens tearfully deciding to return the baby to the adoption agency, and they never again sought out parenthood on the show.[1]

The Kramdens' foray into adoption in 1955 was part of the growing acceptance of adoption in the United States at the time. The sitcoms *Leave It to Beaver* and *Father Knows Best* also featured episodes in the 1950s about adoption. Likewise, a number of couples on the big screen pursued adoptive parenthood, including Cary Grant and Irene Dunn in 1941's *Penny Serenade*, Cary Grant and Betsy Drake in 1952's *Room for One More*, and Doris Day and Richard Widmark in 1958's *The Tunnel of Love*.[2]

The attention paid to adoption in popular culture reflected Americans' growing preoccupation with the nuclear family in the decades just after World War II. During the postwar baby boom, which took place between 1946 and 1964, Americans across lines of race, class, and ethnicity married younger, divorced less often, and had more children than they have before or since.[3] The nation's television shows, magazines, and movies celebrated family togetherness as the most promising path toward meaning and happiness. As the baby boom roared on, adoption became a more common way to build a family, especially for couples that were infertile. Much like the Kramdens, men and women who applied to adopt during the 1940s and 1950s longed for children—so much so that they were willing to turn to social workers and the state, with their intrusive questions and legal formalities, to form the kind of family they desired.

This book uses the experiences and ideas of adoptive applicants as a lens into the role that nuclear family membership played in people's everyday lives during the baby boom. Most couples that applied to adopt during the postwar years were unable to have children or to have as many children as they wanted. They found themselves on the margins of an increasingly family-centric social world. These men and women often felt excluded and isolated as their friends and relatives enjoyed a socially sanctioned sense of purpose and meaning that eluded them. Their adoption applications highlight the intense social, cultural, and personal pressures that fueled the baby boom, as well as the resourcefulness of ordinary men and women in achieving the kinds of families they desired.

By examining the unique experiences of adoptive applicants, *Everybody Else* also uncovers the family's intimate connection with the many demands, pressures, and inequalities of the world outside the household. Examining couples' efforts to adopt brings to light an array of external challenges that limited their ability to support and nurture each other and their children as they wished. Just as Ralph and Alice worried that their small income and working-class household would signal to their social worker that they could not provide adequate financial support for a child, many adoptive parents faced myriad social and economic disparities that affected their day-to-day family lives. Applicants turned to public authorities to build families they believed would make them feel happy, fulfilled, and included. In the process they revealed the many ways the baby boom family was connected to larger political issues of opportunity and inequality in American society. This book, therefore, is a history of adoption, but it is also, more importantly, a history of the changing political significance of the family for ordinary men and women in the decades after World War II.

In telling the stories of those who applied to adopt children during the baby boom, this book adds to the rapidly growing literature on the history of infant adoption in the twentieth-century United States. I shift the focus, however, from birth mothers and social workers, who dominate much of the scholarship, to the expectations and ideas of diverse adoptive applicants.[4] Though one might assume that everyone who applied to adopt during the postwar years was white, wealthy, and generally privileged, that was not necessarily the case. A few agencies, including the Illinois Children's Home and Aid Society (ICH&A), whose history and records are analyzed in this book, solicited applications from African Americans and working-class whites so that they would have diverse parents available for the diverse children in their charge.

To add even greater range to the families under consideration, this book also examines the experiences of couples that applied to provide temporary foster care for pre-adoptive infants. These families were not part of the public welfare system but instead part of ICH&A's adoption program. They went through a similar screening process as adoptive applicants, but they received a modest stipend for caring for infants awaiting adoption, so many who chose this path were working-class couples and families of color who sought to boost the household income. For many foster parents, however, providing care for a pre-adoptive infant was also a desirable way to have more children in the household than one could have by birth or to try out parenthood in hopes of adopting later.

By focusing on diverse adoptive and foster care applicants, *Everybody Else* adds a crucial new layer to scholars' understanding of adoption history. While this approach pays less attention to the other key players in the adoptive triad—birth parents and the children they relinquished—it allows deeper insights into the motivations and ideals of those who sought parenthood at a moment when American pronatalism was at its peak. It reveals the strategies applicants used to gain approval, as well as the tactics of social workers seeking to ferret out those they believed would not make good parents. It also uncovers the experiences of those who have often been overlooked in adoption history—African American and working-class families.

Working-class and African American families have often been overlooked in the broader history of the postwar family, and it is here where this book makes its primary and more significant contribution. When one thinks of the 1950s, one usually considers the exploits of June Cleaver and the Beav, the promises of Levittown and other newly developing suburbs, and elaborate photo spreads in magazines such as *Life* and *McCall's*, touting the benefits of family "togetherness." One conjures up happy baby boom families with two or more children, families that were white, suburban, and well on their way to middle-class affluence. But not everyone enjoyed these privileges. For those who could not have children or have as many children as they wanted, the postwar baby boom proved a source of social stigma and personal pain. Further, in 1950 roughly one in three Americans had a less than middle-class income, and over fifteen million African Americans lived under Jim Crow segregation.[5] Many of these families could not afford a suburban home, and families of color were often barred from the suburbs altogether. These families' stories have rarely been told. By considering the family ideals of those who were unable to embody the domestic ideals of the day for reasons of infertility and inequality, *Everybody Else* reveals the essential role the family played in determining ordinary people's assessments of social, economic, and racial disparities.

This interpretation fundamentally reshapes how historians think about the politics of the postwar family by showing the many connections between the family and the world outside the household. Scholars have traditionally linked the postwar period's distinct pronatalism with a pervasive ideology of "domesticity" that tied together the national and personal rewards of the nuclear family and, particularly, confined women to homemaking and child care. The historical literature suggests that in response to the upheavals in family life and gender relations wrought by the Great Depression and the war effort, domesticity promised a family that was well ordered and secure. The family was posited as the key to happiness, comfort, and fulfillment. It also served as an antidote to Cold War anxiety. Just as U.S. foreign policy sought to "contain" communism abroad, ordinary men and women sought to soothe their worries and fears about the uncertainties of the nuclear age by "containing" their aspirations for happiness within the household. Consequently, the postwar family's political significance rested in its very separation from the realm of politics: domesticity's promises of security and fulfillment encouraged men and women to focus their energies and expectations on an increasingly privatized domestic sphere and to adjust to the status quo rather than challenge it.[6]

This kind of family stability was available, however, only to those who had access to a comfortable home, a successful breadwinner, and a predictable and orderly household—most of whom were white and middle class. But the baby boom occurred across all racial, ethnic, and demographic groups, and many baby boom families did not have access to these amenities. Historians have generally assumed that diverse Americans aspired to embody this "mainstream" model of domesticity, but they have given little consideration to how men and women from different backgrounds actually related to this ideal.[7] I contend that when we look beyond the white picket fences and white faces of suburbia and into the family lives of everyone else, distinctions between the private sphere of the family and public sphere of politics blur. The family was not a sanctuary of safety and calm apart from the problems of the outside world, but instead where economic and social inequities were made tangible.

This analysis builds on recent work that has expanded historians' understanding of family and gender norms of the time by highlighting the many instabilities and contradictions implicit in the postwar sexual order. Rather than a contained and secure refuge from Cold War anxieties, scholars now see the postwar family as a site of considerable disagreement and uncertainty. For instance, Jessica Weiss demonstrates that the middle-class white suburban couples that most ascribed to the dictates of postwar domesticity had much greater equality in their marriages than one might anticipate. Further, as these couples and their children grew older, they made a range of choices, including getting divorced, prioritizing their careers, and pursuing a variety of divisions of labor within the family, that distinctly challenged postwar family ideals.[8] Similarly, Rebecca Jo Plant has suggested that there were significant crosscurrents in American culture regarding motherhood by the 1950s. Scholars think of this period as one in which white middle-class motherhood was deeply romanticized in the press and among ordinary men and women, only coming under fire with the emergence of second-wave feminism in the 1960s. But Plant shows that a powerful anti-maternalist discourse had already undermined an idealized vision of motherhood in American culture well before the 1960s.[9] Studies of middle-class women's neighborhood activism, the growing popular interest in sexology and sexuality, and the experiences of a range of women who did not fit the "domestic" mold, such as lesbians, artists, and women on welfare, have also complicated historians' understanding of American conceptions of gender and sexual norms at the time.[10]

These works complement a wider revision of the 1950s that is currently underway. While the contained, nuclear family used to seem a good historiographic metaphor for an apolitical, quiescent nuclear age, that depiction of the 1950s no longer seems so convincing. Important studies of housing and neighborhoods by historians such as Arnold Hirsch, Thomas Sugrue, and Becky Nicolaides have demonstrated that this period was not one of quiet, apolitical conformity, but in fact rife with contests over the meaning of urban, suburban, and domestic space.[11] Likewise, recent work on the civil rights movement in the North has shown ongoing organizing and agitation in African American urban communities on behalf of equality from the start of World War II and into the 1950s.[12] Further, Alan Petigny and others have demonstrated that the supposed social permissiveness that arose in the 1960s in fact had deep roots in the 1950s.[13] Even Lizabeth Cohen's recent work on the "Consumers' Republic" of the postwar period suggests that mass consumption—often seen as having a privatizing and individualizing impact on society—in fact provided black and white Americans a set of concepts and aspirations that became inextricable from their politics.[14] Overall, the postwar period no longer looks as complacent, contained, apolitical, or under the sway of "the expert" as scholars once believed, and domestic containment no longer seems the most important aspect of postwar family ideals.

Everybody Else builds on this revisionist literature to argue that rather than being a diversion from politics, for many people the postwar family was in fact foundational to their politics. The pages that follow introduce readers to diverse men and women as they pursued domestic bliss through adoption and pre-adoptive foster care. These couples wanted children in order to achieve a sense of personal mission and meaning, as well as a deeper feeling of belonging to their communities, which they believed only parenthood could provide. But even as the family offered access to social citizenship, it also highlighted the many inequities they encountered in their daily lives. The infertile expressed a sense of worthlessness and inadequacy in the face of their friends' and relatives' large families. Black couples told their African American social workers that they were fed up with the racism they encountered while trying to support their families, and they planned to teach their children about civil rights. White working-class husbands gave up on class mobility, explaining that they turned down promotions so they would have safer, less taxing jobs and more time for their children. Wives took jobs they hated to help support their families, or gave up jobs they loved in order to care for their children. For these individuals, the family was hardly a refuge from politics; instead, the family was the lens through which they assessed opportunity, evaluated hardship, and coped with inequality. It was, in short, political.

The politicization of the family in the postwar years had profound consequences in later decades. In Ronald Reagan's 1980 speech accepting the Republican Party's presidential nomination, he repeatedly addressed his audience as members of families, promising "to build a new consensus with those across the land who share a community of values embodied in these words: family, work, neighborhood, peace and freedom." He likewise described the challenges the nation faced during the 1970s—"a disintegrating economy, a weakened defense and an energy policy based on the sharing of scarcity"—as affecting Americans not simply as citizens, but as members of a national family.[15] Historian Natasha Zaretsky argues that this rhetoric drew on linkages between American nationalism and the family that had coalesced in the 1970s. As a struggling economy, military defeat in Vietnam, and two oil shocks called into question America's international dominance, the strength and welfare of the nation's families became the discursive site where politicians, policy makers, and ordinary people grappled with their anxieties about national decline.[16]

Zaretsky contends that the 1970s set the stage for the "family values" politics of the 1980s and beyond. Critics of contemporary conservatism often think of these politics, which tie national well-being with "moral" issues such as abortion, homosexuality, marriage, and parenthood, as a distraction from the matters that most affect family security, such as economic opportunity, high wages, good medical care, and a quality education. But, as Zaretsky suggests, this interpretation fundamentally misses the inextricable linkages between the family and larger social issues that were established in the 1970s: "As a political symbol, the family was never just about culture, society, morality, or sexual politics. Nor was it just about the economy, foreign policy, or the nation's world position. After Vietnam, . . . the family was the place where it could all come together."[17]

I argue that, for ordinary people, the important linkages between inequality, politics, and the family were forged in the 1940s and 1950s. Reagan's speech resonated with the American public in part because they had for decades believed there were important connections between the family and the world outside the household. In people's everyday lives, racial and structural inequality, economic opportunity, desirable neighborhoods, and the chance to live a meaningful and happy life were all inextricable from family membership by the 1950s. The family moved to the center of American politics alongside the emergence of second-wave feminism and the sexual revolution of the 1960s, as well as the conflicts over the ERA and the rise of the New Right in the 1970s. But these political developments built on a foundation established in people's daily lives in the 1940s and 1950s.

This book uses Chicago in the 1940s and 1950s as a case study. I focus on families living in Chicago and its suburbs because it offers a lens into the distinctive experiences of a midwestern city whose problems and promises often mirrored those of the nation. Chicago during this period experienced many of the same social, economic, and political changes as the nation's other urban centers, such as the shift from wartime to postwar production and consumption, housing shortages, and suburban expansion.[18] It thereby offers fertile ground for a deeply contextualized understanding of the family within the larger historical changes occurring during the postwar years.

As an ethnically, racially, and economically diverse city, Chicago is also well suited to analyzing family diversity. The destination of many blacks who moved north during the first half of the century, the city played a central role in African American history. Chicago's thriving black community and culture industry in the postwar years is well documented in both scholarly monographs and rich archival resources.[19] Yet even as Chicago's black and white families shared a city, they frequently (though not always by choice) saw themselves as part of distinct and separate communities. Chicago's racial politics were quite different from those of the Jim Crow South, but the city was starkly segregated and faced repeated—and often violent—racial conflicts over housing and neighborhood space.[20] The city's racial fault lines make it a particularly fruitful site for interrogating the relationship between race and family during the postwar years.

The book's primary source is the confidential case records of over 250 working- and middle-class black and white couples that applied to adopt children or provide temporary foster care to pre-adoptive infants during the 1940s and 1950s. These records, all from the Illinois Children's Home and Aid Society, provide a rich resource for understanding postwar family ideals alongside more traditional sources such as sociological studies, films, magazines, television shows, and archival manuscript collections. The case records from adoptive and foster care applicants open up a world that is usually hidden from historians' view, providing a glimpse into some of the joys and hardships that shaped the everyday family lives of diverse Americans in the postwar period. They let us see the expectations and struggles of women and men who most wanted access to whatever delights and benefits family living was supposed to offer, and who had to explain those desires to a social worker. They also record the priorities and ideals of social workers who sought to create the best families possible. Adoption and foster care applications capture a moment where diverse men and women, applicants and social workers alike, were forced to articulate their ideas, desires, and beliefs about "family." With their moving portrayals of the hopes and dreams of those on the outside longing to get in, and their documentation of the standards and practices of gatekeepers who could give or deny a child, these records reveal many of the assumptions, ideals, and experiences that governed everyday family life among ordinary people during the baby boom. (For more information on these sources and how I have used them, see chapter 1 and Appendix A.)

In the following chapters I consider where applicants' and workers' family visions meshed, and where they came into conflict. I also examine the strategies applicants and workers used to convey their expectations and concerns to one another. I particularly focus on how ideals about family expressed in the records intersected with other important aspects of daily life at the time. How did the records portray the relationship between the family and housing? How did applicants' goals and aspirations for their children shape their understanding of social and structural inequality? How did family ideals both inspire and discourage political activism and civic engagement?

By paying such close attention to the experiences and ideals of diverse applicants, my analysis provides a rich understanding of the process and practice of adoption for the ordinary people who mustered their courage and resources to parent a child who was not born to them, as well as for the social workers who guided and judged them. I suggest that adoption and foster care applications offer a particularly fruitful lens into the many social and personal factors that fueled postwar pronatalism. They reveal the agency of the ordinary men and women who were unable to have the families they desired in other ways, and the surprising flexibility of professionals who sought to build families that would be good for both parents and children.

Adoption is central to this study, but my more significant historiographic intervention is in the literature on the postwar family. I offer a rethinking of historians' understanding of the relationship between politics and domesticity during the baby boom. Adoption records reveal in dramatic detail the inter-penetration of supposedly separate public and private spheres. By pulling apart these idiosyncratic but exceedingly rich sources, I reveal the many subtle but crucial everyday social and personal benefits conferred by membership in a heteronormative nuclear family at the time. The postwar family played a central role in pulling diverse men and women into the national fabric by promising personal fulfillment and social adulthood. At the same time, however, it reified important social and political divisions along lines of gender, race, and class, for the very centrality of the family during this period made it a site where social and structural inequalities were often painfully experienced.

This book unfolds in three sections. I begin in part I, "The Ideal Family," by unpacking the context and content of both applicants' and social workers' fam-ily ideals. Chapter 1 considers the promises and contradictions embedded in the practice of child placement in the postwar years. As applicants pursued their domestic desires, and as social workers policed the placement of children, both parties struggled with adoption and foster care as diverse and untraditional family forms in and of themselves: these were families created in public and related by law, not by blood. Chapter 2 explores the role the Great Depression, the Great Migration, and World War II played in individuals' beliefs about their families. These major historical events cemented the family as the primary unit through which people navigated hardship and uncertainty, and thereby set the stage for the important connections between the family and the world outside the household during the postwar years. As I discuss in chapter 3, applicants and their social workers articulated in the case records a consistent set of ide-als about the importance of family membership to one's purpose and meaning in life, and they suggested that an inability to fulfill these ideals often led to a profound sense of self-doubt and social exclusion. Diverse applicants pursued adoption or foster parenthood in order to achieve personal happiness, while also claiming full social inclusion and citizenship.

In part II, "The Obligations of Domesticity," I consider the important frac-tures in these shared family ideals. Although applicants from a variety of back-grounds professed similar beliefs about why the family was so important to people's personal and social well-being, their daily family lives were quite dif-ferent from one another. In chapters 4 and 5, I examine the day-to-day lives of diverse men and women, paying particular attention to their gendered obliga-tions to their families. I argue that men's and women's domestic responsibili-ties varied in important ways along lines of race and class. There was not one model of domesticity but many, and they were inextricable from the era's rapidly changing economic, gender, and race relations. Although men were universally considered breadwinners and women caregivers and nurturers, these roles took on distinct contours in different social locations, giving intense personal significance to economic and racial inequalities.

The final part, "Family Inside and Outside the Household," considers the role family ideals played in shaping people's interactions with the world around them. In chapter 6 I argue that family ideals were integral to how ordinary men and women evaluated their domestic and residential spaces. By examining the intersection between people's ideas about family and their ideas about housing, I suggest that, during a period when racial conflicts over housing erupted across Chicago, domesticity was crucial to shaping the meaning and value many placed on their homes and neighborhoods. Likewise, in chapter 7, I reflect on the linkage between family ideals and good citizenship. Applicants looked to their communities to help support their private family goals and desires, while at the same time they were motivated by a commitment to their families to help mold their communities so as to best serve their family interests. Yet even as a devotion to family and parenthood drew diverse men and women into the fabric of community life, it also reinforced for them the role economic and racial disparities played in one's ability to effect social and political change.

I conclude that, during the postwar years, domesticity served to both erase and highlight social differences for adoptive and foster applicants in their everyday lives. Heteronormative family ideals promised personal fulfillment and social belonging, and their eager embrace by men and women across lines of race and class tied diverse individuals into the social fabric. At the same time, however, the widespread embrace of family ideals also made family a site where economic and racial disparities became real and visceral. While some found a sense of confidence, privilege, and empowerment by organizing their lives and labors around their families, many others found their efforts to support, nurture, and advance the interests of their families thwarted by racial and class inequalities. As individuals pursued the best lives possible for themselves and their children, "family" itself became the lens through which they assessed their inclusion in, or exclusion from, the full benefits and promises of American prosperity and citizenship. Postwar domesticity thereby reinforced profound social cleavages and political tensions that came to the fore in the social movements and political realignments that defined the 1960s and beyond.

PART I

The Ideal Family

ONE

The Difference of Adoption
Domestic Diversity and Adoption Practice in the Postwar Period

On November 14, 1955, Senator Estes Kefauver, a Democrat from Tennessee and chairman of Judiciary Committee's Subcommittee to Investigate Juvenile Delinquency, opened the second in a series of hearings to investigate the country's supposedly rampant black market in babies. The growing popularity of adoption, alongside the era's fierce pronatalism, meant that far more couples wanted to adopt than there were children available. Authorities feared that desperate couples would pay whatever was necessary to procure an infant, thereby providing an incentive for crooked baby brokers to pressure young unwed mothers to give up their babies or, worse yet, kidnap children outright so they could sell them to adoptive parents in distant states. The potential for criminal activity in relation to adoption was important to the subcommittee, Kefauver explained, because those unhappy and uncared for children who had been placed in the home of the highest bidder, rather than the family most suited to their needs, were "ripe subject[s] for juvenile delinquency." A rash of bad adoptions was "undoubtedly . . . one of the many contributing factors to the wave of juvenile delinquency that we have had in the country."[1]

Several scandals had provoked the Senate's interest in regulating interstate adoptions. The most publicized case involved the Memphis branch of the Tennessee Children's Home Society. In 1950, authorities uncovered the society's widespread illegal practices, which included the use of improper and dangerous foster homes and an arrangement with a corrupt judge to remove children from supposedly unfit parents and to ease interstate adoptive placements. The children were often sold to parents for large sums and without any screening. Due to the high profile of many of the agency's placements (Joan Crawford was rumored to be among the recipients) and the potential connection of judges and other elected officials to the scandal, it was largely swept under the rug by the Tennessee legislature. But the improprieties of the Tennessee Children's Home Society and others like it inspired widespread interest in adoption and its potential connections to a black market in babies.[2]

The spectacle of babies for sale highlighted the public's many uncertainties about adoption as a path to parenthood. Adoption's popularity presented a new kind of domestic diversity to mainstream America. As the practice became more frequent and more tightly regulated in the postwar years, it was celebrated in popular culture as a way to solve the vexing problems of both childlessness and unwed motherhood at a moment when both were frowned upon. But it also raised troubling questions about the bridging of supposedly separate public and private spheres in family making. Parent-child relationships were supposed to be created by nature, not design. Yet adoptive parents were assigned children by lawyers, judges, and a variety of "experts," ranging from social workers and pediatricians to self-appointed (and sometimes crooked) baby brokers, who could make either suitable or careless matches. For the public, the differentness of adoption made it a subject of fascination, for it was full of both danger and promise. For adoptive families and their social workers, however, the differences between adoptive families and those made the "old-fashioned" way were more urgent, as they might lead some to question the suitability and stability of adoptive families. Consequently, both workers and parents tried, with mixed success, to obscure and hide the many ways public forces shaped private adoptive families.[3]

This chapter provides an introduction to the history and practice of adoption in the mid-twentieth century, paying special attention to social workers' and adoptive parents' efforts to navigate the blurred boundaries between supposedly separate public and private spheres in adoptive family making. I suggest that it is this very difference of adoption that makes it a particularly telling kind of domestic diversity, for the process of adopting revealed connections between public and private that affected many postwar Americans—those who adopted and those who did not. As historian and gender studies scholar Laura Briggs puts it in her history of transracial and transnational adoption: "Families are where we live our economic and social relations, and in families formed by law the fiction that families are 'private,' constituted in opposition to the 'public,' is laid bare as the fairy tale that it is."[4] As we will see throughout this book, the postwar family was intimately connected to the world of social and economic relations outside the household in a multiplicity of ways.

⤴

Americans' attitudes toward adoption have long reflected their beliefs about the political, emotional, and social role of the family. Its practice has changed dramatically over time, mirroring broader shifts in family history. Adoption evolved from an extralegal practice in the colonial era, governed primarily by community values and local institutions, to a highly regulated (yet often deeply problematic) process in the twenty-first century that involves an array of legal authorities, experts from myriad public and private agencies, and even diplomatic arrangements between governments. As adoption has become more formalized over the course of American history, it has increasingly confounded distinctions between public and private spheres. Over time, adoption has required ever-greater public and legal intervention in the creation of supposedly private family relationships.

It was during the mid-twentieth century, when adoption was practiced more widely than at any time before or since, that its bridging of public and private proved both a serious problem and a significant opportunity for adoptive families and their social workers. It was a problem because it marked adoptive families as different at a moment when they most wanted to fit into mainstream family norms. It became an opportunity, however, as social workers staked their professional authority on the promise that they could hide the difference of adoption and thereby provide adoptive parents the happy family they desired.

Historians have documented children being raised outside their families of birth for reasons of love, labor, and inheritance since the seventeenth century. In most of colonial America, patriarchal households were the organizing unit of social, economic, and political life, with little distinction between public and private matters. In this context, the exchange of children was simply another aspect of maintaining the welfare of the community. A number of children were formally bound out or indentured to labor for and live with families that were better off than their own. Others were informally taken in by couples and relatives who formed relationships with them and who left them substantial sums in their wills. There are also a few known cases where children's names were legally changed to formalize the family relationship, but generally colonial-era adoptions did not require severing legal ties with a child's biological parents.[5]

During the nineteenth century, adoption for reasons of affection—rather than labor or inheritance—became more frequent. Legalized name changes also became more routine and the state played a growing role in managing the family relationships of parents raising children who were not born to them. These changes reflected larger shifts in middle-class family life, and particularly changing definitions of public and private in relation to the family. As the U.S. economy grew more complex in the early decades of the nineteenth century, the household ceded its place as the central location of production and increasingly became defined as a separate, private sphere dominated by women and children. The family's personal and social role changed from a place where public duties and responsibilities were discharged to one of emotional support and caretaking, thereby making it more important to provide legal sanction to bonds of affection between parents and children to whom they did not give birth.[6]

Informal, undocumented adoptions were still common in many places, but the modern concept of adoption—where parents take on the responsibility for rearing a child whose legal relationship to his or her biological family has been severed—took hold in the early decades of the nineteenth century due to these larger transformations in the relationship between family and society. Families caring for children who had not been born to them increasingly petitioned state legislatures to pass private adoption acts to give legal protection to their family relationships. Massachusetts was the first state to respond to the growing number of private adoption acts by passing the nation's first modern adoption law in 1851, which made the process more efficient by outlining the transfer of the custody of a child to a legal guardian who was not a birth parent. The Massachusetts law and those that followed it made the state a regular participant in the creation of adoptive families.[7]

There was not a straight line, however, between the emergence of modern adoption laws and the widespread embrace of adoption as means of caring for children whose birth parents were unable to raise them. It was also during the middle decades of the nineteenth century that orphan asylums, almshouses, and other institutions for the care of impoverished, orphaned, or half-orphaned children (those who had lost one parent) became more common. As urbanization, immigration, and industrialization led to a growing number of families who were unable to care for their children, the spectacle of needy children requiring public assistance garnered greater attention from reformers and politicians. Reformers generally deemed large institutions the most cost-efficient and effective means to retrain children from the supposedly degenerate classes to become productive members of society. Yet despite the growing popularity of these institutions, critics soon charged many of them with failing to provide adequate physical and moral care for the children in their charge. They pointed out institutions' crowded conditions, their mixing of children with adult criminals, and their harsh discipline, which seemed antithetical to raising productive, independent citizens.[8]

In response to the undesirable conditions of many institutions, Progressive Era reformers increasingly pushed instead for the "placing-out" of children with foster families that could offer the individualized care and morally upstanding environment that seemed impossible to provide in a large and impersonal institution. Reflecting a growing sentimentalization of childhood during the Progressive Era, placing-out became the preferred strategy for dealing with orphaned and half-orphaned children, even as difficulty finding foster families meant that institutions remained common. Placing-out, however, was not the same as modern adoption. Reformers suggested that poor and needy children should be raised in a family setting, which in the long run made adoption a more acceptable way to deal with children whose birth parents could not care for them, but at the time they did not advocate that these children be legally adopted—even when their placements were to be permanent. The popularity of eugenic thinking at the time led many to assume that poor children would inherit the feeble-minded or even criminal traits of their parents, particularly if a child was born out of wedlock. Therefore, social workers and many families were reluctant to form legal kinship ties to the children placed for care.[9]

Although placing-out was different from adoption, its popularity eventually led to the public protocols and regulations that shaped adoption practice in the twentieth century. A number of reformers worried about the potential dangers of placing-out, for they believed that simply placing a child in a private home did not ensure proper care and guidance, and could even expose him or her to abuse and exploitation. Placing-out was also more likely than institutional placement to permanently break natal family bonds, which raised the stakes for finding high-quality homes for needy children. Reformers argued for greater public scrutiny and investigation in child placement to protect their vulnerable charges. They contended that when natal family ties were to be permanently severed by a distant or permanent placement, the circumstances of the child's birth family and potential foster parents be thoroughly investigated so as not to break up families unnecessarily. They therefore pushed for greater public oversight of adoption and foster care by creating a more formalized legal process for placing children with families to whom they were not biologically related.[10]

At the same time, eugenic fears began to fade and couples increasingly desired to form legal ties to the children in their care. This shift toward permanent legal placements also heightened the stakes for investigating adoptive families. States began to enact laws that dictated minimum standards for prospective adoptive homes and required licensing for those who placed children. The first minimum standards law was passed in Minnesota in 1917, and by the middle of the twentieth century most states had created a child placement system that relied on licensed nonprofit child welfare and charity agencies to investigate and approve potential homes for foster and adoptive children.[11]

The history of the Illinois Children's Home and Aid Society (ICH&A), the organization whose records form the primary source for this book, illustrates this trend well, as it quickly carved out a place for itself within Illinois' growing investigative and supervisory framework. Illinois legalized adoptions in the 1870s, but the first regulations requiring the licensing and approval of homes for adoptive and foster children were not enacted until the Boarding Homes Act of 1919. This law mandated that foster homes housing two or more children be licensed. Founded in 1886, ICH&A had always devoted considerable resources toward screening potential homes and supervising adoptive and foster placements. In 1919, the state's Department of Visitation of Children immediately accepted the organization's investigations as acceptable for the licensing procedure, making it among the state's first legally recognized placement agencies. Illinois bolstered the legal regulation of adoption within its borders in 1945, when it passed its first adoption law requiring the investigation of adoptive homes and creating a six-month probationary period prior to legally finalizing a placement. ICH&A continued to exceed state requirements by generally overseeing placements for a full year prior to finalizing adoptions.[12]

Adoption had long straddled distinctions between public and private spheres, but it was with the passage of increasingly strict investigative and minimum-standards laws in the first half of the twentieth century that it came into its own as a formalized and legally regulated means of family creation that routinely involved public authorities in the building of private families. Although most adoptions were still conducted independently by physicians, members of the clergy, or commercial adoption agencies well into the postwar period, the regulation of adoption tended to increase social workers' control over the process, as they became the primary licensed and legal public authorities charged with investigating and managing birth parents, their children, and potential adoptive parents. Even when other professionals placed a child, many states required social workers to observe and approve the placement before the adoption could be legally consummated. Working on the front lines to carry out state mandates, child placers began engaging in more formal and elaborate record keeping, delving more deeply into the pasts and family backgrounds of both children and potential parents, and increasing the length and scrutiny of post-placement supervision. Because there was usually little oversight of their work, social workers and local agencies had a great deal of autonomy in determining placement practice within the dictates of the law.[13]

Even as states and social work agencies secured their oversight of adoption practice, the popularity and visibility of adoption diminished a bit during the trials of the Depression and World War II because fewer families had the resources to pursue it. But as the war ended and the baby boom began, adoption rates skyrocketed. The annual number of adoptions climbed consistently from the 1940s to the 1960s, peaking nationally in 1970. Likewise, the demand for adoptable white babies, which had exceeded supply since the 1920s, became nearly insatiable by the mid-1940s.[14]

The greater acceptance of adoption among America's families and social workers in the 1940s, 1950s, and 1960s reflected the pronatalism of the baby boom. Adoption was widely understood as a second chance for unwed mothers and their "illegitimate" babies, and for couples that were unable to have biological children. Adoption became a positive choice for solving a wide range of personal and social issues because it theoretically allowed for all of these parties to partake in postwar affluence in ways they had been previously denied. White middle-class unwed mothers were increasingly encouraged to relinquish their babies to the homes of infertile middle-class white couples and to move on to a new life in which they would supposedly remain chaste until marriage gave them the opportunity to have a "legitimate" family. Meanwhile, childless couples were given access to the children they so ardently desired. Further, children who would otherwise have been condemned to the stigma of being born out of wedlock and raised by an unwed mother were spared potential shame when they were placed with married adoptive parents. This pattern kept the sanctity of the nuclear family intact on all sides of the equation. In contrast to the many promises attached to adoption among white families, however, black families rarely adopted and black unwed mothers were often encouraged to raise their children themselves.[15]

The growing popularity of adoption during the postwar years proved an opportunity for social work as a profession. The largely female ranks of social workers had been struggling to gain professional authority and status in the eyes of the American public and their (often male) peers in psychiatry since the early decades of the century. Most social workers in the first decades of the century lacked professional training beyond a college degree, although by the 1930s and 1940s a graduate degree was becoming more standard. They also lacked legitimacy because, as women involved in a "helping" profession that often involved families, women, and children, their work was viewed as more feminine and thereby requiring less skill and recognition. The field of child adoption was therefore a crucial arena for social workers' professionalization: in many states, they had been given significant legal authority to evaluate homes and make placements. In addition, adoption was a potentially positive, joyful exercise in family formation that as the adoption scandals at the time confirmed, could go terribly wrong if put in corrupt or simply inexperienced hands. Even as adoptions arranged by other professionals, such as doctors or lawyers, remained common, the social work profession saw in the realm of adoption an opportunity to prove the benefits of their expert knowledge to the public by creating happy, well-adjusted families in accordance with state law.[16]

Social workers particularly emphasized their specialized training and expertise in educational materials they created for the public about adoption, promoting themselves as the public authorities most skilled at creating private families. They encouraged potential parents to use adoption agencies staffed by trained social workers, boasting that they could provide reliably better outcomes than placements arranged by other professionals. For instance, in a University of Chicago Round Table pamphlet recounting the dangers of "The Gray Market in Child Adoption," experts warned of placements made by "a doctor, lawyer, nurse, clergyman, or others doing it with good motives or perhaps just for a favor, but certainly without any knowledge of the important consequences involved." Professional social workers, they insisted, were better able to ensure that the birth mother was ready to relinquish her child and that all legal steps for relinquishment were completed, thereby protecting adoptive parents from potential court battles over custody. They also were able to provide the proper study and counsel to make sure the newly formed family was "a happy family, both for the child and for the family involved."[17]

At ICH&A, agency leaders sought to professionalize the adoption staff by encouraging them to continually read new social work and psychological theory. Although in its early years ICH&A social workers—like most child welfare workers—had limited training and relied on moral and religious criteria to evaluate social problems, by the 1940s the agency focused on hiring and retaining caseworkers who had graduate social work training. Agency leadership also arranged regular workshops and sessions with outside experts to continually enhance the staff's knowledge and skills, and to generally promote a commitment to cosmopolitanism and scientific accuracy among agency workers.[18] The agency's orientation was also increasingly psychodynamic during this period. Psychodynamic psychology encompassed a range of theories—mostly originating from the insights of Freud—that assumed a dynamic or repressed unconscious and a psychological explanation for thoughts and behavior. Workers trained in psychodynamic psychology were encouraged to approach clients therapeutically in order to address and resolve personal and family problems rather than judge, criticize, or reject clients based on their problems.[19]

Professional social welfare agencies also developed fee structures to regulate the cost of adoption and eliminate the taint of baby selling. In the 1940s and through the early 1950s, ICH&A relied on voluntary contributions to the agency from adoptive families. In 1957, however, the agency began using a sliding-scale fee structure based on adoptive parents' incomes. They continued this practice into the 1960s. The fee was anywhere from a few hundred dollars to over a thousand dollars, and was charged when a child was placed. Parents were told that the fee was to help cover costs, and while some worried about their ability to pay, many were grateful to give something back to the agency for their services. The fees were also usually less than the thousands of dollars often charged for black-market babies. Although the fee was reduced or waived completely when it was simply out of reach for qualified applicants, social workers used applicants' willingness to pay a fee as evidence that parenthood was important to the couple and evidence that they would be willing to make sacrifices for their child.[20]

In order to solidify their status in the public's mind as family authorities, however, social workers had to do more than simply publicize the many distinctions between their services and the vagaries of the black market. They also had to accommodate the ideas and expectations of clients who might otherwise turn to other sources for their adoptions. Workers therefore had to take into account applicants' expectations and values even as they attempted to carry out their professional obligation to find the best placement for each child in their care. Applicants generally desired an efficient application process, as well as one that would result in the placement of a child they could trust would fit in with their family.

One of the major benefits of working with an agency was "matching," the process whereby social workers did their best to "match" children's coloring, IQ, and ethnic and religious background with those of the adoptive parents. In part, social workers believed that their efforts at matching would make adoption more socially acceptable, since adoptive families would not inspire curiosity due to dramatic differences between family members. Moreover, they felt matching would make it easier for both parents and children to feel like they fit with each other. Parents would be able to adopt a child most like one they might have had themselves, and children were spared undue pressures to perform for parents whose expectations for intellectual abilities they could not meet. Workers and applicants sought to create families that would blend in, presuming that likeness was crucial to creating the feelings of love and intimacy that characterized family relationships. By trying to mimic nature, matching was a way to hide the difference of adoption, and particularly the role of social workers and the state in creating adoptive families.[21]

Adoption experts published widely in the popular press about the benefits of matching. An article in *Tomorrow* magazine in 1949 explained that the delays associated with using an agency were worthwhile, as they stemmed from "the agency's policy of attempting to find the child most perfectly suited for the parents." Matching, the author continued, ensured that "a child with a low I.Q. would not be placed with people of above-average intelligence." Likewise, "Brown-haired, brown-eyed children are given, whenever possible, to parents with the same coloring. A family of redheads would not be likely to get a brunette, and tall parents are seldom given short, chubby children." Matching was not simply cosmetic, the author explained: "There is an important psychological reason behind this policy of simulated resemblance: to some extent, at least, children who look like their new parents will feel more secure than those with marked physical differences."[22]

Applicants generally agreed that matching was an important part of the agency's services. A number of applicants requested children who looked like them or their other children. Elmer and Beatrice Arnold, an African American couple, contacted ICH&A after abandoning a private adoption through lawyers. They preferred using the agency because the lawyers "have no matching and . . . the couple would not know anything about the natural background or have any assurance that the health of the child was best." Beatrice also described a family she had known with adopted children in her native Kentucky, noting that "the resemblance between these girls and their adopted parents was very striking." The social worker continued, "She pointed out that actually it is very important that the resemblance be close not so much for the particular family group as for the help and support of the people in the neighborhood and outsiders."[23] Similarly, Marvin and Barbara Adams, a white couple, told their social worker that they were quite happy with ICH&A's services because of the good match the social worker created for the family. Barbara "expressed understanding and appreciation of what it meant to know the family and why it was important, saw the value of matching the child, how well matched . . . [their son] is and they're pleased that people think he looks like them which they feel as strengthening the placement and making him more comfortable as well as pleasing them."[24]

Matching required a small army of pre-adoptive foster homes, whose case records I use in this study alongside those of adoptive parents. Pre-adoptive foster parents were necessary for creating well-matched adoptive families because they agreed to care for an infant for up to a year or more while social workers studied the child's complexion and his or her intellectual, emotional, and physical development in order to make sure that he or she went to the proper parents. Unlike the public foster care system, which involved the temporary placement of children whose families could not care for them but who did not wish to relinquish custody, the pre-adoptive foster care records I am using in this study were from an in-house program created by ICH&A as part of its adoption department to provide care for infants who were available for adoption but for whom no final placement had been made. The same corps of social workers who studied adoptive applicants also studied potential foster parents, and the process for gaining approval was quite similar. (I discuss these similarities and differences in more detail in following chapters and in the appendices.) Many of these foster homes received a modest stipend in exchange for caring for an infant, however, and were more likely than adoptive applicants to be struggling financially. Many of them also deeply desired more children and entered the program as a means of having a young child in the home even if it was only temporary.[25]

In addition, matching necessitated an ample and diverse pool of potential adoptive parents to meet the needs of diverse youngsters. Therefore, the agency had no set income requirements for placement since they believed some children from less privileged backgrounds would actually do better in a lower- or working-class family. Workers sought families with stable incomes, but they did not require a large income or any additional assets. Social workers at ICH&A particularly sought to address the needs of Illinois's—and especially Chicago's—diverse population. The agency formed a "Colored Children's Auxiliary" in 1920 that cared for and placed black children, and starting in 1942 its Chicago headquarters always had at least one African American social worker on staff to work with black children and families. In the 1950s, ICH&A also worked closely with the Welfare Council of Metropolitan Chicago to develop a Negro Adoption Project to better reach and evaluate potential adoptive families in the black community.[26]

The assumption that only those families who appeared "natural" would be able to fully partake in the benefits of postwar family membership was implicit in the exercise of matching. As historian Ellen Herman explains, "According to the matching ethos, the best adoptive families never betrayed their adoptive status by declaring their difference. . . . Exacting specifications aspired to create families that appeared to be authorized by nature rather than society. Successful matching erased itself, making the social design of adoption invisible."[27] Matching attempted to hide the difference of adoption in order to create families that were supposedly just like any other, even though many parents and children who were related by birth were in fact quite different from one another. To be a full part of the postwar domestic order one needed to mimic the ideal—a heteronormative nuclear family of parents and their birth children—as closely as possible.

Moreover, the practice of matching also covered up the role that state actors played in pairing adoptive parents with children. Matching, paradoxically, empowered professional social workers as the most qualified authorities to make crucial family decisions while at the same time hiding their role in family making. It justified publicly licensed social workers' role in creating families by suggesting that they could make families that would seem most natural or authentic rather than giving that authority to birth parents, adoptive parents, adoptees themselves, or even close friends, doctors, or clergy who knew all parties involved.

Just as they embraced matching, adoption experts and applicants also lobbied for greater legal protections for adoption records and the birth certificates of adopted children. In order to protect unwed birth mothers from stigma and the newly formed adoptive family from scrutiny, adoption records and the original birth certificates of children placed for adoption went from being legally confidential, and thereby hidden from the public, to being inaccessible to even the very parties most affected—adoptive parents, adopted children, and birth parents. States reissued birth certificates listing the adoptive parents' names, eliminating all evidence that the child had a different birth mother. Likewise, adoptive parents, birth parents, and adopted children were not able to access their case files. These practices hid the documentary proof of adoption and prevented any contact between birth and adoptive families, removing any indication that families related through adoption were different from any other.[28] This practice also made lawyers, judges, legal mandates, and all of the other regulations attached to adoption disappear from view, thereby eliminating the role of the state in creating an adoptive family.

These practices, however, elided not only the very public factors that went into creating families by law rather than by birth, but also the social relations that shaped adoptive and foster families. In her history of adoption in English Canada, Veronica Strong-Boag ruminates on this aspect of adoptive family making by exploring the parallels between nation building and adoption. Strong-Boag notes that, throughout the history of adoption, adopted children have been much like immigrants arriving in a new country. They have had to adapt to the culture of a new family just as immigrants have had to adapt to the culture of a new nation. Their parents, meanwhile, like a nation accepting new migrants, have had to adjust to whatever needs and differences lingered from the child's experiences prior to adoption. She draws out the analogy further, noting that a variety of personal, political, and economic factors have long influenced who immigrated and to which nation they moved, just as they have influenced which children have been relinquished for adoption and which individuals have been allowed to adopt them. Likewise, these same factors have dictated how much difference could be tolerated within the nation, or within the family. They have shaped what aspects of the past had to be forgotten or remembered as part of the larger project of nation—or family—building.[29]

Under the postwar model of adoption practice, much was lost, forgotten, or erased even as a new family was formed. Most importantly, birth parents, and their reasons for relinquishing their child, were eliminated from the child's legal record, and adoptive families were given only scant knowledge of their children's birth relatives. Instead, children were matched with adoptive parents who were deemed by social workers similar to their birth parents in terms of race, ethnicity, religion, and, to some extent, class. These parents were to replace a child's birth parents completely, and to offer the child a similar or better (but never worse) standard of living than the birth family could have provided. The economic, gendered, or racial imperatives that led this child to be available for adoption, and these parents to be available to adopt him or her, were wiped from the slate in the process.

Of course, despite social workers' efforts to cover up the most obvious differences between families related by adoption and those related by birth, the differences remained for adoptive families. New parents reckoned with their feelings about raising a child who was related not by birth but by law. They wondered about their child's origins. They also wrestled with the question of which family members and friends should know about their child's (or children's) adoptive status. For many, the hardest part was figuring out how to tell the child himself or herself.

Some of the differences were also impossible to hide. Many of these couples had struggled with infertility, and were therefore older than many of their peers when they had their first child, which set them apart from their peers. They also were never pregnant, making the sudden appearance of an infant potentially an open question for friends, relatives, and neighbors. Further, most wanted several children, but were at the agency's mercy in terms of how many children they would eventually have.

Meanwhile, families providing temporary care for pre-adoptive infants often sought to earn extra money by taking in foster children, but many of them also wanted more children in their home and many hoped to go on to adopt. These families dealt with the ongoing anxiety of knowing a child to whom they were attached would almost certainly be removed. No matter how well matched a child was with his or her foster or adoptive family, the differences between families made by law and those made by birth were undeniable—and they shaped the daily emotional tenor of people's family lives.

Attempts to hide the difference of adoption were also relatively short lived. During the 1960s, interracial and international adoptions became more common. As single parenthood became more acceptable, white unmarried mothers in particular faced less pressure to relinquish their children for adoption and more often chose to raise them themselves, leaving fewer white babies available for the many white couples seeking to adopt. Matching complexions and IQ also became less important to social work professionals and to adoptive parents as Americans generally became more tolerant of differences, including those of race, ethnicity, and ability. Further, political shifts in American welfare and family policies created greater justification for taking children of color from their families of origin and placing them in supposedly more stable white families. By the late twentieth century, both social workers and adoptive parents increasingly looked across both racial and international borders in pursuit of available children. It became difficult—and unnecessary—to hide the very public nature of adoptive family making.[30]

⌒

During the postwar years, the most obvious difference between families created by social workers and those related by birth was the rigorous process of applying to have a child placed in one's home in the first place. While couples faced no screening at all to become pregnant, they faced a number of bureaucratic hurdles in order to become adoptive and foster parents. Even as applicants benefited from the increasing acceptance of adoption, they also faced greater competition for available adoptable infants and tighter screening procedures. To make the best possible placements at a moment when the demand for adoptable babies far outstripped supply, social workers employed a thorough application process to make their decisions. Further, given the mandate to match children with the most similar parents available, the application process was often quite drawn out, as workers studied both child and parents for signs that they would be a good fit. Adoptive and foster families faced a level of scrutiny usually reserved for those suffering from family problems such as domestic abuse or a need for welfare. In order to become parents, they had to open up their homes, reveal their finances, and share their hopes and dreams with social workers who had the power to grant or deny them a child. As they went through the process, applicants could not deny the public side of adoptive family making.

This demanding application process is also what makes this study possible. A thorough knowledge of it is therefore important to understanding how the case records of adoptive and foster care applicants illuminate the domestic ideals of those who never set foot in a social worker's office or even considered adoptive or foster parenthood. These case records offer rich descriptions of the daily lives and values of ordinary people, but they also were produced under very unusual circumstances. A closer look at the process of adopting or taking in a foster child, as well as the relationship between social worker, applicant, and case record, reveals the utility, as well as the limitations, of this particular archive and family form for interrogating postwar domesticity.

For prospective adoptive and foster parents, the "home study" was at the heart of the application process. To perform the home study, a social worker formed a relationship with the applicants over the course of several months in an effort to fully understand their personal and familial backgrounds alongside their hopes, fears, skills, and any persistent personal or family problems such as unemployment, inadequate housing, or ongoing disagreements within the family. The process was designed to ascertain the couple's fitness for parenthood as well as the type of child that would fit in best with their family. The social worker interviewed the couple together and individually, generally interviewing the wife more often than the husband. In the written record, the worker sought to best reconstruct the conversations in the interviews as they had happened, including nonverbal cues, and noted her reactions and evaluations of the couple. She also visited the couple's home in order to get a better sense of them in a more comfortable environment. She sought to formulate an impression of the type of life they would be able to offer a child in terms of the neighborhood, furniture, cleanliness of apartment or home, condition of building, and so on. The home study was complemented by letters of reference from, or meetings with, the couple's friends, family, or neighbors, as well as written verification of income and job history from employers.[31]

All of this information was recorded in great detail in an applying couple's case record. Historian Karen Tice's study of the role of case records in the professionalization of social work in the first decades of the twentieth century argues that there was a great variety in the content and tone of case records across the helping professions. Tice suggests that, in most instances, the case records of social workers included more details about the subjectivities of clients than similar records created by those in more male-dominated helping professions like psychology and psychiatry. Early social workers were "able to grasp certain realities of clients' lives in a deeply contextualized fashion." Though their representations of clients were "far from innocent of the privileges emanating from race, class, and professional authority," they were "less likely to frame clients with the terminology of professionally significant syndromes and less likely to reduce them to categorical types than medical and psychological practitioners." Instead, "social case records were more typically encyclopedic renderings of selected details, impressions, and events snatched from the daily lives of clients."[32]

This dedication to capturing the texture of the daily lives of applicants continued into the postwar years. At ICH&A in the 1940s and 1950s, social workers were expected to produce case files documenting an array of interactions with, and information about, adoption and foster care applicants. These records, which were anywhere from ten to over fifty typed, single-spaced pages long, were supposed to document every conversation, letter, or other contact between applicant and worker, from the applicants' initial inquiry with the agency until the end of the supervisory period. Although some social workers were likely more diligent than others in their efforts to fulfill these requirements, on the whole the case records were generally overflowing with numerous details about applicants' lives and their encounters with the agency.

The case records were used extensively in ICH&A's daily operations. They were shared among colleagues and supervisors in order to best match children with potential foster or adoptive parents. Likewise, if a worker left the agency or for some reason could not continue working with particular applicants, or if a family reapplied at a later date, the case record introduced the new worker to the applicants' situation and helped her get to know them. Records were also part of the supervision and monitoring of social workers by the agency. Staff workers met with their supervisors every other week about their caseloads and faced annual reviews, and they relied on case records when reporting to superiors.[33]

Given the circumstances in which they were produced, we might expect these records to be simply a recounting of social workers' biases and agendas as they imposed their values on clients seeking parenthood. In actuality, however, they are much more complicated. Case records document the complex interplay between social workers, who certainly had their own biases and agendas, and applicants, who came to the exchange with needs, desires, and expectations of their own.

For their part, social workers tried (although not always successfully) to moderate their own personal, if not professional, biases within the records. On the one hand, their efforts were simply a way for individual workers to protect their own credibility among their colleagues. Records circulated among a variety of agency workers and supervisors, and applicants were frequently transferred among staff members. Consequently, a social worker's depiction of any given couple had to be accurate and thorough enough in the case record that, regardless of the worker's personal feelings, her peers would respect her professional judgment when they met the couple themselves.

But eliminating personal bias from the records was also integral to workers' larger project to professionalize adoption practice. Social work research at this time frequently noted a particularly complex relationship between social workers and adoptive applicants. Several studies noted the possibility that social workers would "over-identify" with applicants and not be properly critical of them because adoptive applicants were likely to come from similar social and educational backgrounds as the worker. Although in my study workers often possessed at least some educational and class advantages over applicants, as a number of African American and working-class applicants in my study did not complete high school and many did not go to college, applicants' often stable and orderly households likely appeared to many social workers as more like their own than those of other clients. In addition, adoptive and foster care applicants did not come to the agency for help with any personal problems aside from a desire for children. Whereas most other clients required assistance with family troubles, adoptive and foster care applicants were instead offering to help the agency by taking in a child. Due to these factors, research at the time assumed that adoption social workers were less likely to feel they had a moral, educational, or class advantage over their clients than workers whose clients faced more personal, occupational, and social disadvantages and hardships. Workers therefore had to take special care when evaluating applicants for adoptive and foster parenthood, as their own biases might make them overly generous or excessively harsh with them. In a profession that prized self-awareness, working with adoptive and foster parents required social workers to submit their reactions to their clients and their relationship with them to even greater scrutiny than usual.[34]

Applicants for adoptive and foster parenthood also brought their own needs to the table throughout the home study, and thereby profoundly influenced the process and the records that were left behind. Some applicants asserted themselves in ways that frustrated or even angered their social workers. Some resisted workers' attempts to pry into their lives and intervene in household affairs by avoiding questions or disobeying worker requests. Others voiced their doubts about workers' reasons for asking personal questions, their need to contact employers, friends, and family members, and their insistence on having so many interviews prior to placement. A number rejected workers' advice about how to best parent their children, and most adoptive parents refused to tell their children that they were adopted despite persistent strong encouragement on the part of workers that they do so.[35] Foster mothers were often incompliant when workers removed beloved foster children from their family, one going so far as to gather neighbors on the lawn to physically prevent the social worker from going inside to remove the child. These families also experienced divorce, alcoholism, unemployment, infidelity, and even child abuse. From the African American woman who started running a numbers game from her apartment to make extra income while her husband was on strike to the white family who led to the death of a foster child by leaving the child unattended in a car while going shopping, families engaged in a range of activities of which social workers did not approve.[36]

Applicants also influenced the process in more subtle ways. In her work on the history of family violence, historian Linda Gordon has demonstrated that members of poor and working-class families who interacted with aid and charity workers often had their own agendas and ideas about what they wanted from the exchange. She contends that scholars should not see charity and child protection organizations as simply agents of social control, with their caseworkers using their greater power and authority only to manage and restrict the activities of their clients. Instead, Gordon suggests, "the participants in family violence, both victims and assailants, were by no means passive recipients of social-control policies. Rather, they struggled actively to get help they considered useful from charity and social-work agencies as well as kin and neighbors." In short, these families were "subjects," not "objects."[37] Although many men and women who looked to agencies for help did not end up getting the kind of help or relief they necessarily wanted, Gordon argues that "it is a mistake to see the flow of initiative in these social-control relationships in only one direction, from top to bottom, from professionals to clients, from elite to subordinate. In fact, clients were not usually passive but, rather, active in arguing for what they wanted."[38]

The same pattern holds true for adoption and foster care applicants and their social workers. Applicants desired parenthood, and they used whatever resources they could muster to achieve that goal. Applicants' agency when interacting with social workers is, on the one hand, a real opportunity for the historian grappling with these records because it allows one to glimpse their wishes and desires. But it also raises a whole host of questions and potential problems, for applicants had a strong incentive to distort the truth in their interactions with social workers.

Couples' most-used strategy for getting a child was to try to please or impress their social worker—and they engaged in deceptions that ranged from mild exaggeration to outright lying to do so. On the milder side, some offered overly rosy tales of family harmony and glowing descriptions of the loving care they provided to darling nieces and nephews. Others showed off their furnishings, bragged about their incomes, and boasted of the opportunities they could provide a child. As they tried to connect with workers, they relied on positive spin to portray the very best version of themselves and their lives.

Many also likely engaged in more elaborate fabrications or tried to hide aspects of their lives that they feared would doom their applications, a concern that also plagued social workers at the time. Social workers sought to find the best homes they could for their charges and saw the home study as the best, if imperfect, means to ascertain parental fitness—but it was difficult to know what a couple might be hiding. In a discussion of this problem in relation to the selection of foster parents, two workers from ICH&A acknowledged that "applicants are not motivated to reveal the family problems; on the contrary, they usually are motivated to present their best selves." While not wishing to "minimize the reality of this dilemma as an obstacle to obtaining a full and adequate understanding of the applicants," they urged their colleagues to not "be intimidated by it." They argued that there were four ways for the social worker to confront this difficulty: "1) the establishment of a friendly, professional relationship with the applicants; 2) the establishment of a mutual understanding of the purpose of the study and what the study will entail; 3) clarity on the part of the caseworker of the areas of information to be covered; and 4) appropriate timing of exploration of sensitive areas in relation to movement of the relationship."[39]

In this model, workers who expressed "a genuine depth of appreciation and respect for the applicant as a human being" would over time win the trust of the applicant and have access to more intimate information. Similarly, when the applicants truly understood the importance of the worker's full knowledge of their situation, "they too develop[ed] an investment in sharing a more intimate picture of themselves to determine with the caseworker whether foster care is really good for them and the foster child." When applying for adoption, a longer, more in-depth home study also ensured that applicants who were tempted to present only the rosier side of their lives would have difficulty maintaining that tactic consistently, as workers saw it as their duty to ferret out inconsistencies in people's accounts of their family lives. From the workers' point of view, all of these tactics best ensured that the responses given were as genuine as humanly possible under impossible circumstances.[40]

From the historian's point of view, these records still raise questions. Despite social workers' care when evaluating potential parents, applicants' lies (or failures to tell the whole truth) certainly pervaded the process. I suggest, however, that applicants' honesty is not central to the utility of the records for understanding postwar domesticity. These records are useful because these couples were forced to articulate aspects of family life that no one else had to. It is their very difference—and the potential for deception—that makes them telling. Unlike most other Americans who wanted to have children, adoptive and foster care applicants had to explain why they wanted children and talk about their own childhoods, their current marriages, and what their intimate relationships meant to them—and to try to appear their very best while doing so. Applicants often did not know what workers wanted to hear or what kinds of questions they would be asked; they only knew what they believed those workers wanted to hear. Most had never talked to a social worker before and claimed to have read very little about adoption and foster care beyond what they had seen in movies or read in sentimental articles in popular magazines. Many also claimed they had not read Dr. Spock's popular book on infant and child care and were not well versed in issues of parenting and child psychology.

Their attempts to persuade their social workers, then, reflect their best guesses as to what would make them appear to be good prospective parents. Their stories provide a lens into ideals about family that were circulating among the applicants' peers and communities, regardless of their veracity for any particular family. I read these records not as the absolute truth about individuals' family lives, but instead use them as a lens into the available language, ideas, and images people used to talk about their families. I focus my attention on the expectations, ideals, and desires applicants invoked rather than assuming that they (or their social workers) were expressing an absolutely factual account of their lives.

Social workers and applicants navigated their way through what was, for both, a complicated and very high-stakes interaction. Each party strategized, cajoled, and made judgments about how to best proceed to achieve their desired ends. The case records that remain from their exchanges were written by social workers and privilege their point of view, but they do not simply document the imposition of social workers' professional agendas on clients—or, for that matter, applicants' attempts to mislead social workers in order to get a child. Instead, what is left on the written page is a joint construction that reflects the agency and the assumptions of both social workers and applicants. It is this interaction between a public, family-making authority and potential parents that makes these records such rich sources about diverse and competing family ideals during the baby boom.

⌒

Adoptive and foster care applicants could not ignore the many ways their families differed from others. From their social workers' regular visits to inspect their homes and parenting techniques, to their trip to the courthouse to make their family relationships legal and valid, to the economic and social relations that had led their child to be available to join their family in the first place, these men and women were daily confronted with the many ways public forces profoundly affected their private families. Their social workers, as public authorities tasked with building the best families possible, likewise reckoned with the many ways adoptive and foster families differed from the "normal" and "natural" families they were hoping to mimic. Both applicants and workers dealt with the differentness of these family forms largely by trying to re-create families related by birth, and to thereby hide the public's intrusion into the supposedly private realm of the family.

Their efforts to create well-matched families who would not betray their adoptive status, however, only reified the differentness of adoption because they required such an elaborate application and screening process. The rigorous protocols involved in applying for and placing a child—and the records created in their wake—are what make this study possible, for they capture the inextricability of public and private in postwar family life in ways that go far beyond the intrusions of a social worker into a couple's supposedly private household. Adoption and foster care make explicit what for many families was implicit: social and economic relations shaped *all* families because no one became a parent or raised children in a vacuum. It is this interpenetration between public and private, and its consequences for individuals, families, communities, and ultimately American politics, that is the subject of the rest of this book.

Embracing Domesticity

The Great Depression, the Great Migration, and World War II

Ronald and Irene Lawrence, a young white working-class couple, applied to adopt in 1949. During their first formal interview with an adoption social worker, the worker asked the couple how they had met. Irene "laughed and said, 'We'd better not tell them that [story], or they may think it was kind of silly and rule us out.'" While still a teenager during World War II, Irene had signed up with a pen pal program that encouraged people to write letters to servicemen abroad. Ronald had found one of her letters on the ground while stationed in Europe and decided to write back. They corresponded for nearly two years, finally meeting in person when he returned to the States. They began dating and were married a few months later.[1] Although their chance meeting was so unusual that they had even been interviewed on a radio show about it, the Lawrences were like many Americans who rushed to the altar at the war's end: they hoped marriage and parenthood would provide happiness and security in the wake of wartime uncertainty. Further, like many of their fellow applicants to the Illinois Children's Home and Aid Society at the time, they emphasized in their application the centrality of the war to shaping their commitment to their families and their interest in foster and adoptive parenthood. Applicants also mentioned the Depression and, among African American couples, migration from South to North as important factors in their decision to focus on their families.

The post–World War II rise in marriage rates and birthrates was not an inevitable result of the return of prosperity and peace after the Depression and the war. Previous U.S. depressions and wars did not produce similar demographic explosions.[2] But in people's daily lives, the Depression, the Great Migration, and World War II had an enormous impact on their options and opportunities, and they proved essential to the power of postwar domestic ideology. In the case records, the trials and tribulations of economic deprivation, migration, and war served as the narrative foundation for applicants' hopes and dreams for their postwar family lives. As they tried to explain to their social workers why they wanted and deserved a child, applicants highlighted their experiences during these events. The hardships of depression, migration, and war informed their commitment to forming families of their own, and shaped their expectations for what kinds of rewards and meaning their families could provide in their lives. Likewise, their stories about these events were central to social workers' assessment of their clients' motivations. These events therefore provide the necessary context for understanding the politics of the family in the postwar era, for the domestic ideals of the 1950s were rooted in the upheaval and adversity of the decades before. The family was a means of coping with inequality, suffering, and struggle, and this connection between the family and the world outside the family continued into the more prosperous and peaceful postwar years.

∽

Chicago was hit hard by the Depression. Though it was a city known for its broad industrial base and vibrant immigrant workforce, its workers faced massive hardship during the 1930s. By 1933, only half of those employed in the city's manufacturing sector in 1927 still held jobs, and company payrolls were reduced to a quarter of 1927 levels.[3] Likewise, the 1931 unemployment rate in the city was already 30 percent, which was considerably higher than the national rate of 25 percent in 1932–33, the deepest years of the Depression.[4] Homelessness, Hoovervilles, and hunger became increasingly pressing social problems. Private charities and public coffers had difficulty keeping up with the demand for relief.[5] Many of the city's residents responded to the crisis by organizing in resistance: they joined newly formed Congress of Industrial Organization (CIO) unions, created neighborhood councils, protested for greater aid, and even forcibly prevented evictions.[6] Although the 1933 World's Fair provided a brief diversion from the suffering at hand, Chicago was a changed city during the Great Depression.

Chicago's families struggled to cope with the hardships of unemployment, inadequate housing, and poverty. In their 1938 study of white families in Chicago during the Depression, researchers Ruth Cavan and Katherine Ranck found a number of ways Depression-era conditions forced greater family reliance and intimacy. Some families relocated to smaller quarters or shared housing with relatives, including adult children, which meant more time spent in each other's company. Family members also spent more time together as other forms of recreation grew too expensive. Many individuals were unable to afford presentable clothes to wear to church, transportation to visit friends, and even telephone service, which limited people's social contacts to other members of the household. Cavan and Ranck suggested that in some families this degree of forced intimacy led to conflict and quarrels, while in others it led to greater unity as family members adjusted to the limitations on their lives and reorganized their activities and priorities in order to assist and support one another. Some couples also increasingly focused on their children's lives and accomplishments in an effort to spend a family's resources most meaningfully. These families funneled their limited funds into educational and artistic opportunities for their children and found pleasure in providing for their children's futures despite current deprivations.[7]

Similarly, sociologist Glen Elder studied the lifelong impact of the Great Depression on those who experienced it as children. Elder found that when these children reached adulthood (and became the parents of the baby boom), those who experienced economic deprivation tended to value family life more than other aspects of their lives. According to Elder, "experiences during the depression did more than simply intensify the desire for a more rewarding family life, children and all; it provided examples of the family as an adaptive resource in times of economic trouble." Although "the parental family in deprived situations did not present an attractive model for emulation," it did offer an example of the ways in which family roles and structures could adapt to care for family members. In short, the family was "a means of coping with economic hardship—as an emotional haven, a production unit, and a source of alternative forms of economic support." The stresses of the Depression made family particularly valuable because they made "rewarding, secure relationships difficult to achieve and therefore scarce."[8]

The case records further highlight the range of ways the Depression shaped Chicagoans' family lives and heightened their interest in meaningful family relationships. A number of applicants emphasized the contributions they had made to their families' survival, even at a young age. Many who were children or youths during the 1930s had left school to work to help support their families and to care for the house and younger siblings. For instance, John Malone, a young white applicant, explained that when his father died of a heart condition in 1933, he had done his best to support his mother and sister, but the family ultimately had to request public assistance.[9] Similarly, several men across race who had been the oldest boys in their families claimed that they had become so accustomed to earning income while also helping with cooking and child care during the Depression that they felt they were more competent housekeepers than their wives.[10] Workers noted these youthful sacrifices favorably as evidence of applicants' willingness to put their families first.

Slightly older applicants, who had married during the 1930s, described their experiences during the Depression in terms of the personal and emotional value of working with one's spouse to achieve economic survival. For example, Robert and Evelyn Pearson, a white couple, described at length their difficulties during the Depression after Robert lost his job. The family was forced to go on relief until he eventually found a low-paying position as a school janitor. In the meantime, the pair worked together to start their own business to help lift the family out of poverty. Their social worker noted in 1941 that Evelyn believed that "because of the experience on relief . . . she and her husband were drawn more closely together and that probably because of this experience they took more pride in their home and their present situation than they might otherwise. She said that they feel they 'deserve a pat on the back'" for having managed to provide so well for their family under such difficult circumstances.[11] The social worker agreed with Evelyn's assessment, later adding that she thought this couple would be good foster parents because they seemed "to have been able to accept the reversals in their life without bitterness or lack of faith in their ability to improve their way of living." She also reported approvingly that this family's experience with a relief caseworker during the Depression would likely make them easier to supervise.[12]

Social workers also recorded the stresses that the Depression could place on family relationships. For instance, George and Mary Branch, who were white, waited two years for economic conditions to improve before finally deciding to wed in spite of the Depression. Unfortunately, Mary explained, "if they had a hard time before they married it was nothing compared to what happened after they had been married about 6 months." George lost his job and could not find work, and as Mary reported in 1949 with some hostility, his fairly well-off family had refused to help support them. Her parents, however, who were struggling themselves with her father's unemployment, helped them get by until the young couple could get back on their feet. The experience created an ongoing rift between Mary and her in-laws, but the pair claimed that it had ultimately solidified their closeness to one another.[13]

Many put a positive spin on the financial and emotional strains of the Depression years by emphasizing that it was Depression-era hardships that taught them to prioritize friendship and emotional intimacy in their family lives. For example, Richard Payne, a young African American applicant, suffered a divorce during the Depression that profoundly shaped his attitude toward his second marriage. Richard had struggled with being away from his first wife on long-distance trucking runs. The job was the most lucrative he could find in Depression-era Mississippi, but the couple fought frequently because he rarely had the time, money, or energy to take his wife out in the midst of working so hard to support them. He eventually learned that his wife was having an affair and filed for divorce, blaming both her lax morals and the circumstances of the Depression for the breakup of their marriage. But Richard did not give up on marriage altogether and later chose to marry Elizabeth, this time being much more attentive to his wife's interests and expectations. He felt that, before marrying, "couple[s] should discuss attitudes and have understanding of one anothers [sic] views beforehand, re: what they want and expect in marriage." Richard had told Elizabeth what he wanted out of marriage: he "liked home life, quiet life, didn't run around, wouldn't want her to, didn't drink." Elizabeth had told him that she wanted him to "respect her, be kind, considerate, understanding." This couple got along well, had similar values, and talked things over. Richard appreciated the greater intimacy and unity in their partnership partly because of the strains the Depression had put on his first marriage.[14]

Depression-era deprivations also helped applicants explain and put into context their commitment to their families long after the Depression was over. Applicants whose spouses had had difficult or deprived childhoods due to the Depression frequently mentioned hoping to provide their spouse with a fresh start and a better and happier life together. Roland Martin's troubles had begun in the 1920s, when his father passed away while he was still a young boy, and the family's finances only grew worse during the Depression. His wife felt bad that Roland "had to take care of himself at a very young age and has been responsible for himself for many, many years." She hoped their life together would help make up for his past, and she believed that he deserved "to have some of the nicer things now since he did have so much difficulty when he was a young child." Likewise, Ann Robbins's parents had struggled financially while she was a teenager during the Depression, and she had often been sad that her friends had new dresses when her family could barely keep food on the table. Her husband, Lloyd, explained that in response "he had tried all during their married life to make up to his wife for her unhappy childhood, that he wanted to give her whatever she wanted, whether it be clothes, a house, or anything else."[15] For these couples, the postwar family offered a remedy for past hardships by serving as a source of the comfort and support that was lacking in their earlier lives.

The Depression played an important role in applicants' explanations for their postwar interest in marriage and parenthood, and social workers reiterated the Depression's significance in shaping applicants' postwar values. Workers' careful recording of applicants' tales of Depression-era hardships and the important lessons they drew from those experiences suggests that social workers too believed that these were fundamental to their clients' interest in their families long after the Depression had ended. The Depression provided worker and applicant a common language of scarcity, sacrifice, and putting family first. As applicants sought to convince their social workers of their genuine dedication to their families, they suggested that the experience of living through the Depression had made them accustomed to organizing their lives around the needs of their families and dedicated to the importance of the family as a source of security and stability.

᠆᠊

Chicago, like many northern cities, was the destination of many black southerners who migrated north in search of jobs and greater opportunity in the twentieth century. During the first wave of the Great Migration, in the years around World War I, Chicago's black community grew 148 percent from 1910 to 1920, with an influx of 65,355 migrants. A second, even larger wave of migrants headed north during and after World War II. Although this wave caused a smaller percentage increase in black population in Chicago than the first, in absolute numbers it dwarfed the earlier one, with over five hundred thousand African Americans coming to the city between 1940 and 1960.[16]

For many black Chicagoans, the experience of migration from South to North proved important to their priorities and values, and served as a frequent touchstone in the communication between black applicants and their (often black) social workers. Applicants suggested that the harsh conditions in the Jim Crow South made the black family a locus of support and security prior to migration, and the uncertainties involved in moving so far from home tended to further strengthen family bonds. In addition, the records described the move north as central to applicants' hopes and dreams for their family lives, since many longed to provide their children with more opportunities than they themselves had had growing up in the South.

Scholars have offered a range of interpretations as to the impact of migration on the black family. In a 1930 study of black household patterns in Chicago based on census data from 1920, researchers from the University of Chicago considered the crowded conditions and general poverty of many of the city's black families as the first wave of migration north was coming to a close. They argued that residential patterns suggested "family solidarity," noting that "the presence of so many related individuals and families in these Negro households, especially married sons and daughters, is another indication of tendency to help one another out, and for kin to stick together." Likewise, black mothers often worked, leaving their children unsupervised or in the care of other family members and friends. The researchers suggested that "all the evidence points to the fact that these mothers work with the principal object of keeping the home together, and not because they prefer the greater independence of a wage earner to the duties of home making."[17] They concluded that a reliance on family unity was crucial to coping with conditions in the urban North.

Several prominent researchers working later in the decade found contrary patterns. They suggested that migration weakened black family life, particularly among the lower classes. In his 1939 *The Negro Family in the United States*, E. Franklin Frazier suggested that as men and women left the confines of rural life, many also abandoned all sense of sexual respectability and personal responsibility. Frazier argued that individuals who migrated without the company of family members were often pulled into lives of impropriety and crime. Unschooled in city ways, they found themselves baffled by the complexity of the urban North and vulnerable to exploitation. Frazier described both northern and southern black urban communities as plagued by single mothers, deserting fathers, and intractable children and youths. Likewise, in their groundbreaking study, *Black Metropolis: A Study of Negro Life in a Northern City*, St. Clair Drake and Horace Cayton portrayed Chicago's Black Belt during the 1930s and early 1940s as troubled by the disorganized family lives and lax morals of the black lower class. Although all of these scholars contended that most middle-class and elite black families were in fact models of family devotion, they suggested that lower-class family patterns were a significant problem for the black community—and that migration was primarily to blame.[18]

Recent historical scholarship has overturned many of these conclusions. It has shown that the experience of migration tended to intensify black Chicagoans' ties to family and close friends. For instance, historian James Grossman suggests that the Great Migration was deeply connected to family and institutional networks that reached black communities on both sides of the Mason-Dixon Line. Job advertisements and editorials in Chicago's chief African American newspaper the *Defender*, correspondence from family and friends, and even relocations of entire church congregations all shaped southern blacks' decisions to migrate northward and their experiences when they got there. Many found housing and work upon arrival in Chicago with the help of hometown family and friends, and they relied on these individuals for assistance. The centrality of personal and family connections to relocation meant that many aspects of southern values and culture—and even entire communities—survived in the urban North.[19]

Black applicants described migration as crucial to their conception of family life. For those whose entire families had migrated, parents and adult siblings often lived near one another and visited back and forth frequently. Relatives who had made the journey together were described as a primary source of support and friendship. Likewise, crowded housing conditions in the Black Belt usually made nuclear family privacy impossible, which tended to encourage more intense (though sometimes more volatile) relationships with in-laws and other kin living in the household. For those who had left parents and siblings in the South in order to come to Chicago, the experience of migration could foster close relationships with other relatives living in the city and family friends who had migrated first.[20]

Further, many couples maintained strong relationships with their families despite the distances involved. For instance, Henry and Virginia Franklin, a young pharmacist and his wife, left Virginia's family, who owned a restaurant, in Texas. When the couple was unable to visit them one Thanksgiving, her family sent a whole turkey for the couple to enjoy and throughout the year sent cookies and cakes.[21] For others with relatives still in the South, a yearly visit back home was a priority, and southern relatives also tended to come to the city every year or two for a stay of at least a month.

Families' closeness in the North built upon already strong family relationships developed in the Jim Crow South. African American applicants with southern roots frequently described long histories of helping to support their families, noting that educational opportunities were fewer and the need for family labor more persistent in the South. Even before the Depression, those from poor black communities frequently relied on each other for support. For example, Charles Clark explained that in his large family in Georgia in the 1910s and 1920s, "as was the custom, the older children assumed responsibility for the younger ones as soon as they were able to help in any way. None of them ever resented having to work as his parents taught them early that it was the duty of each member of the household to share whatever he had or could offer to the other. . . . When he grew older his clothing was shared with the other siblings without question." His experiences growing up were considered by applicant and worker alike as evidence of his sincere commitment to his family.[22]

Applicants had often left the South in order to pursue better jobs and to escape the confines of Jim Crow. These goals were believed to particularly benefit one's children, and parents' dreams of offering a better life to their children often justified the move. Applicants placed special emphasis on giving their children both the emotional and educational opportunities they had missed growing up in segregated communities and often in grinding poverty. For instance, Florence Reed had grown up at a boarding school because her single mother had had to work as a live-in domestic in the South and had not been able to keep her daughter with her. Although Florence appreciated that she had been able to stay in school and receive an education, she also regretted that she had missed building a close relationship with her mother. Further, the family's poverty meant that while all of the other students at the boarding school received care packages and frequent visits, her mother was unable to provide these things. Florence vowed to provide more for her own daughter after moving North. She told her social worker that "if . . . [her adolescent daughter] hadn't been such 'a good child' she thinks she might have spoiled her because she tried so hard to give her everything she didn't have from her own mother."[23]

Raising a child outside of the South also allowed for better educational and social opportunities. Leon Nelson wanted his son to "be able to do some of the things he had not done" when he was growing up in the South. His social worker recorded that he had come "from a poor family in a small town with poor schools. The school was [open] for six months out of the year for Negro children. He seemed to feel bitter because white people control[led] the town and arranged for their children to go to school for nine months a year. The Negro children had to stop in order to work on the farm." Leon believed that his son would receive better and more equitable schooling in Chicago.[24]

Yet Chicago was an intensely segregated city, and black migrants did not always find the welcoming opportunities they had anticipated. Chicago's black neighborhoods were physically and culturally separate from the white neighborhoods surrounding them, and any expansion of the Black Belt faced fierce resistance. Further, the city's Black Belt had been integrated into the city's Democratic political machine through a strong black submachine in the 1930s, which meant that the community's fortunes rose and fell based on the whims of the local Democratic Party. Though African Americans made some gains under the relatively friendly administration of Mayor Edward Kelly, who was in office between 1933 and 1947, Kelly's successors felt less compelled to cater to the black vote in the city. While Kelly had pushed for housing integration, Martin Kennelly, who took office in 1947, and Richard J. Daley, who succeeded Kennelly in 1955, frequently ignored the black community's demands even as they relied on their votes. Though life in Chicago was for many preferable to the Jim Crow South, poverty, discrimination, and inferior housing and education continued to plague Chicago's black families.[25]

Despite these ongoing hardships, many black Chicagoans focused on the positives the city offered for their children. The story of the McKays, a poor black family who lived on Chicago's West Side, demonstrates the importance of children to migrants' feelings about their decision to leave the South—even when conditions remained difficult in the North. The McKays were studied extensively as part of a research project under the purview of the University of Chicago's Allison Davis, an African American anthropologist and education professor. Known as the Washington family in Davis's published work about them, the family struggled to support their children in the North, but they still believed that they were better off than they would have been in the South.[26]

The McKays faced a number of hardships in Chicago. In 1945, the family had eleven children, ranging in age from newborn to twenty-four years old. The parents, Claude and May Della McKay, were in their forties and had moved to Chicago in approximately 1922 after marrying several years before in Kentucky. The couple believed that the older children in the family had benefited from the move north. These children had music lessons, a piano, and the chance to go to school rather than pick cotton.[27] The situation of the younger children was less hopeful, however. The family had fallen on hard times during the Depression, and they called the children born after 1930 "rats" or "panic children." The family usually had ample (though monotonous) food during the Depression, but they struggled to keep the children clothed well enough to attend school. They had difficulty keeping all of the children in shoes and warm winter coats, and even the loss of a comb would lead to days of unkempt hair because they could not afford to replace it. The couple's furnishings were poor, there was minimal plumbing, and the family could rarely afford soap, but family members did what they could to get along. Claude worked long hours at his job, and the older children also contributed to the household income. May Della worked outside the home for pay occasionally and was often busy at home running a numbers game that brought in extra income.[28]

The couple believed that Chicago was a hard place to raise a large family but that the deprivations were worth it to escape southern racism. Even during the comparatively flush war year of 1943, Claude complained of the difficulty of supporting such a large family in the city. A researcher quoted him as saying, "Children in a city is too hard on one man. Back in Kentucky in the country kids any size can get out and chop cotton and pick cotton and help out some, but here in town a kid ain't got nothing to do but eat and sleep and go to school and they don't even want to do that." Yet Claude himself had never returned to the South—even to visit—after having left twenty-four years before, and he suspected that his children would not fare well there: "I know if my boys was in the South, they'd get lynched, cause I'd get lynched myself. White folks down South will lynch a man for nothing, just the least little thing."[29] He later explained, "Sometimes I wish I was back on the farm with this big family I got. That's where I need to be with all these children. It's too hard to raise children in a big city like this. But I wouldn't go back there now. Them white people don't treat colored people right."[30] Even though their lives were not terribly comfortable in the North and their children no longer had the kinds of opportunities Claude and May Della had hoped to provide, the move from South to North was still justified as good for the family because it spared the children southern racism—if not northern poverty.

Black men and women highlighted the journey from South to North as crucial to the African American experience in Chicago, and they suggested that the experience was intimately related to their commitment to their family lives. They described migration as strengthening family bonds and improving children's educational and social opportunities. Although ongoing racial inequality in the North was never far from parents' minds, conditions in the South were never distant either. Building on a long tradition of placing the family at the heart of African American culture, black Chicagoans pointed to experiences of racism in both locations, and the family as a site of resistance and support, as integral to their commitment to their families during the postwar era.

⌒

Along with the Depression and migration, applicants also asserted that the onset of World War II solidified their devotion to their families. In many cases, the family unit continued to be crucial to providing economic support during the war, just as it had during the hard times that came before. But World War II also had a unique impact on the American home front—from the everyday inconveniences of food and gas rations, to the struggles many men made as they transitioned from worker to soldier, to the experiences of women as they were recruited to contribute to the war effort. World War II permeated daily life and American culture more thoroughly than any war since the Civil War.[31] Facing such profound disruptions in their usual routines, the emotional aspects of family took a different cast for many during the war.

Historians have suggested that wartime media presented carefully controlled images of family life on the home front in order to soothe wartime anxieties and contain the potentially disruptive impact of war on postwar gender relations. For instance, Wendy Kozol has demonstrated the importance of domestic and family images to *LIFE* magazine's coverage of the war. Kozol suggests that "government propaganda and the mass media . . . turned to the private obligation of domesticity to encourage Americans' participation in the war effort." At the war's end, "*LIFE* focused on reconversion in terms of male employment, economic stability, and domestic happiness when soldiers returned."[32] Likewise, Maureen Honey has demonstrated that propaganda encouraging women's war work emphasized the sacrifices and obligations of women's citizenship rather than the potential of paid work to provide women with autonomy and independence.[33]

Despite the promotion of well-ordered, patriotic wartime families and smooth postwar reconversion, many magazines also pointed out the potential family problems that could arise from war. Women's war work was a primary source of concern. In a 1944 article entitled "Mothers . . . Our Only Hope," FBI director J. Edgar Hoover encouraged readers of the *Women's Home Companion* to stay home with their young children rather than go into war work, in order to stem rising juvenile delinquency rates. Hoover deemed undernurtured and unsupervised children a greater long-term threat to the nation than the war itself, and he reminded women of their patriotic and social duty to focus on their responsibilities as mothers first and foremost.[34] Likewise, as soldiers returned home, an array of commentators sought to ease spouses' readjustment to one another in order to avoid social disruptions. A former soldier suggested in 1945 in the *Ladies' Home Journal* that wives of returning servicemen should be supportive and understanding if their husbands seemed distant or aloof after the war. Seeking to limit marital squabbles and potential divorces, he explained that soldiers had become accustomed to doing without the comforts of home and family during the war, and it would take time for them to settle back into the routines of civilian life.[35]

Scholars at the time also fretted over the impact of the war on the American family. Sociologist Earnest Burgess believed that the war would have a far-reaching impact on the structure and purpose of the American family. He suggested that the looser morals (and particularly the prostitution and venereal disease) associated with military camps, the large numbers of women engaged in war work, and the prospect of children and youths left without parental supervision would create a fundamental change in American values. Burgess presciently predicted that in the decades after the war families would become more companionate, women more empowered, and children more often in the care of nurseries and day-care professionals. He also contended that there would be liberalization in sexual mores and greater family instability.[36] In addition, Burgess noted the potential difficulties of family reintegration at war's end. Families experienced significant stress when women were forced to leave jobs they enjoyed when soldiers returned home—particularly among couples that had married hastily before or during the war and did not have an especially strong bond with one another. Burgess also feared the Depression would recur at war's end, adding financial strain to already tense family relationships. To combat marital strife and a rise in juvenile delinquency, Burgess argued for greater education and counseling on family issues in the years after the war.[37]

In Chicago, the war dramatically altered the rhythms and patterns of everyday life. The city witnessed the shortages of goods and supplies that plagued a number of communities at the time, yet many people found themselves with better jobs and higher pay than they had seen since before the Depression. The city was a major center of wartime production, receiving $9.2 billion in war supply contracts, which was fourth highest in the nation after New York City, Detroit, and Los Angeles.[38] Chicago's central location also made it a hub for both soldiers and military supplies in transport. With new jobs being created, a transient population of soldiers passing through, and the widespread stress of wartime rationing and loved ones in service, Chicago offered its residents both opportunity and anxiety during the war.[39]

Ordinary men and women in the city reckoned with the upheaval the war created. Adoptive and foster care applicants primarily recounted the deep sense of unease, fear, and doubt they felt during the war, and the centrality of marriage and family relationships to dealing with those feelings. For instance, James Hurley, a white teacher, had been thinking about marrying his girlfriend Helen before heading overseas but had decided not to propose before he left because "he saw men on all sides of him married and then feeling so terribly miserable about leaving their newly acquired wives in America." He "knew too that the 'world was kind of cockeyed' and he wanted to be sure about things before he offered marriage." However, like many men in service, he began to change his mind after heading overseas. According to their case record, the couple's wartime correspondence made them realize how much the relationship meant to them. Overcoming his doubts about the potential of marriage in an uncertain world, he proposed to Helen and they wed soon after he returned.[40]

The Hurleys were certainly not unique, as many couples rushed to wed in response to a boyfriend's military status. The prospect of wartime separation and the uncertainty of military service reinforced for couples the emotional benefits of family and encouraged many to cast their doubts aside and marry quickly. This trope was repeated throughout the adoption and foster care records and in the popular culture of the time.[41] Although many social workers were, like Burgess, concerned about the haste of wartime marriages, workers emphasized that, for couples whose unions remained intact in the postwar period, the war was an important turning point in solidifying their commitment to building a family together.

Social workers noted that the upheaval and instability of military service encouraged men in particular to prize the security and stability of family life. Thomas Wilson, a white doctor who was glad to provide his service in the war because he had received government assistance with his medical training, contended that the long periods of separation from his wife during the war made them both more eager to settle down into "the stability of a home and family."[42] Likewise, Albert Booth, a white small businessman, had had a particularly harrowing war experience, witnessing many deaths. Albert elaborated that "the Army made him realize it was kind of silly getting all worked up over little things and the next day he might not even be here." He decided that a simple life with a home and family was the best way to cope with the uncertainties of life. As the social worker explained it, "He just developed the philosophy of taking things as they come and trying to work out your life in such a way where you could have some measure of financial success, have a happy marriage and some children with whom you could try to instill in the best way you could—this wasn't such a bad world after all." Further, his domestic aspirations gave Albert a reason to regain control over his life and tame his "wild side." He explained that "when he got out of the army he didn't know quite what he wanted to do, in the army there wasn't much to do except to have fun, drink. When he first started seeing his wife he thinks that she thought he was a little on the 'wild side,' she being a more conservative type, and he soon began to realize that civilian life was not army life, and that if he was going to get anywhere he was going to have to go to school and cut out the drinking and settle down. This wasn't so hard to do because he was kept busy and more than that he was in love with his wife and he wanted to get married so he had a real goal to work toward."[43] Applicants and social workers agreed that marriage could provide a purpose and the promise of happiness for men struggling to adapt to life after the military.

Military service was not the only aspect of the war that encouraged people to value family as a source of comfort and financial and emotional security. The records of several black couples recounted the closeness and intimacy that grew between spouses when husbands worked in essential war industries and therefore did not have to serve in the military. These couples used the time to bolster their savings, build their lives together, and generally reported growing closer together from the experience. Raymond Herrington told his social worker "that he won't pretend he wasn't glad [that he was exempted]. After so many years of living together a man and a woman become like this—here, Mr. H held two fingers closely together. He didn't think it was necessary to stand up and wave a flag though he would have been glad to serve if he had been called on in other capacities."[44] Ralph and Betty Shields used the wartime economy to achieve their joint goal of buying property and starting their own business. Ralph, who was deferred from the draft as an essential worker in a steel mill, and Betty, who stayed at home, strictly saved their money while their friends spent their incomes on parties, fun, and clothes. They repeatedly emphasized that it was their steadfast commitment to each other and their joint goal of home owner-ship that inspired them to deny themselves the luxuries others enjoyed.[45]

The stresses of wartime ripped some families apart, but for those couples who managed to persevere through the war and demobilization, the experience affirmed their commitment to each other and to the benefits of family living. Stories emphasizing the importance of emotional intimacy during wartime also resonated with social workers and provided a way of explaining applicants' de-votion to their families. As couples coped with the uncertainties and anxieties of wartime, they looked to each other for support, and they carried those values into the postwar era.

❧

The Depression, the Great Migration, and World War II served as touchstones for applicants and workers as they crafted a joint narrative explaining the role that family played in applicants' lives. Although these events did not single-handedly cause the baby boom, for many they served to focus their attention on their families. When asked about their family lives in the postwar years, ap-plicants highlighted these events, suggesting that they were integral to how they understood their own commitment to foster and adoptive parenthood—or, at the very least, they rightly believed that family narratives about these events would prove compelling to social workers. In either case, their stories suggest that the hardships of earlier decades forged linkages between the household and the world outside its doors that prevailed into the more prosperous postwar period.

Yet even as applicants used these narratives of adversity and suffering to con-vey to workers their sincere dedication to their families, they simultaneously rejected the sense of deprivation and anxiety they associated with these events. Responding to their experiences of scarcity and uncertainty in their pasts, they noted the resiliency of their families while they were growing up, but they told social workers that they hoped their own families would provide greater warmth and security for themselves and their children. As the next chapter will explore, the case records outline distinct emotional, personal, and social benefits to marriage and parenthood during the postwar years. Ideas about family forged in experiences of depression, migration, and war were reinforced as prewar privation turned into postwar prosperity. As they sought to move past the hardships of their own childhoods and young adulthoods, diverse applicants articulated an intensely powerful ideology of domestic fulfillment that shaped their choices and opportunities into the 1940s and 1950s.

THREE

Defining Domesticity
Family Ideals in Everyday Life

Edward Thomas, a young white lawyer living in a Chicago suburb, was applying to adopt a child in 1948. According to his social worker, "Some of his friends with whom he plays poker once a month used to 'kid' about . . . [he and his wife Doris] not having any children." Thomas was hurt by their teasing, with its subtle implication that he was inadequate as a husband and unable to impregnate his wife. His social worker noted, however, that Thomas felt that their jokes "were only natural since they had been married for 6 years and people would assume that they ought to have children."[1]

Thomas's teasing poker buddies reiterated the messages of much of the family-centric, pronatalist popular culture of the time. Although the postwar media were not monolithic in terms of their presentation of conventional gender roles, they tended to emphasize the benefits of family membership. Films such as *The Best Years of Our Lives* and *The Man in the Grey Flannel Suit*, television shows like *Leave It to Beaver* and *Father Knows Best*, and popular magazines ranging from the women-focused *McCall's* and *Ladies' Home Journal* to the more gender-neutral *Look* and *Life* all portrayed family living as the surest path toward personal happiness. Further, social and psychological authorities frequently depicted single men and women as poorly adjusted, and perhaps pathologically so. Single men were tainted with the stigma of possible homosexuality, or, if they were returning veterans, feared as lacking the domesticating and calming influence of a wife to help them settle back into the routines of civilian life. Likewise, single women, and even married women who were infertile, were believed frigid and possibly neurotic.[2]

Thomas's experience at his poker game also points to the role that interactions with friends, family members, and even colleagues played in inscribing and reinscribing the importance of marriage and parenthood. Such interactions influenced people's sense of themselves as being fulfilled and socially accepted adults—or not—during this period. Rather than being driven exclusively by popular culture or Cold War political concerns, the baby boom was also fueled by everyday social encounters in which family ideals were espoused and reiterated. Thomas and his social worker took for granted his friends' ribbing: it was "only natural" for people to "assume they ought to have children" after a few years of marriage. The teasing, while neither mean spirited nor emotionally devastating, made clear to Thomas that his manhood and full inclusion in his peer group rested upon nuclear family membership.

Couples and their social workers articulated in the case records a consistent set of ideals about the role family should play in people's daily lives. The applications of diverse couples recount, on the one hand, remarkably similar beliefs about the personal pleasures and promises of family living, suggesting that it provided individuals a profound source of joy and purpose. Marriage brought love and security, while parenthood added warmth and fulfillment to the mix. These emotional benefits were widely embraced as essential to a meaningful and happy life.

On the other hand, the case records also reveal that applicants encountered these ideals in an array of social, familial, and professional contexts, creating important social benefits to fulfilling family norms. The records make clear that, from poker games, to the shop floor, to conversations with friends and relatives, applicants faced pervasive social pressure to have families in the postwar years. Just as agency workers urged applicants to deeply consider the joys and benefits of marriage and parenthood, a variety of friends, neighbors, and relatives also pushed these men and women to focus on their nuclear family relationships. Applicants for adoptive and foster parenthood often found themselves on the margins of a social world that privileged family membership, and they felt these pressures particularly acutely. Having a family allowed applicants to connect more fully with the social world around them, while an inability to fulfill the era's domestic dictates often led to a sense of social exclusion and personal doubt.

⤳

The case records outline a powerful ideology that depicts family membership as essential to happiness and fulfillment in the postwar era. Applicants and workers located the origins of this ideology in experiences of depression, migration, and war. But they differentiated postwar family ideals from those that had governed their lives in the decades before. Rather than serving as a source of strength and security in uncertain times, as it had in the upheavals of the 1930s and early 1940s, the postwar family was companionate and promised emotional fulfillment and personal wholeness.[3] As later chapters of this book will demonstrate, there was significant variation among people's daily family patterns along lines of race and class, making people's family lives often look quite different than the stereotypical image of "postwar domesticity" would suggest. Yet regardless of race or class position, a shared ideology about the pleasures and benefits of marriage and parenthood prevailed among diverse adoption and foster care applicants and their social workers.

One can attribute the wholehearted embrace of family life portrayed in the records, in part, to their origins. Adoption social workers had dedicated their careers to building happy families, and they were committed to documenting the family practices and ideals of those they studied. Likewise, adoption and foster care applicants tended to be uniquely dedicated to family living. Adoptive applicants were often infertile and eager for parenthood, while foster care applicants often had children of their own already but enjoyed the care and company of children enough that they desired to care for a foster child as a source of further companionship and extra income. Their heightened ardor for children only increased their stake in convincing social workers of the sincerity of their desire, the wholesomeness of their household, and their ability to provide a child with loving care. It is therefore not surprising that the case records would generally portray applicants as deeply committed to the benefits and pleasures of family living. Despite their predictability, the beliefs and attitudes described in the records are still quite useful for analysis. Even if these particular men and women—applicants and workers alike—were more invested in the benefits of family living than the majority of their postwar peers, their descriptions of those desires provide a lens into the ideological beliefs about children and parenthood circulating among a range of ordinary people during a period when there was an explosion in childbirths across all demographic groups.

For their part, social workers envisioned good families as stable, loving, and beneficial for both parents and children. The leaders at ICH&A during the 1940s and 1950s, like their counterparts at most prominent social work agencies at the time, were deeply influenced by psychodynamic theories of human motivation. ICH&A staff members were urged to consider not only applicants' conscious explanations for why they desired parenthood, but also the underlying unconscious drives that would shape applicants' relationship with the children in their care. Workers were to scrutinize both men's and women's descriptions of their everyday lives and their desire for foster or adoptive parenthood for any signs of unresolved psychological conflicts, neurotic tendencies, or repressed hostility toward a spouse, parents, or other close relatives. Ideal families required well-adjusted parents at the helm, for only those with the proper psychic makeup could both create and benefit from the family's proper nurturing atmosphere.[4]

Social workers sought couples that had genuinely warm and happy relationships, and who sincerely desired to care for and love a child placed in their care. In a 1954 conference in Chicago, two of ICH&A's social work supervisors, Marjorie Ferguson and Draza Kline, summarized "the essential qualities which characterize suitable foster parents" as such: "They are a stable couple who have worked out an enduring and satisfying marital relationship, whose relationships with relatives and friends are primarily gratifying and free from severe neurotic conflict; they have found satisfaction in their own children if they have had any, and this satisfaction arises primarily from mature gratification of helping the children grow and develop as individuals separate from themselves."[5] In short, the ideal family provided meaning and succor for both parents and children. Workers sought applicants with the potential to provide loving care to children, and who expected in return only a sense of accomplishment and pleasure.

Applicants, who often had little interest in the subconscious and wished only to convey their sincere desire for a child, also suggested that nuclear family membership benefited themselves as well as their (potential) children. They agreed with social workers that being part of a family provided purpose, meaning, and a sense of personal wholeness. Fleshing out workers' more abstract notions about adjustment and stability, applicants offered vivid stories and images to explain their feelings about their families and their desire to parent adoptive or foster children. Together with workers, they outlined in the case records a coherent family ideology that attached specific personal and emotional benefits to family membership.

This ideology had several key components. First, companionate marriage was at the heart of the postwar companionate family. Marriage was understood as an expression of a deeply felt emotional connection with one's partner, making one happier, more complete, and more fulfilled in life. For instance, Edward Thomas fell for his wife, Doris, "because she was so 'fundamentally right'" for him.[6] Fred Shaw, a white mechanical engineer, and his wife, Josephine, bragged to their social worker that "their friends described [their marriage] as a true 'love match.'"[7] Joe and Thelma Bates, an African American couple, had been childhood sweethearts. Both subsequently married other people "based on things other than real affection" and both divorced in a few years. They then married one another, both "feeling that they were meant for each other." Thelma believed "that opportunity knocked for her twice rather than the usual once." As the social worker put it, "with him she feels she has found enough happiness to compensate for what she might have missed earlier."[8]

Parenthood only increased this sense of purpose and fulfillment. Applicants described having children together as a completion of the stable, loving intimacy of the marital bond. According to a social worker Harold Gibson, a black baker, explained "that it was always his idea that a home was incomplete without a child. He thought that every couple definitely should have a family."[9] Similarly, Irene Lawrence thought, in the words of her social worker, that "the next thing that would really complete their home would be a baby."[10] Likewise, Ruth Pike, the wife of a well-off white construction contractor, felt "that they would like to share the happiness they have with another."[11]

Ruth went on to express another common and related belief—that children were an extension of a loving marriage and offered a degree of fulfillment unachievable through marriage alone: "[The Pikes] feel it would bring so much in to their lives, and altho [*sic*] they love one another a great deal, that a child would fulfill their lives completely."[12] Similarly, Anna Cash, a white laundry worker's wife, professed that "she feels that people's purpose in life is to fulfill themselves by having children. She further added that a child is an expression of love for one another."[13] Shirley Hall, the wife of a black factory worker, "said that she thought it would add to their marriage to have a child in the home, and that they were taking him purely as a source of joy and as a companion, and that they felt that they were so happy they should share some of the love they had with someone else."[14] The Farmers, an African American chef and his wife, wanted to adopt because "a childless home is not a home."[15]

As an extension of the love couples had for each other, the records suggested that children strengthened a marriage and heightened the intimacy of the marital relationship. Upon seeing the child they would adopt for the first time, the Farmers told their social worker, "It's just like we were courting again, Miss Church. Since we have seen the baby, we are so happy we seem to be closer together."[16] Similarly, after adopting her first child, Ruby Douglas, the wife of a black small business owner, "wonder[ed] how [her] marriage was held together" before they had a child. She and her husband Stanley had both had jobs and many interests, so they had rarely had quality time together. Ruby believed that having a child had brought them closer together: "Now both of their interests center around home and family which they find satisfying. . . . Both enjoy a richer and new life."[17]

Similarly, the case record of Marvin and Barbara Adams, a white pharmacist and his wife, likened becoming parents to getting married, noting that both parenthood and marriage required valuing someone else's happiness as much as or more than your own. Barbara felt that parenting created "a feeling of unity, that it is similar to being married in that one begins to feel at one with the other person and they think of themselves and things together." She believed that the daily care and attention a child required also brought the couple closer and smoothed over any difficulties in their marriage: she was "amazed at how much being parents will 'tide things over.' If parents [are] disagreeing over something inevitably . . . [their son] will be into something or need attention and in going to him they forget all about the disagreement and it just blows over." She felt it "enriched their marriage in that . . . [their son] is something they share together in their concern."[18] Being part of a family unit, and particularly raising children, was portrayed as giving individuals a larger sense of purpose and creating a stronger bond between spouses.

Children were also a source of companionship for lonely stay-at-home wives, and a distraction for those facing marital distress. Some records recounted the stories of women who were so certain that a child would create intimacy in their marriage that they wished to adopt or provide foster care simply to ease their marital problems. These applicants hoped having a child in the home would be of interest to their distant husbands, and thereby make these men more companionable for their wives because they would have a joint project. For instance, Gladys Bond, an African American woman, had married her husband when both were in their mid-thirties. She told her social worker that she "felt that perhaps when older people marry, it was more a matter of convenience for both of them and less of a romantic match." She believed, said her social worker, that "'in our situation, we need a baby.' . . . [because] a baby could be both of theirs and bring them closer together." Although her marriage turned out not to bring her the kind of fulfillment and companionship she had hoped for, she believed a child would solve the problem—thereby investing further in the domestic ideal even when it had already let her down.[19]

In addition to showing how parenthood might complete the family unit and heighten its emotional rewards, the case records also depicted parenthood as providing a sense of purpose that would make life more meaningful. A social worker noted in shorthand the series of reasons that the Pruitts, a white union construction worker and his wife, gave for wanting a child: "Both want children. Feel that life and energies somewhat unfulfilled without. Feel that they want to invest their energies and their strivings, etc. in something 'that matters'. Material achievement success, possession, etc. not fulfilling enough—not significant enough. Both just love children."[20] Likewise, Carl Scott, a young white graduate student, explained why he would not mind a child's interruptions to his studies: he "felt that even though he had to spend a lot of time studying, men with a happy home life actually produced more than those who only had the carillon bells as company."[21] Similarly, Florence Reed, a black optometrist's wife, believed children "made life different and worthwhile," while Willie Reynolds, a black factory worker, and his wife, Annie, felt "that they would not have much purpose in life if they did not have the children to care for."[22]

Applicants also suggested that becoming parents would make them into better people. Children had the paradoxical effect of making their parents both more mature and more youthful. On the one hand, having children was supposed to make one a more responsible and caring adult. One social worker suggested that parenthood made Howard and Patricia Allen, a white factory worker and his wife, less selfish and materialistic. She wrote: "until . . . [the child's] placement life had little to offer and they spent money foolishly and for nonessential things. Now that they had purpose and direction Mrs. A was no longer self-centered, didn't spend money on clothing she didn't need in that all her efforts and attention were to [son]."[23] Similarly, Doris Thomas emphasized that "it means something when you stayed up all night with a child when it's been feverish and sick and worried about it as well and watched it grow through various phases." She felt she had grown by attending to her daughter's needs rather than simply her own. She went on to describe how, on a recent trip to a nature museum with her daughter, she had held and fed a snake even though snakes give her "the 'willys'" because she did not want her daughter to be as afraid of them as she herself was. She was delighted to find that her daughter "thought it was a wonderful thing for her mother to do and wanted to do the same thing."[24] Louis Brown, a black salesman, and his wife, Eleanor, felt that having a child would be the true mark of settling into mature, caring adulthood: "for years they have satisfied themselves in the things that they want to do," but they were now ready for a child, including all of the "washing of diapers, fixing formula, seeing that he had school clothes, washing behind his ears, as well as fussing at him sometimes."[25]

On the other hand, a child also kept an adult young and flexible. For instance, Alfred Roberts, a white executive, explained that "one cannot long remain a 'stuffed shirt' if he has a child around him very much of the time." He supposed having children made people easier going and more fun, and realized that if he became a parent he would have to adjust to toys scattered around the house and a baby crying.[26] Likewise, Louise Howe, a white woman, mentioned that "people who do not have children are apt to get selfish and crabby. She remarked that children 'keep you interested in things and give you something to live for,'" while her husband Norman, a factory worker, "added that 'they keep you from getting old fashioned—if you do the kids will tell you about it.'"[27] Similarly, Anna Cash felt after becoming parents that she and her husband William "never are grown up, also enjoy belly flopping on the hills, skating, etc."[28] Stanley Douglas, an African American small business owner, relished picking out elaborate gifts, such as a Pony Express bicycle and Hopalong Cassidy outfit, for his son—reliving the childhood he wished he had had through his son's excitement with each new toy.[29]

The case records further suggest that the promises of parenthood—a greater purpose in life, an improved character, and a more rewarding marriage—made men and women eager to organize their lives around their children's activities and daily care. A number of records describe applicants anticipating daily involvement with their children. Arthur Carter, a white printer, confessed to the social worker that he and his wife, Norma, pretended that their child had already been placed, and imagined enjoying her daily care: "in a rather embarrassed manner [he] told worker that they play a game sometimes while they are eating dinner. He will say 'Its [sic] your turn to wipe her mouth' or she will say 'she wants more milk now.'"[30] Kenneth Hanks, a black factory worker, asked his wife if "the baby could be able to eat breakfast with him or eat supper with him, and he had already been fantasying about what they would do with the youngster."[31] Further, the imagined pleasures of parenting were also distinctly gendered, with girls and boys providing different kinds of fulfillment. Across race and class, fathers imagined taking their future little boys hunting, fishing, and to ball games, while mothers dreamed of sewing dresses for little girls and doing their hair.[32]

The accomplishments of growing children were also depicted as providing an unequaled sense of pride for their parents. The social worker of Jack Blevins, a white executive, commented that "what they want in a child is really to be able to share the love they have between them with children because both of them feel that marriage without children can be successful but that the different kind of happiness in sharing [a] child's illnesses, watching their development, taking pride in whatever achievements they have and even if they don't achieve, just taking pride in them as a child."[33]

Embracing family togetherness, parents expected to enjoy partaking in their children's activities. The Henrys, a white laundryman and his wife, admired friends who had a "lively" family life, in which "they all seem to get along together and they think this is because the parents enjoy the children so much and both participate in their activities together."[34] Lawrence Tompkins, a black factory worker, hoped to adopt a daughter who was "desk high" so she would be old enough to go places with him and talk to him. He hoped to expose his imagined daughter to new things, such as museums, the beach, and music lessons. His wife Phyllis, meanwhile, told her social worker when the adoption was consummated that she felt "she would be 'able to close her eyes in peace' if she could see . . . [her daughter] grown and married happily with a family." Like others, she valued the joys of family life so much that she deeply wished for the same fulfillment for a daughter who was barely out of diapers.[35]

Case records describe a child-centered life as the surest path to happiness — and, in many records, the more children a family had, the better. Although social workers tended to prefer that families focus their energy and attention on one child, many applicants feared raising an only child and thought that having more children was better for both the children and their parents. Some couples simply wanted the joy of raising more than one child, and they particularly wanted one of each gender. But others felt that the stakes were higher, fearing emotional problems for themselves or their children if they had only one. Several mothers of only children applied to adopt or board foster children because they feared smothering their kids with too much attention, and wanted a distraction so as to feel less anxiety about giving them more freedom. These mothers particularly worried when their only child was a boy, for they feared that without multiple children they might unintentionally make their sons timid and weak through too much maternal attention. Gloria Rice feared she had waited too long, for the fact that her son was a bit effeminate and a "mother's boy" was widely known among friends and neighbors. She felt that he needed "a real boy around" and hoped that by being around a boy who was "a little tougher," her son might become a bit more masculine.[36]

Children were idealized as an emotional asset to the family—a financial responsibility that paid back its costs in the priceless emotional rewards provided to the child's parents and siblings.[37] Many men and women asserted that if one child helped foster intimacy and a stronger connection within the marital couple, then additional children would certainly emotionally enrich the entire family. They felt, as Herbert and Pauline Winter put it, that there was "a richer kind of family life for a child if there is a brother or sister."[38] Further, parents who had siblings remembered the experience fondly and wanted their own children to have the same experience. Siblings also taught children to get along with others, which parents believed would help their children later on in life. Warren and Grace Matthews "thought that there was an advantage for a child having a brother or sister in view of the fact that it gave them an opportunity to learn to share." However, they explained that "some of their friends have limited themselves to one child because they want that child to have just everything." The Matthews were staunchly in favor of multiple children because they believed that "material values are not nearly as important as emotional values for a child," and it would be a mistake to only have one child so as to spoil it.[39]

Regardless of the number of children in the family, applicants proposed that their families would be much more child and family focused than those in which they grew up. Margaret Wilson felt that her own mother was "'nasty neat' in that she couldn't allow ashes to be in an ash tray for more than a minute, was constantly reminding the children to pick up their clothes or to put them away, instead of really just relaxing and being a mother in more sense of the word than getting the meals on time or having the house clean." She believed that "from her own experiences [with her mother] that she would be a good deal different in relationship to the child; would rather not be so concerned about the housework, committee meetings."[40] Likewise, Samuel Pappas said that "he would like to spend more time being a pal to his child and sit down and talk with him." He realized "that a child sometimes would 'get in my hair'" but expected to spend most of his time with a child showing him new things and providing him with "constructive outlets for his energies."[41]

Above all, parents expressed a desire for their children to feel comfortable talking to them and wanted an intimacy they believed they lacked with their own parents, emphasizing that the emotional rewards of the postwar family were its most important quality. For instance, Warren Matthews echoed a very common sentiment when he explained that "he had been raised in a period when children were to be 'seen and not heard.' He said that he felt there were too many restrictions on children in his day that made them feel rather self conscious and unnatural and he would prefer to bring up a child a little less strictly."[42] Likewise, Melvin Walker, a black father, felt that "children should be taught to confide in their parents" and hoped for a close relationship with his future children.[43] The passing of the era where children were expected to be "seen and not heard" was embraced by many of these potential parents.[44]

⤺

The records outline a range of personal benefits to family membership. By pursuing adoptive and foster parenthood, applicants sought a stronger marital bond, a greater sense of meaning in their lives, companionship, and even an improved demeanor. This dense nexus of emotional promise and personal fulfillment through family living both inspired and pressured people to organize their lives around their families during the postwar period. Its promises of greater happiness and purpose in life made men and women eager to gain these joys for themselves. But it also subtly insisted that one's life was intrinsically less complete, meaningful, and happy if one was not married and raising children. The records suggest that people often identified and connected with relatives, neighbors, and friends through their shared embrace of family ideals, and that those who did not fit its dictates found themselves socially marginalized. Consequently, social belonging itself became increasingly contingent on family membership, and it provided even further motivation for men and women to place their families at the center of their hopes and aspirations.

First and foremost, marriage became essential to one's social status as an adult during the postwar years. Couples married at ever-younger ages in response to social and ideological pressures. As historian Jessica Weiss has pointed out, "Before the war, marriage had signified the end of youth, whereas by 1945 American youth embraced marriage."[45] Early marriage was especially appealing to young people because it conferred adult legitimacy and sanctioned sexual activity. Yet as more chose to marry at younger ages, the very meaning of marriage shifted. Men no longer had to be self-sufficient, and young women increasingly expected to work outside the home before settling down to have children.

No longer requiring adult responsibility but still granting adult status, marriage became a particularly desirable option for young couples. Eugene and Catherine Rothman had married very young because they had wanted the autonomy of adulthood. As Eugene put it, "he married at age 20 and as he looks back, his wife was really a child since she was only 15. They both wanted to be adults but through the years learned to assume adult responsibility." Like many who married young, "marriage was a growing up experience for [the Rothmans] . . . and in the early years of marriage . . . it was stormy, both were young and did not have the maturity they have now." It took several years before "everything seemed to fall into place" for this couple, and Eugene contended that their lives had improved after they had settled into a more mature adulthood by attending church, buying their first home, and giving birth to their first child. He believed "it was very fortunate that they did not have children before this because they were not ready to assume the responsibilities entailed in bringing up a child."[46]

Similarly, Louis and Eleanor Brown, a young black couple, had married when Eleanor was sixteen and Louis nineteen. They had spent their first years of marriage renting a cheap kitchenette so that they would have plenty of money left over for fun. As the social worker describes it after talking with Eleanor, "Anything she wanted, he got for her; they had a good deal of fun going to the beaches; eating hot dogs and chili for dinner rather than having her cook; going to the movies etc." However, after several years they decided "the honeymoon was over" and Eleanor wanted a place of her own. They found an apartment in a building with a number of older tenants and began to lead a much quieter life. As the social worker put it, quoting Louis, "They are often referred to as 'the oldest young people.'"[47] Couples desired and felt pressure to marry young in order to establish their social adulthood—but they could wait a few years before fully embracing adult responsibility. They emphasized to social workers their growing maturity and stability, which were the required attributes for parenthood, but it was marriage that had conferred adult status.

The social pressure to marry, however, also encouraged many women to stay in marriages that did not fulfill their hopes for happiness. As historians Elaine Tyler May and Jessica Weiss have noted, the steady divorce rates of the 1950s differ sharply from the overall growth in divorce rates over the course of the twentieth century. May contends that many postwar couples lowered their expectations when their marriages did not provide the joys and benefits they had hoped for, while Weiss points out that some of the couples that staved off divorce during the 1950s finally parted ways as laws and public ideologies about divorce changed in the 1960s and 1970s.[48]

The experiences of applicants support these claims. Although a number of African American men and women in particular had divorced during the Depression and later remarried, very few couples in the records of any race or class split up during the postwar years. Instead, many chose to stay together despite a less than ideal marital life. One affluent white couple stayed together even after the husband's molestation of a foster child was uncovered, while others fought regularly but viewed it as part of their routine.[49] Similarly, some women were willing to put up with infidelity in exchange for an adequate balance of companionship, reliable financial support, and the social status of marriage. Rose Baker, an African American woman, revealed to her social worker in 1951 that her husband Clarence had had a child with another woman during their marriage, and had been supporting this other woman and her son for years. Clarence had always "given a lot of trouble about women" but Rose "made little or no complaint since foster father provided well for his family and gave her a great deal of his time." Further, "he was always 'discreet with his affairs', and since foster mother wanted to 'hold the home together I made no complaints.'" Rose believed that a husband's affairs were "part 'of a woman's burden', but 'why complain when your husband is good too.'" Rose had not told their daughter about Clarence's affairs because her own father had cheated on her mother, and she was glad she had not known about this until adulthood. But she had also learned from her mother that "men will chase around but if they are good too—forget it." Rose's patience and acceptance were well rewarded, for she believed Clarence was particularly generous with both his time and his luxurious gifts for her because he felt guilty about his extramarital activities. By shifting her expectations to the kinds of rewards and privileges her marriage did provide—and ignoring those it did not—she was able to overlook her husband's unfaithfulness and appreciate the stability and social belonging that came with being part of a family.[50] She also, presumably, hoped to impress upon her social worker that her home was a stable and supportive one, despite her husband's infidelity.

In addition to the pressure to marry and stay together, people also experienced significant social pressure to have children—and childless couples frequently felt marginalized in an increasingly family-centric social world. The pervasiveness and power of the social pressures of family ideology are clearest when one considers those who had difficulty fulfilling its dictates. As Elaine Tyler May puts it in her study of childless Americans, during the postwar period "polls indicated that virtually nobody considered the ideal family size to be no children, and only a tiny minority said that they did not want children themselves."[51] As the baby boom roared on and the number of childless adults dropped, "Childless women and men struggled to find their place in a society that wrapped happiness and meaning around having children."[52] The situation was particularly difficult for infertile couples. As May suggests, "During the years of the baby boom, when couples without children felt the sting of exclusion from the parent-centered culture, their extreme social isolation heightened the private anguish of infertility."[53]

The escalating pressure to have children certainly affected infertile adoptive applicants. These men and women had all envisioned having children as part and parcel of their reasons for getting married, and felt shock and grief when their infertility was identified. Edith Blevins's mother had waited until just before Edith's wedding to tell her that she was infertile because she had been afraid her daughter would close herself off into a "shell" and not date. Although Edith and her husband Jack decided to wed in spite of the news, Jack was not only surprised and but also disappointed "because every man likes to think when he is contemplating marriage [that] children will be the natural result." However, he "was honestly more sorry for his wife [than] he was for himself because she was so broken up about it."[54]

This couple, like nearly all the others who faced infertility, told their social worker that they were happy with their decision to stick together regardless of their infertility, but that the experience did force them to acknowledge that they both had implicitly assumed they would have children after marrying. Leroy Mitchell, an African American man whose wife was infertile, pulled his social worker aside during one interview to explain why they had applied to provide temporary foster care rather than to adopt, since it was clear they both deeply desired the chance to raise a child to adulthood. He told the worker that they believed they had a better chance of being approved to provide foster care rather than adopt because of their small income. He explained that his wife Bernice had already had several miscarriages, adding, "I guess she has had so many disappointments already, that she is scared to death that this will fall through."[55]

Infertile couples often described themselves as more than childless—they were also lacking an essential aspect of personhood. They contended that they had failed to provide a fundamental obligation and expectation of marriage, that of reproduction and the subsequent joy of childrearing. Many felt they had let their partner down when they were found to be infertile, and several suggested that their spouses might have been better off marrying someone else (although their spouses never agreed). Feeling like personal, marital, and social failures, infertile men and women frequently believed themselves to be abnormal, and less of a man or a woman because of their infertility.

The records recount a range of feelings of inadequacy around infertility. Marion Peters, a white woman, explained that she "was brought up and accepted the idea that girls get married and have babies." At first, "she was saddened and in despair because of her inability to have a child." She was also "embarrassed, sometimes even ashamed, wondering if and almost as if she were a depreciated person, but gradually with the help of her husband she came to feel that she wasn't too different from others, it was something that she couldn't control and she accepted her childlessness like she might have any other problems you might have had to face."[56] Lloyd Robbins, who was white, believed that "if he had known he could not have children, he never would have married, because he felt it was depriving . . . [his wife] of motherhood." His wife Ann, however, disagreed and was glad they had wed. She felt "they have a very deep relationship that she feels has only been enhanced by this unfortunate thing."[57] One social worker wrote that her client, Esther Jacobs, "felt she was not fulfilling her duty as a wife and a woman" because she was infertile. She explained, "Having wanted children she was naturally disappointed that she couldn't have any of her own, but even more than that was the feeling that she just wasn't being a good wife." However, Esther had finally gotten over her guilt about her infertility and appreciated that "her husband was able to show her, not only in words that he loves her even if she can't have children of her own."[58] Beatrice Arnold, a black woman who had had a series of miscarriages, found her inability to have a child "traumatic," and felt it was "somewhat a reflection of her inadequacy." She admitted to the social worker that, after her first miscarriage, she had been "feeling sorry for herself and somewhat jealous of women who could have natural children."[59] For their part, social workers recorded these stories and occasionally noted that applicants would need to accept their infertility if they were to fully embrace adoptive and foster parenthood.

Childless applicants also often felt like outsiders in everyday social interactions, and they longed to fit in with their relatives and friends who had children. These couples wished to emulate those they knew who had children, and many had been inspired to apply to adopt because of their experiences being around other families with children. In particular, many couples frequently socialized with adult siblings who had children, and caring for nieces and nephews was usually the most regular close contact childless couples had had with young children. Clara Richards, an African American woman, wanted children in part because all her siblings had children, including her twin sister.[60] Likewise, Andrew and Jane Holmes, a white couple, became convinced they wanted to seriously pursue adoption after caring for Andrew's sister's children.[61] Couples also believed that having children would give them more in common with their adult siblings and relatives. For instance, the Robertses noted that "most of their relatives now have children of their own, and their interests center in their children and their homes." Alfred Roberts "thought it would be nice if he and his wife could have a similar interest in a child of their own, so that they would then have more in common with other members of their family."[62]

This couple also brought up another common theme for childless couples hoping to adopt: the realization that one's parents would not be around forever and the potential loneliness of being childless into later adulthood, which increased couples' desire to create a new generation of the family for themselves. Alfred "commented that his mother-in-law's recent death brought home to him the advantage of having children in the family. He explained this by saying he realized for the first time how alone he and his wife would be when their parents were gone if they had no family of their own."[63] Frank Pike said that "it was a sad prospect to think of becoming old and to have no family."[64] Charlie Frank, an African American man, "hated very much to think of growing older without a child." He also regretted having no one to inherit his and his wife's home, and he hoped to have a child who could benefit from their inheritance.[65]

Likewise, family-oriented holidays such as Thanksgiving and Christmas made people feel even more marginalized within a culture that glorified parenthood and family membership. For example, Nancy Graham, who was white, explained that "with the holidays coming up both she and her husband particularly feel the need for a family. Somehow it seemed to bring things more sharply to focus because families were getting together and were planning for Thanksgiving and Christmas and they were planning with their family too, but their family is a family that they know is not going to be with them too much longer. [Her husband's] father is 75 yrs old and he feels quite healthy and has a good number of yrs ahead of him but his life is waning nonetheless. Her family too are older and somehow she feels that there is no growth and change to look forward to the way there is in a family with children."[66] Louise Howe similarly "remarked that 'it is too lonesome' in a home without children, and added that holidays and other special occasions are always so much more fun if there are children around to enjoy them." She and her husband realized that "'they were not getting any younger' and the sooner they got their family going the better."[67] Clifford and Clara Richards, who were black, had always given each other toys for Christmas as a way to make the holiday seem more fun and meaningful. They explained that their deepest wish was to have a son or daughter to give those toys to instead.[68] These couples saw having children as a way to continue traditions within their own families, and to strengthen family bonds between themselves and with their relatives. Their feelings of sadness from facing these holidays without children of their own demonstrate not only the power of the belief that one could only achieve real happiness and purpose through child-rearing, but also the ways in which that belief also made those who did not fit its dictates feel limited to a social world of aging family members and potential loneliness.

Further, in contrast to the social marginalization of unmarried or childless men and women, those who were able and willing to mold their lives to the dictates of family ideology were rewarded with a variety of social contacts. Family membership drew people into a rich social network of meaningful relationships with relatives, neighbors, and friends—for the same ideological pressures that encouraged people to look primarily for purpose and meaning in family membership also created a bond between those who enacted the normative family models of the day. Embracing family ideology provided postwar men and women with a more extensive familial and social network, making family membership increasingly essential for social belonging.

First and foremost, marriage brought together more than just two individuals—it frequently brought together two family groups. Marriage pulled each spouse into a new network of relatives and potential friends, and as the social pressures for family membership grew, relatives were often eager to welcome new in-laws into the family fold. While certainly some individuals experienced these relationships as an obligation rather than an advantage of marriage, they still emphasized to social workers that they appreciated the companionship they found with their in-laws. At a minimum, applicants believed that they were *supposed* to be grateful for the benefits of extended family relationships, even if they did not always genuinely feel this way.

Working-class whites tended to stay particularly close to their in-laws and extended family members throughout their marriages. As Mirra Komarovsky suggested in her 1962 study of working-class marriages, "there is hardly any function of [blue-collar] family life to which relatives make no contribution." Komarovsky further found that working-class women in particular stayed close to their families, and only 27 percent of their closest friends were not related by blood or marriage.[69]

The case records reveal a similar pattern. Many working-class applicants chose to share their homes with their in-laws for much of their married lives, and even turned to their relatives in times of marital discord. For instance, when Billy and Rita Hawkes, a mechanic and his wife, began arguing in the mid-1940s, both parties retreated to the homes of extended family members. Their social worker had difficulty getting in touch with the couple themselves, but often found herself on the phone with Billy's sister and Rita's mother. Both parties blamed the other's family for being too involved in the marriage and stood up for their own relative's innocence. This couple eventually reconciled, but their families continued to be integral to their marriage.[70] Similarly, in an exceptional example of the close bonds that could form among relatives, Irene and Ronald Lawrence, the young welder and his wife who had met by letter during World War II, saw Irene's twin sister and her husband almost every day. The two couples had married in a joint ceremony and then gone on their honeymoon together. They also worked together on building a garage for the Lawrences' new house, and they frequently babysat their nephew. Ronald explained that the couples were truly friends, and he sincerely liked his in-laws and believed his brother-in-law felt the same way.[71]

African American couples placed similar value on their relationships with their in-laws. Floyd Rivers became very concerned when his wife's mother became ill with arthritis and diabetes. He eventually suggested that they move in with her to help care for her. Floyd and his mother-in-law became "so close that people in church would ask Mrs. R.'s mother, 'How's your son?'" He was devastated when she eventually passed away.[72] Further, crowded conditions in the Black Belt, the experience of migration, and the stresses and strains of discrimination also inspired many black families to form close relationships with in-laws and other kin.

Many middle-class whites also enjoyed close relationships with in-laws. Some spouses formed especially close bonds with their parents-in-law, particularly when their own parents were not around. Barbara Adams's parents had moved away soon after she had married at age twenty, so she had become especially close with her husband's parents because she missed her own. When his mother became gravely ill, Barbara used her skills from her job as a nurse before marriage in order to help care for her mother-in-law at home until she passed away.[73] Similarly, Doris Thomas cultivated a relationship with her in-laws because she had "always been very close to her mother and father, brothers and sisters and she wanted to be a part of her husband's family." While her husband Edward was overseas in the service she had lived with her own parents but had dinner with his one night a week. Soon after his return, Edward's mother became quite ill with cancer and the couple visited her each evening together until she died. Doris "felt that it was sharing experiences like this which brought people very close together."[74]

Like marriage, parenthood also pulled couples into closer relationships with in-laws and parents. Having a child gave a married couple more in common with their own parents while also drawing the entire extended family unit together in their love for the new child. Just as they hoped parenthood would give them more in common with their siblings who had children, many couples could not help but feel proud about making their own parents grandparents. For their part, grandparents were often eager to help welcome a child to the family by knitting snowsuits, sewing clothes, and helping prepare the baby's room. If the older generation lived elsewhere and was unable to come to Chicago soon after the placement, the child's first trip was often to see one or both sets of grandparents. Further, some couples considered requesting a boy rather than a girl because they wanted someone to carry on the family name.[75] As an extension of their love for one another, children were also seen as an extension of the family line.

Marriage and parenthood also brought women and men into new kinds of social contacts with friends and neighbors. For many, the very fact of being married became central to organizing their social activities with other married couples. Although many men and women reported having a peer group of single friends before marriage, once they married they rarely socialized apart from their spouses, and maintained previous friendships only if the friends also married and couples could socialize as a group. Likewise, some couples became very involved with the "young marrieds" clubs at their churches. Others formed bridge clubs with neighboring couples and had a regular weekly or monthly gathering to play cards. Consequently, unmarried individuals not only failed to fully fit in with the expectations and lifestyles of their relatives, they also were often unable to turn to their peers as a source of social support. Further, even when spouses socialized apart in single-sex groups, they still often bonded about their status as husbands or wives or as parents. For instance, the example of Edward Thomas, the young lawyer who was teased by his fellow poker players for being childless, shows not only the ways in which he was socially marginalized for his childlessness, but also the ways in which his marital status at least allowed for some social bonding and inclusion within his peer group.[76]

Having children created even more new opportunities for meeting others, forming friendships, and socializing. Although the nuclear family unit became the center of many couples' activities once they became parents, these families also socialized as a unit with other families. Group picnics with friends or relatives and all the children were a common weekend pastime for many families. Company picnics and carnivals sponsored through a husband's workplace also created opportunities for the whole family to meet and socialize with others. Further, parents were more likely to get involved with the PTA and other activities in which their children participated, such as scouting, where they met other parents and formed friendships.

Women in particular based many friendships around their identity as a mother. Some women who were upset over their childlessness had pulled away from their friends with children, but renewed their friendships once they adopted. Joyce Montgomery, a young white woman, had initially withdrawn from a women's social club where she had many long-standing friends "because when she went most of the women were talking about their children and she felt very much out of things." After adopting, she was eager to rejoin the group and started looking up many old friends. Further, Joyce, like several others in the records, felt that she met more neighbors through her son than she ever would have alone. She was very shy and found it difficult to meet new people on her own—so she appreciated that her son tended to attract attention and bring her into contact with new people. Ethel Banks found it hard to break into a cliquish suburban neighborhood and felt she had made her only acquaintances there through her children. Similarly, Beatrice Arnold, a young African American mother, planned to join a local mothers' club. She had met some of the women in the group, who had told her that "they enjoy the club because they compare notes on children, play a few cards, gossip and the like."[77]

Overall, then, marriage and parenthood provided a platform from which many men and women built relationships with relatives and friends, providing a meaningful source of connection and identification with those around them. Alongside the ideological promises of personal fulfillment and happiness and the social pressures to conform to family ideals, the extensive social and familial networks that emerged from marriage and parenthood reinforced the centrality of the family to organizing men's and women's lives during this period.

∽

For applicants and their social workers, the family was so valuable because it offered a sense of purpose in life. It also provided a meaningful connection with friends, relatives, neighbors, and colleagues. Domestic ideals were social:

they circulated in a wide range of contexts, from urban black ghettos to wealthy white suburbs, and in daily encounters at work and at home. Rather than identifying popular culture or Cold War politics as the most important sites of the ideological production of the family, adoption and foster care records reveal that the importance of the family was produced and reinforced for many ordinary men and women in their everyday lives. A multitude of everyday social interactions reiterated this powerful family ideology, giving momentum to the postwar rise in marriage rates and the baby boom.[78]

The very social pressures that made family membership so essential, however, also made it a site where inequalities were acutely felt. For even as applicants from very different backgrounds espoused a common family ideology, their everyday family lives and labors were in fact quite different. Shared family ideals did not translate into equal opportunities for oneself or one's children, particularly for African American and working-class white applicants. One can begin to get a sense of the inequalities embedded in postwar family life by examining postwar gender roles within the family. As the following two chapters will suggest, family living offered distinct benefits to—and required distinct sacrifices from—men and women. But gender was not the only factor influencing individuals' family responsibilities. Racial and class inequalities also fundamentally shaped men's and women's different gendered obligations to their families, and informed their sense of inclusion in, or exclusion from, the promises of America's postwar prosperity.

PART II

The Obligations of Domesticity

FOUR

Providing Anxiety and Optimism
Domestic Masculinity

In his study of a working-class suburb in the late 1950s, sociologist Bennett Berger considered a group of white California autoworkers who uprooted their lives in an urban, industrial area to follow their plant to a nearby suburban community. Seeking to understand the social and political meaning of the vast growth of suburban tract housing at the time, Berger wanted to know if these working-class families who bought in the new suburban developments close to their plant would acquire "middle-class behavior, beliefs, and aspirations as a result of the suburbanization process."[1] He concluded, in part, that although working-class men saw their transition to suburban home ownership as making them "better off" and allowing for more comfortable lives, they were not in fact "*socially* mobile." In their own assessment, these men had "achieved a standard of living beyond which most of them do not expect to rise, and, perhaps, beyond which they feel they have no further *right* to aspire."[2]

Berger described the situation from the point of view of a white, suburban working-class man as such: "The [suburban workingman's] rationale probably goes something like this: 'Here I am the son of a sharecropper with a ninth grade education and no really salable skills, and look at me: I'm paying off a nice new home, have a good car (often two), my kids and my wife are decently dressed; she has a washing machine, I have some power tools; what more do I have a right to expect?'"[3] Berger's account is notable for its distinctly gendered and domestic cast: the prototypical husband in his study assessed his progress in terms of the suburban home and the consumer items he could provide for his family, not his rise through the ranks at the plant. The suburban workingman judged his place in society in relation to his role as a family provider and breadwinner, not as a worker—and his verdict was that his place in society was adequate but stagnant.

Berger's suburban workingmen were adjusting to a postwar America that saw itself as a place of abundance, promise, and increasing affluence. As memories of the Great Depression and wartime sacrifices lingered, changes in policy, politics, and American business culture created a new social landscape for both work and consumption. Rising incomes, alongside the growing consumer economy, made more goods and services available to more people, and thereby elided some traditional markers of social status and class distinction. The GI Bill also opened up new opportunities for home ownership, job training, education, and small business loans to working-class veterans for whom they would have been out of reach before, while big labor succeeded in winning significant wage increases for blue-collar workers.

As these workingmen well knew, however, America after World War II was not solely a land of growing opportunity. The blue-collar sector experienced some stress, as employers responded to higher wages and growing union power by moving blue-collar jobs to less unionized areas in the Sun Belt and, as the trend intensified in later decades, outside the borders of the United States. Likewise, media such as *Life* magazine depicted workers and unions as part of mainstream American life but in ways that often hid the ongoing deprivations workers faced. Meanwhile, white-collar work expanded as the ranks of corporate middle management grew, but the increase in low-status office jobs also meant that white-collar work no longer always garnered the status and income it had before. In addition, although some African Americans managed to capitalize on wartime wage increases to enjoy some degree of greater affluence and opportunity, racial inequality and persistent discrimination in employment and education still plagued the black community in the postwar years.[4]

Alongside these changes in the organization of social class and the ongoing importance of racial hierarchies, ordinary Americans were also coping with changing gender ideologies about men's and women's roles within marriage. Growing numbers of married women were working outside of the home, while prescriptive literature and magazines also urged men to spend more leisure time with their families and to be more involved in their children's lives. Although husbands and wives continued to divide family labor along gendered lines of a male provider and female nurturer, they increasingly accepted and even encouraged greater overlap in their shared duties and obligations to their families.[5]

Just as Berger's working-class subjects struggled to come to terms with the changes taking place in their work and family lives, social workers and applicants wrestled with the changing postwar landscape of gender, race, and class in the case records. They offered conflicting visions for men's and women's domestic roles and responsibilities, and differing assessments of the importance of race and class in shaping those roles. In this chapter and the next, I explore workers' and applicants' conceptions of men's and then women's gendered responsibilities to their families. I suggest that gendered roles within the family varied in important ways along lines of race and class. Although men were universally considered breadwinners and women caregivers and nurturers,

Chicago was a racially and economically divided city, and these roles took on distinct contours in different class and racial locations. They gave intense personal significance to social and racial privileges and inequalities.

Social workers and applicants agreed that the husband and father should be the family's primary breadwinner. Men were expected to support their families financially and to earn an income large enough to provide comfortable housing, nutritious food, decent clothing, and educational opportunities for their children. But workers and applicants differed in their understanding of the role breadwinning played in the daily life of the family. When evaluating applicants, social workers' psychodynamic orientation encouraged them to focus on men's personalities and ability to be steadfast family leaders. As long as they believed a man would support his family reliably, social workers gave relatively little interpretive weight to his work life. Instead, they sought to understand a man's potential emotional role within the family based on his character and personality. Would he be supportive and confident? Passive and insecure? Dictatorial and harsh? Workers' ideal husband and father was reliable, engaged, kind, and self-assured as he led his dependents through the complicated emotional terrain of daily family living.

Much of the evidence presented by applicants, however, emphasized the emotional and practical impact of male breadwinning on family interactions. Applicants highlighted the interconnectedness of men's economic and emotional responsibilities to their families, as well as the inescapable impact of race and class on their efforts to support and care for their families. The records of white middle-class applicants emphasized ambitious male providership and upward mobility with few other domestic responsibilities. In contrast, the applications of working-class white families noted husbands' limited room for economic advancement and instead prioritized men's involvement with their families. Those of African American families highlighted the impact of persistent racism in employment on family well-being, and they emphasized men's racial pride alongside their strong determination to be reliable providers in the face of adversity. Breadwinning made unique demands on men—and their families—along lines of race and class, with important ramifications for the emotional tenor of everyday family life and men's participation in day-to-day family affairs. Shared family ideals led to starkly different family experiences, which in turn informed men's assessment of the privileges and inequalities that shaped their own and their children's lives.

The case records reveal the many ways domestic masculinity was embedded in the larger changes taking place in postwar America, as some men found new opportunities for upward mobility while others encountered growing economic dislocation and systematic discrimination. Applicants' stories go beyond the usual depictions of postwar masculinity as described in films and literature at the time: that American men were trapped in a world of gray flannel suits and organization men, becoming alienated by and often angry about the emptiness of their lives and labors. Instead, the records depict men who navigated work and family to find meaning and purpose in a rapidly changing postwar society, even as many of them also encountered frustration in their attempts to get ahead.

↩

For social workers, gender was an important aspect of their evaluations of applicants. Their chief message to potential fathers was clear: their primary job was to support the family financially. Men's breadwinning was so assumed as to be nearly taken for granted by workers. A man did not have to earn a sizable income in order for his home to be approved, but social workers did need to be convinced that he could adequately provide for the household and be able to offer educational opportunities for his offspring.

Despite the centrality of breadwinning to men's role within the family, workers gave relatively little consideration to this responsibility once they were certain a man would be able to meet their expectations. Instead, reflecting their interest in the influence of the unconscious on family dynamics, workers zeroed in on men's character and personality. They paid particular attention to the emotional contributions each man would presumably make to daily family living. They looked for clues to a man's future family behavior in his upbringing, his attitudes and preferences, and his fears and anxieties. Workers had a specific definition of well-adjusted domestic masculinity: ideally, men were to be authoritative without being authoritarian, and to bring a sense of easy confidence to family relationships.[6]

Workers approved most heartily of men they believed would be stable breadwinners while also adding masculine competence to the emotional life of the family. They looked for evidence of these qualities throughout the home study. Workers scrutinized men's style of dress and posture in order to assess their self-confidence during interviews. Frederick Richardson, a young African American applicant, was described by the worker as "well dressed in a business suit, gives the appearance of being clean cut, quite masculine." She continued, "He seemed to sit in a casual position, without really lounging but you have the feeling that he is making himself at home." After the interview was over, the worker noted in the "impressions" section of the record that, based on his performance in the interview, he seemed a good candidate for adoptive fatherhood. She noted, "Mr. R seems to have considerable self-esteem, poise, and basically seems forthright and open."[7] Even the subtlest aspects of men's posture and dress carried important meaning for workers.

Social workers also praised men who seemed comfortable and knowledgeable in their roles as husbands and fathers. A worker made favorable comments about Vernon Whitaker, "a very proud father," who, when applying to adopt a second child, expressed a relaxed and confident attitude toward childrearing. While his wife Emma was very worried about following the advice of experts, Vernon did not express "the same over-concern that his wife showed about doing what the book said." Instead, the social worker noted, "There seems to be much natural warmth and feeling toward his boy and spontaneous enthusiasm in talking about him."[8] Vernon exemplified good fatherhood to his social worker: he was eager and engaged in the application process and in parenting, while still bringing a sense of ease and self-assurance to daily domestic affairs.

Once a child was placed in the home, fathers were to model men's roles and responsibilities for their children. For those with daughters, men were to embody the ideal of protective masculine stability—to be the kind of man they hoped their little girls would someday marry. For those with sons, they were to engage their boys in sports and masculine activities around the house. For example, when evaluating the Booth family for a second child, the worker noted approvingly that Albert Booth had appropriately modeled manly behavior for his son. The boy was "beginning to identify with his father in definite masculine play activity like ball, being interested in his father's carpentry work, putting up a storm window."[9]

Involving a child in putting up storm windows was about more than simply making sure boys learned all the skills they needed to be good husbands; it was also about instilling in them proper masculine interests and qualities. Workers' attentiveness to male applicants' masculinity was integral to their interest in developing these same qualities in the boys they placed in these men's homes. Little boys, even male infants, were approvingly described as husky, masculine, and sturdy, and workers fretted about the gender identity of boys who seemed overly sensitive.[10] While workers were very sympathetic with the emotional lives of young children and expected even the toughest of boys to express fear, anxiety, and vulnerability, they sought potential fathers who they believed could help boys learn to manage these feelings in an appropriately masculine manner.

In practice, however, most male applicants could not live up to these many expectations. Many men were quite nervous during the home study and did not handle the situation with the confidence that workers desired. Generally, these lapses in confidence did not doom a couple's application. A man's anxiety about the process was sometimes interpreted by workers as simply an indication of his strong desire for a child. Workers also considered nervousness due to inexperience with children a common and quite natural aspect of masculinity, since men (unlike their wives) were not assumed to have had much opportunity for contact with young children prior to becoming parents themselves. As long as a man seemed to genuinely care about his family, to be secure in his relationships, and to be a reliable provider, he was still deemed an adequate potential father who would likely relax into his relationship with his child over time. For example, Glenn Emerson asked his social worker when applying for a child "if he would have to 'change pants'. When W[orker] replied 'of course' he was quite amused at himself in this situation." The worker was not troubled that Glenn clearly had no experience—or interest—in changing diapers. After the child had been in the home almost a year, she noted that he had become an excellent father and wrote that "there is every indication that he will continue to be a very active, good father person to this masculine little boy." She added playfully, "His reluctance to 'change pants' has been amusing in the real life situation as it was when he discussed the possibilities during the study."[11]

Throughout the home study, men also presented considerable evidence that complicated workers' neat view of domestic masculine competence by explaining the persistent impact of their income-earning work on their sense of themselves and their role in day-to-day family affairs. Instead of seeing breadwinning as separate from men's personalities and emotional engagement with their families, male applicants and their spouses emphasized the centrality of men's duties as breadwinners to daily family life. They suggested that it was this responsibility that shaped nearly all of men's relationships with their family members—including their involvement in childrearing and the everyday emotional life of the household.

In particular, applicants highlighted the many ways differences of race and class played an important role in the emotional, physical, and economic resources that men brought to marriage and parenthood. Diverse men had different access to various types of jobs, and their experiences with their work shaped their expectations about the quantity and quality of time they would spend with their families, as well as their hopes and dreams for their children. Historian Robert Griswold has shown that, despite the ongoing importance of breadwinning to American fatherhood, the meaning of even this most ubiquitous male responsibility has varied across time, as well as across social and racial locations. He explains that in the twentieth century, "Breadwinning did not mean the same thing to an immigrant working class plagued by un- and underemployment, periodic layoffs, and pitifully low wages as it did to financially secure Anglo middle-class fathers working in the businesses and professions." The meaning of breadwinning was also different to "black men coping with the crop-lien system and Jim Crow or to the thousands of black men who moved to Northern cities to be greeted with persistent discrimination, segregation, and menial work." Griswold concludes, "Even their anxieties were different."[12]

The case records similarly suggest that the worries, pleasures, and demands of breadwinning did indeed differ in important ways along lines of race and class. Social workers certainly recognized some of the barriers men of color faced as breadwinners, and they sought to encourage diverse families to apply by publicizing their acceptance of diverse living situations. They made an especially concerted effort to recruit more African American applicants by running articles and advertisements in the black press and distributing literature emphasizing that one did not need a large income or to own one's own home in order to become an adoptive or foster parent.[13] Yet despite their emphasis on racial and class differences in their recruiting and evaluation materials, they did not link these inequalities with men's daily emotional involvement with the family. Applicants themselves, however, presented the many ways that men's roles as husbands and fathers were shaped by the important social and economic inequalities of the world outside the household.

⇐⟩

For white applicants, class was a key axis of difference in men's expectations for fatherhood. Potential fathers' domestic obligations, as well as the satisfactions they expected from their home lives, depended greatly on their income and type of work. Social workers and applicants portrayed middle-class white men as committed and ambitious family providers. The privileges of education, race, heterosexuality, and gender made an array of high-paying and high-status jobs open to these men, and interactions with their families revolved around their responsibility to be dependable providers who enjoyed success at work. Further, because so much of these men's talent and effort went into successful breadwinning, their families sought to provide in exchange a comfortable, pleasurable home life that did not make too many demands on their time and energies. These men's emotional participation in the household revolved primarily around leisure activities that would provide a respite from the demands of work.[14]

The case records from working-class white male applicants, however, echoed Bennett Berger's findings in his study of workingmen: these men and their families appreciated their accomplishments, but also reckoned with their limitations as breadwinners. Lacking the education and skills to move into white-collar employment, these men prioritized jobs that avoided some of the more dangerous or stressful aspects of blue-collar work. They also recognized that there was limited room for career advancement within the blue-collar sector, and they therefore placed greater value on emotional involvement with their families and personal contentment.[15]

Applications from middle-class white families linked masculine competence with advancing one's career. These men repeatedly described themselves as ambitious and energetic breadwinners. For example, Vernon Whitaker had worked his way up from being a trainee to an executive at a major retailer. When applying to adopt his first child, he told the worker that he enjoyed the challenge of rising up the ranks at his company, explaining that "he was finally in almost the spot he wanted to be," but he hoped to rise a bit further. His interactions with his supervisors reinforced the importance of career advancement to his sense of pride and promise: "He told . . . [the social worker] with some pleasure that one day his boss came over to him & asked him what his goal at . . . [the company] is & he was free enough to tell him I want your job. This personnel manager is getting toward retirement age & Mr. W & he get along very well so that he is quite hopeful that some day he will be able to achieve that."[16] As he tried to impress the social worker with his suitability for fatherhood, Vernon emphasized his professional ambition as one of his chief qualifications.

White middle-class wives reinforced the importance of their husbands' professional success by repeatedly expressing to social workers that their husbands were exceptionally hardworking and successful. When Gordon Russell, a traveling salesman, began joking about what he would do when he retired, his wife Vivian "replied with a little smile 'you'll never retire—you like the business world too well!'" The social worker noted that Gordon "looked a little sheepish at this, and then said actually he thought it was better for a man to continue working as long as he could, because he felt this helped keep a person young. He had known some men who retired before they really were at the point of becoming inactive, and he had noticed how they began to 'go down hill just as soon as they stopped working.'" Vivian "agreed seriously, and added that she thought it didn't hurt a person to keep on working as long as he was able and really wanted to."[17] Like Vivian and Gordon, both men and women often equated masculine satisfaction and pleasure with hard work and fulfilling the role of successful provider.

Career achievements frequently came at the expense of family time, however. Business trips and company functions compromised men's ability to spend quality time with their wives and children. Men justified the costs to their families by pointing out their successful breadwinning and explained to social workers that they felt good about their hard work because it allowed them to provide well for their families. For instance, Philip Cross, who directed an insurance agency, described himself to the social worker "as a person who loves to work, works perhaps more than he has to or more than he should but he does it not for material advantage but because he enjoys it and feels that he is providing well for his family."[18] Even as Philip disavowed an interest in "material advantage," he acknowledged his sizable earnings—over $25,000 a year in 1958—by explaining that the real benefit of his income went to his family. Though working so hard limited a man's emotional participation in daily family living, it offered other family benefits.

Despite the demands of breadwinning, middle-class men told their social workers that they expected to be involved in their family's activities. But their expectations were limited, and they planned to engage with their families primarily in ways that would affirm their status as family providers rather than require their energy and attention. Embracing a family ideal that promised personal wholeness and emotional intimacy through the family, many middle-class white men expressed a sense of entitlement to the attention and warmth of family members when they were at home. For example, Calvin Mott, an accountant, expected, as the provider, to receive the benefits of his wife's attention when he got home each evening. His wife Eva told their social worker that "he becomes irritated if he sees her doing any housework. He says he wants her companionship when he is there."[19]

These men also considered themselves involved fathers and expected the attention and respect of their children—but their involvement mostly consisted of a brief period of play when daddy came home from work rather than a sustained engagement in a child's daily care. Wives, in fact, spent considerable energy crafting opportunities for their husbands to spend relaxing, pleasurable time with their children at home. Wives discussed their strategies with social workers, describing how they would go into the kitchen to wash dishes after dinner to give their husbands and children some alone time together reading the funnies, or how they would suggest tasks like raking leaves that fathers and children could do together on weekends.[20] Their efforts reinforced their husbands' expectations that home should be an enjoyable break from their work lives because they encouraged men to participate in their children's lives as pals, rather than insisting they help with their children's daily care and discipline. James Hurley, a teacher, and his wife Helen combined "playtime" with their daughter each day at five o'clock with a cocktail hour. As they explained it, "they gave their daughter their complete attention at this time and she likes having them watch her do things and to play with her." However, the cocktails mattered too, the social worker noted: "Sometimes she will climb onto their laps and try to jump and then they have cautioned her not to spill their drinks."[21] Involved middle-class fatherhood was carefully designed to complement a father's busy work schedule and his need to relax at home.

Middle-class men's supportive home lives and their career success were linked, and a man's failure as a breadwinner could easily seep into his sense of self and lead to the deterioration of family relationships. Wilma and Peter Laumann, who had adopted in the mid-1940s, returned to the agency in 1953 seeking advice because Peter and the children constantly fought. Wilma felt her husband's insecurities caused him to hold the children to too-high standards and made him quick to accuse them of being disrespectful. When meeting with a social worker, Peter explained that he "wishes that he were able to live in isolation without the pressures of 'keeping up with the Joneses, etc.'" He was an immigrant to the United States and was a skilled artisan who taught at a university, but he felt he had never managed to get ahead as he wished. He was "concerned about his height, his slight accent, and what he calls 'false standards' in the world." He also worried "about the physical weakening of middle age" and felt "that he has no mastery at home." His feelings of inadequacy as a provider affected his relationship with his family, ruining his ability to be a fun, caring father, and further exacerbating his feelings of emasculation.[22]

Like Peter, many working-class men also encountered diminished prospects for career advancement and larger incomes, which affected their participation in the daily life of the family. During the postwar period, Chicago faced a slow economic and industrial decline. Though the city was home to a number of manufacturing and transportation concerns, the city's wartime industrial boom began to wane as more regional businesses moved their factories and corporate headquarters to the city's suburbs or left the Midwest entirely for the Sun Belt.[23] Even as manufacturing jobs remained plentiful in the 1940s and 1950s, the city's workingmen reckoned with gradually shrinking opportunities for blue-collar labor.

Working-class men reported to their social workers very different conditions of work than their middle-class counterparts. These men struggled with the inconvenient hours, physical dangers, and bodily exhaustion of many blue-collar jobs. They described working long hours, and often nights, in jobs they found tiring and stressful. They did not enjoy their work, were often unable to brag about their abilities as providers, and were also unable to spend quality time with their families. For instance, Joseph Levitt, whose job at a steel mill was quite dangerous to himself and others, went to bed early every night so as to be alert and energetic enough to perform his job.[24] Likewise, men who drove milk trucks often worked six or seven days a week, and had to be up before dawn for work.[25] Further, men who worked nights usually slept all day, leaving their wives struggling to keep their own and their children's activities quiet during the day.

Many of these men also reported vulnerability in terms of their health and safety at work, but they persevered in their commitment to provide for their families. Robert Pearson, who had been injured at work in a machine shop, felt he could not stay out of work for as long as the employer's doctors required, so he quit and began working elsewhere before he was fully recovered.[26] Likewise, Chester Taylor, a cabinetmaker, began having profuse nosebleeds from breathing in Formica dust at work. His doctor suggested he stop this kind of work, but his family needed the money so he kept it up, even adding side projects for extra income during his days off.[27]

The physical demands and long hours of blue-collar work shaped working-class men's definition of a desirable job, encouraging them to focus on working conditions, shorter hours, and less physical and emotional stress when choosing employment. These aspects of work were more important to many men than a higher income. For example, Samuel Pappas, a factory worker, talked about his short career as an assistant foreman, which had taught him why the foreman was always so "crabby"—he was apparently under "tremendous nervous strain." He described the family-oriented concerns his colleagues brought to the workplace and how stressful it was to weigh their competing demands: "the men would beg the foreman to give them more work as they needed a high paycheck this week for their family or for one thing or another, and how even the receptionist and the girls in the office were afraid of being laid off should there not be enough work, and everyone was looking to the foreman to straighten the whole thing out. Should a man be sick and off for a couple of days it would be that much less work to be distributed, and the whole air of tension in the plant was one that fell completely on the shoulders of the foreman." Samuel was offered a permanent promotion to the foreman position but he turned it down and asked to be returned to the factory line. He explained that "he does not feel that any job is that important—that is [to] sacrifice your personal happiness and put that much uncomfortableness upon yourself. . . . He felt that his total happiness was more important than a few extra dollars."[28]

In his 1955 study of autoworkers, sociologist Ely Chinoy discovered similar sentiments among blue-collar workers in an unnamed auto plant. Chinoy found that, among unskilled workers, the most-sought positions in the plant entailed a "regularity of employment and the relative absence of physical and psychological strain." Because work in the auto industry was often cyclical and very physically demanding, men deemed jobs that offered a steady paycheck and some degree of control over their own work more desirable than higher-paying jobs that were less reliable, required significant physical repetition, or entailed too much pressure or stress.[29]

These men's limited aspirations for career advancement were integral to their blue-collar status, emerging "from a process in which hope and desire come to terms with the realities of working-class life."[30] Chinoy noted that as men moved through their careers, many recalled initially believing that their work in the plant would be temporary, and they therefore had little reason to put their energy into climbing the occupational ladder. But opportunities to leave the plant, or even rise within its ranks, were few and far between for men with limited skills and families to support, so many ended up prioritizing a steady paycheck and reasonably comfortable job while abandoning other ambitions.[31] Breadwinning was central to their identities, and it defined their responsibility to their families, but climbing a career ladder, or even making more money, were less important than finding a job that was stable and safe.

The records reveal that working-class wives played a crucial role in reinforcing a working-class masculinity that valued personal safety and control over one's work over greater pay. Women recognized that there were negative family implications when a husband had a stressful or unpleasant job. Herman Jennings explained that during the war he had "given up the job on which he had worked for a number of years and on which he had been promoted to a job of foreman or its equivalent in responsibility." He had been losing sleep and becoming quite irritable with his family: "He worried about the responsibility and his inability to satisfy his superiors under the difficulties that existed in the war conditions, mainly shortage of materials and shortage of help." His wife Julia believed he had become "so anxious" that she had "feared a breakdown." After moving to a new job with less responsibility, he began to relax again—much to the relief of the entire family.[32] Realizing that husbands with jobs they enjoyed made more reliable providers and engaged spouses, wives tended to support their husbands' quests for work that was more fulfilling.

Working-class wives also repeatedly made financial and personal sacrifices in order to help their husbands find more stable and fulfilling work. Elaine Benson encouraged her husband to attend night school training to become a machinist because she felt "that it is important that he learn and work at what interests him, rather than just make a living at any thing just for the sake of earning a living."[33] Similarly, the Rushing family decided that it was worth it to go into debt so Dale Rushing could leave farming, which he hated, in order to train to be an electrician. The Rushings moved from their Iowa farm to Chicago, Dale went to school, and within two years they had paid off their debts and he had moved up the ranks to foreman.[34] Likewise, Louise Howe understood her husband's reluctance to give up a low-paying warehouse job for a more lucrative factory job because of his distaste for the constant pressure and scrutiny of factory work. She explained that "she did not mind a factory job herself, but it was different with her because she knew she would not be working all her life, whereas her husband would be and therefore he ought to have a job which he liked."[35] These women emphasized their husbands' happiness rather than their potential to get ahead financially by pursuing new jobs that were more challenging.

Further, both husbands and wives knew that the one real avenue many unskilled workers had for promotion—becoming foreman—could be a mixed blessing. Although Dale Rushing enjoyed his job as a foreman, many men—as the mention of the "crabby" foreman above suggests—believed that being a foreman was not necessarily a cushy or comfortable job. It was, in fact, a uniquely stressful position because it often meant overseeing men with whom one had once identified, but without the power to make decisions about plant management.[36] Many men were also too old or too poorly educated to ever receive a promotion to foreman anyway, and even when they did, a foreman was unlikely to ever rise into the ranks of senior management. C. Wright Mills suggested that a promotion to foreman was the end of the line for most unskilled workers because they lacked a college education. Even worse, the worker-foreman was also left socially isolated in the workplace: "No longer belonging to labor, not 'one of the boys in the union,' the foreman is not secure in management either, not of it socially and educationally."[37]

Consequently, even as many men enjoyed the rising incomes available to working-class whites during this period, they also understood their limited potential for further economic upward mobility and instead focused on job stability and better working conditions. As breadwinners facing limited options, they also prioritized spending time with their families. Just as Berger's suburban workingmen tended to evaluate their economic progress in relation to their domestic lives rather than their upward mobility within the plant, applicants also looked to their quality of life outside the plant, rather than their unfulfilling jobs within it, for their sense of well-being. They therefore looked to their home lives to provide the sense of purpose they often lacked at work.[38]

In contrast to the conventional wisdom about the middle-class bias of family togetherness, these men's working-class status made them particularly eager to spend time at home and to focus on the quality of their domestic lives.[39] Blue-collar workers were the most likely in my sample to turn down or adjust their jobs so that they would have more time and energy for their families, and their wives supported these choices. For instance, several men who usually worked days were offered promotions to foreman or supervisor on the night shift. These men resigned and changed jobs instead because, as Kathleen Maxwell, whose husband Martin had turned down such a job, put it: working nights "would spoil the family life which the group enjoys now."[40] Likewise, Bill Underwood briefly accepted an evening shift, and his wife Audrey described how she kept their daughter up until eleven each evening to see him when he came home because otherwise they would not have any time together as a family. They were very relieved when the company believed Bill's threat to quit unless he was put on the day shift and changed his schedule.[41] Though these men might have hoped to please social workers by emphasizing how much they valued their family lives, it seems just as likely they would have felt pressure to emphasize their success as stable, upwardly mobile providers, which was the path most of their white-collar counterparts took. It therefore seems probable that they were being truthful in their accounts of thinking about their employment in relation to the amount of time they had left over to spend with their families.

Working-class men also looked to their families to give meaning to their work in ways that went beyond income. For instance, William Cash—who, after stints as a worker in a steel mill and as a laundry truck driver, eventually found a job he enjoyed as a bakery driver—could not help but explain his personal satisfaction in relation to his family. He particularly enjoyed sharing his job with his young son: his son wanted "to drive a truck just like his dad's which he calls a 'hot bread truck.'" He also recounted that he had "taken . . . [his son]

down to the place on a couple of occasions and how thrilled . . . [the child] has been and that often times when he gets home . . . [he] inquires about what has happened in the business."[42] Likewise, men enjoyed recognition from their employers that they could share with their families. Harvey Fulton looked forward to an upcoming banquet honoring his twenty-five years at the company, which his whole family would attend. Arnold Hampton showed off the gifts he had received from the company for ten and then twenty years on the job.[43]

These men defined themselves by their breadwinning, but—knowing the unlikelihood of ever climbing a career ladder—they made the most of their existing class position and focused on their family's quality of life rather than further advancement. According to his social worker in 1952, Harry Pruitt, who was a union representative and a foreman at the construction division of a major company, "thinks people are happier if they associate with others of their own kind rather than moving into the [wealthy, suburban] North Shore or Oak Park set. Some of those North Shore and Oak Park people are real nice too but just have different living situations that are unrealistic for laboring people."[44] Embracing a more "realistic" understanding of their potential earnings, and likely enjoying increasing working-class incomes already, these men fulfilled their obligations as providers while also fulfilling the growing emphasis on fathers spending quality time with their families.

These men's experiences suggest that even as working-class incomes rose during the postwar period, there were important continuities from prewar family patterns. In his evaluation of the centrality of immigration and kinship in working-class politics, historian John Bodnar argues "that for the rank and file in the twentieth century labor issues were essentially family issues." Bodnar contends that family welfare dominated workers' concerns into the 1930s, encouraging Depression-era workers to fight for "job security more than social equality . . . because equality and even mobility were largely personal goals while job security was the key to family sustenance."[45] This link between the family and the workplace lasted into the postwar years as blue-collar workers continued to prioritize family welfare while also taking on an additional commitment to spending quality time with their loved ones.

Spending time with one's children and sharing work accomplishments with them, however, did not necessarily mean that working-class white men were deeply involved with their children's physical care. These men professed a greater commitment to emotional engagement with daily family life than their middle-class counterparts and were eager to play with their children, but they shared a reluctance to take on the dirtier and less entertaining aspects of their children's daily care. Although Kathleen Maxwell, a working-class foster mother, "spoke with pride that she 'got the biggest kick' in watching her husband change diapers" for the infant in their care, most wives assumed certain limitations in men's involvement with their children.[46] In fact, both male and female white working-class applicants often articulated a belief that it was the husband's duty to provide while his wife stayed home to care for the family. For instance, when asked about his wife's good qualities, Wayne Ford, a machinist, noted her domestic skills rather than her winning personality: "He considers . . . [her] a good wife and mother and likes her cooking, the way she keeps house, etc. He feels that she keeps things neat and comfortable without being too particular so that they can be comfortable in the house."[47] Marilyn Lewis explained that her husband seemed "quite contented to let . . . [her] assume the major responsibility in rearing the girls, although, of course, he is the one who supplies the funds for the undertaking."[48]

White men across class also tended to leave discipline to their wives, although there is limited information on discipline in the files because many case records ended when the children were too young to require much discipline. When applying, both working- and middle-class couples often told their social workers that they intended to always agree on discipline in front of their children, and to support each other's punishments. Once a child was placed, however, things were more complicated. A few couples put fathers in charge of discipline. But most files that describe the enforcement of discipline report that fathers were away at work most of the time, leaving their wives to take care of most disciplinary matters. Jay Clifton, a well-off white doctor, captured the phenomenon well when he explained to his worker: "you know how fathers are. They are away from the child all day long and when they come home, they don't want to scold [the] child." Jay's wife Rosalie smiled when he made this comment, and he added that his wife did not think he was strict enough with their young son.[49] Other families left the most serious discipline to fathers, while mothers handled most of the daily punishments. For instance, Dora Kern did the majority of the punishing in their working-class household, but she sometimes resorted "to threats of 'wait until your father gets home.'"[50]

Applicants' class status did, however, shape their ideas about what kinds of careers their children should pursue. Middle-class white men's focus on successful breadwinning shaped their ambitions for their children—and particularly their sons. (Their hopes for their daughters will be examined in the following chapter.) These men saw bright futures for their sons, and believed their skills as providers would help get them off on the right start. They hoped to raise sons who fulfilled the same qualities of middle-class masculinity to which their fathers also aspired: they dreamed their sons would grow into men who were successful, responsible, hardworking, and ambitious, and who advanced in their chosen careers.

Middle-class white couples first and foremost claimed that they wanted their sons to follow their dreams into careers they truly enjoyed, regardless of their status or pay. Yet at the same time they also hoped their sons would be particularly successful at their chosen careers by embracing their fathers' sense of dedication and drive. For example, Maxine West, whose husband was a vice president at his company, explained that she would prefer that her child attend college, but "if a son of theirs had mechanical aptitude, she would want him to be an airplane mechanic rather than work in the local garage. She thinks a youngster develops his own interests and she wouldn't want a child to do the easiest thing. She thought she would encourage a child to go in more for the better trades."[51] Alfred Roberts, who was an executive at his company, presented a similar set of expectations for a son: "he would like to give a child of his the opportunity of going to college if he wanted to, but he would certainly not feel that this was absolutely necessary. He added that if his child wished to be a plumber, he would feel this was alright. He said with a smile that he might want his child to own a plumbing business of his own, but otherwise he would feel that the child's career or occupation should depend entirely upon his own choice."[52]

These couples were among those in my sample who were most familiar with postwar parenting advice that advocated choice and self-expression for children. So perhaps, while speaking to social workers, they felt pressured to downplay their hopes for economic and academic achievement and instead acknowledged childrearing ideologies that promoted self-direction and personal fulfillment.[53] They also might have hoped to appear that they would support a child who was quite different from themselves and who desired to pursue a career that differed from that of the father. Even if that was the case, however, these middle-class fathers had also embraced a similar set of expectations for themselves—for they too had pursued their own sense of personal pride and fulfillment in their work—and they hoped their sons would find the same kind of joy and sense of masculine achievement through their occupations.

Middle-class men also saw their own rising affluence as fundamental to their sons' future success. For example, Oscar Davis, a printer who had quit school as a young man against his family's wishes, told his social worker that he felt he had "'muffed' his early life as far as education was concerned . . . 'You know, how young boys are.'" When Oscar got out on his own he realized he needed more education, and struggled to go to night school while working. He found the experience trying due to his busy schedule and because it was difficult to return to school after so many years away. But he successfully moved to management at his firm, making over $5,000 a year in 1947, and had bought a home in an affluent suburb by the late 1940s. He hoped his own son would not follow his example and would stay in school, adding that "a small community like [the one where they lived], where his son will grow up with his friends and a regular school life would be the accepted thing, would be more conducive to what might be called a normal way of living these days."[54] Oscar had clear aspirations for his son to be firmly ensconced in the upwardly mobile middle class, and he hoped an affluent suburban childhood would provide his son with the background needed for greater success. Embracing an ideology of middle-class masculinity that prized career success, middle-class families sought to raise boys who would find happiness and accomplishment through their careers—and presumably the same comforts and privileges their fathers enjoyed when at home.

Most working-class families also desired that their sons have successful and meaningful careers. Many hoped they could provide their sons with college, which would allow them to pursue a white-collar occupation, but they were also supportive of their sons moving into blue-collar careers. Perhaps rising union wages, as well as the advancement they themselves had seen in their work after additional GI Bill training, made blue-collar men aware of the benefits of blue-collar work. Perhaps they instead simply doubted that their sons would be able to advance much further than they themselves had. In either case, however, they envisioned their sons with decently comfortable financial lives. Howard Allen, a metal spinner who loved his work and had not attended college himself, felt with his wife that "college was a nice thing and a desirable achievement. If . . . [their son] so wishes to go to college and is capable of doing college work they are very willing and eager for him to do so." However, if the child was unable or uninterested in going to college, Allen felt "that Industry has [its] satisfactions and if the child is not interested in education beyond the high school that there are good training schools available and that a comfortable living and a satisfying life can be had in Industry."[55]

In many cases, the conditions of work were more important to working-class men's wishes for their sons' careers than money. Just as their own sense of masculine accomplishment relied on finding comfortable jobs with adequate salaries and time left over for their families, these men envisioned a similar future for their sons. Two different motormen on the city's streetcars both hoped their sons would have better jobs than their own, and they both explained their hopes in terms of the conditions of work itself. To Allen Dixon, the social worker "remarked at some point that she supposed . . . [his son] wanted to be a streetcar motorman like his father. Mr. D replied laughingly, 'I'll break his arm if he does.' He said he'd like . . . [his son] to be a dentist and added that he thought this was such a nice job, the dentist making his own hours." Although Dixon clearly hoped for upward mobility for his son, he still articulated his wish in terms of his son's quality of life on and off the job and in terms of setting his own hours rather than in terms of income.[56]

Meanwhile, Roland Martin, another motorman, who had himself always wanted to be a doctor but had left school when his family could not afford his education, had a startlingly similar response, according to his social worker: "I said his son might want to be a streetcar motorman and his quick response was that he sure would talk him out of that. It would be all right for him to be a streetcar conductor I learned, but Mr. M. just can't understand why anybody would want to be a motorman. Being a conductor you see all sorts of people, being a motorman you only have trucks in front of you and something always getting in your way. He thinks the nervous strain of a motorman job is a hard one. You can only work a certain number of hours etc." Although Roland went on to admit that it would be nice if his son became a doctor, his main concern was that his son's work was pleasant.[57]

These fathers certainly wished for professional careers for their sons, but they remained cautious about their sons' prospects and placed most emphasis on them finding stable, reasonably interesting work. It is hard to know if they were simply pessimistic about their sons' potential for upward mobility, or if they were instead invoking deeply held values about the relationship between labor and quality of life. At the very least, however, men who had assessed the limits of their own class mobility and chosen to focus on their families hoped they would be able to provide enough opportunity to allow for a comfortable living—if not greater affluence—among the next generation.[58]

Although social workers' evaluations of applicants suggested a separation between men's breadwinning and emotional roles in their families, applicants themselves posited a much tighter relationship between these two obligations. White men described a variety of ways their work lives—be they particularly successful or particularly trying—intersected with their duties as fathers and the rewards they sought from their home lives. They overwhelmingly expected their families to be a fulfilling respite from work, which would provide relaxation and enjoyment while not making many demands on their time and energy. They also hoped that their sons would, in many respects, emulate or improve upon their father's experiences in terms of the satisfactions they could expect from their employment.

Despite white male applicants' shared belief in the importance of breadwinning for shaping the pleasures and rewards of family living, class played a crucial role in shaping these men's engagement in their families' day-to-day lives. Many white-collar workers put in long hours at the office in the hopes of achieving upward mobility, and they described their rising incomes as their most important obligation to their families. Their professional accomplishments went hand-in-hand with their often-limited emotional participation in everyday family affairs. In contrast, blue-collar workers suggested that they had limited room for job advancement and instead described their health, safety, personal contentment, and time and energy to spend with loved ones as their essential contribution to family welfare. These men offered a secure—if modest—income, a reliable (and, it was hoped, healthy) breadwinner, and an involved participant in the less-taxing activities of the household. For white men, their role in the daily texture of the family depended greatly on their class and occupational status.

꙳

The case records of African American families offered sharp contrast to those of both working- and middle-class whites. Across class, black men confronted a very different set of circumstances than white men when looking for work and providing for their families. Facing discrimination in hiring and wages, they almost always made less money at less secure and more physically demanding jobs than whites.[59] Black potential fathers, therefore, described everyday lives infused with the limitations and frustrations of racial inequality, and their gendered family obligations revolved primarily around coping with the injustice of discrimination.

Black men described a determination to be reliable providers in the face of adversity, linking their efforts to be adequate breadwinners to their hopes that their children would have more opportunities and more comfortable lives. They described a deep sense of racial pride, pointing out repeatedly to social workers the inequity of pervasive racial discrimination. They hoped their hard work would allow the next generation to both overcome the impact of racism themselves and to help others by engaging in racial uplift. Yet their labors were bittersweet, for their struggles to support their families often failed to lead to financial stability, and they cost men valuable time with their wives and children. Black men's commitment to support and provide for their families made the consequences of inequality all the more heart-wrenching.

Most of the black families in my sample were better off than many black families at the time but worse off than many whites. They embodied the paradox in postwar black communities of people who were simultaneously working- and middle-class. In terms of national trends for work and income, they were solidly blue collar and working class, but within the black community they held respectable jobs, were comparatively financially secure, and had access to middle-class privileges like home ownership. Only eight out of seventy-seven African American men in my sample held white-collar jobs: one dentist, one optometrist, two lawyers, one salesman, one pharmacist, one executive of his own company (a training school that grew out of his work in a skilled trade), and one retired minister (who also did blue-collar work while preaching). Otherwise, these men held a variety of skilled and unskilled blue-collar jobs. There were skilled factory workers such as welders and pipe fitters, as well as a few skilled tradesmen such as a tailor and a shoe repairman who had been trained at Tuskegee. Among those who were less skilled but still had reliable and adequate incomes, a number worked for the post office as custodians, laborers, or letter carriers. A number of earlier applicants worked on railroads as porters or cooks. About 20 percent of my African American male sample held an unskilled occupation such as laborer or janitor.[60]

These men, regardless of their education, type of work, or class status, faced repeated encounters with racial discrimination in the labor market. Even a white-collar job did not ensure an upwardly mobile career for black men. For example, the career of Lester Reed, the optometrist, had started out quite promising—he was one of only a few African Americans in his class to be making it in his own private practice. Despite this success, he was constantly networking to find more patients and always felt a bit insecure about his business. Although Lester hoped that in time his practice would become firmly established, his wife—who also worked outside the home—wished he would abandon optometry and go to dental school, believing it would provide a more stable and lucrative career.[61] Similarly, Walter Bennett, a lawyer, had trouble getting his practice off the ground, and the family repeatedly pursued other investments as a way to secure more income. Eventually his wife, Viola, who was a nurse, went back to work three nights a week to help boost the family's finances.[62] These families, though at the top of the professional ladder, relied on two incomes to maintain their class status.

In the records, black men identified the systemic inequality of racism as the root of the problem for their failures—for they encountered a myriad of forces arrayed against them. Many had been forced to repeatedly abandon career goals and dreams due to racism, and they described to their social workers their regret that they only worked to earn a living and support their families rather than pursuing interesting and fulfilling careers. Leon Nelson had always wanted to be a doctor and had been pre-med in college, but he had abandoned his medical aspirations for a degree in education because he could not afford more training. Upon graduating and coming to Chicago during the Depression, he had found that he could not earn a reasonable wage teaching because his southern agricultural alma mater was unaccredited. Leon instead took a series of unskilled jobs and then, feeling he lacked other options, enlisted in the navy early in the war. He found the navy a nice change of pace because it took advantage of his skills and intelligence. He was assigned to the hospital at a naval training base where he gave immunizations and provided doctors with information on new patients. He boasted to his social worker that he had even stitched up an injured man's head, and was very proud of the responsibilities with which he had been entrusted. His military service was the closest he had ever come to being a doctor.

When Nelson left the service, he found a job in a company's laboratory. His social worker recorded, "He enjoyed this job because of associations with professional people. Though his job was janitorial he was allowed to help with some of the experiments and had quite a lot of satisfaction in this." He was so inspired by this experience that "he then decided to go into the school of pharmacy as this was nearer to medicine and did not require as long a time. He worked part time at the post office, received the G.I. Bill and attended school." Unfortunately, Thomas could not manage the schedule because "the hours were quite long from 10 in the morning until 12 at night. He found this rather tiring, and his school work was failing. . . . He finally discontinued in school and has been working at the post office for the past 10 years."[63] Feeling stuck in his menial job as a night laborer for the post office, he described his job as monotonous, saying "that it was not professional. To him it was a matter of security and receiving a regular paycheck." The social worker explained: "He worked at night for two reasons. They gave additional compensations for working at night, in addition there was a larger demand for men to work then as more mail came in at night." Overall, "He seemed to feel that it was simply a matter of earning a living."[64] Nelson still wished he could become a doctor, but his professional ambitions were frustrated by his inability to afford a quality education. He instead settled for an unskilled, tedious job to earn enough money to support his family. His demoralization about his unfulfilling work and his inability to get ahead pervaded his application to adopt.

Men also frequently described incidents of racism in the workplace. Veterans of World War II were particularly infuriated by these experiences. Many black men discovered that their wartime skills and training were trumped by the color of their skin. Roger Gates, who had built airplanes during the war, used his GI Bill benefits to continue his training. He then applied for a job at an airline and was told over the phone to come in first thing for an interview by someone who "practically assured him a job." The social worker noted, "He said with a wry grin that when he got to the employment office, I should have been there to see the run around which he got. Official came to him with many apologies stating that they had no opening although felt that they could give him a job 'washing planes.'" Roger instead found work as a welder, and then, getting as close as he could to his real dream of being a doctor, went into business with his pharmacist brother running a drugstore. He worked eight to ten hours every day welding, came home for dinner, and then worked at the store each evening until eleven.[65]

Black men knew what they were up against in the labor market, and this had a profound impact on their approach to their jobs, their expectations about their treatment in the workplace, and the kinds of satisfactions they looked to work to provide.[66] Unlike middle-class white men, who focused on career success, or working-class white men, who focused on the quality of their working conditions and their ability to share their time with their families, African American men instead focused on their income as the marker of good breadwinning and successful masculinity. When hoping to impress their social workers, they proudly presented earning a consistent income as evidence of their skill and ingenuity in coping with racial inequality in order to support their families. For example, Stanley Douglas, who had founded a successful business and training school with his brother, boasted about his income, revealing how his financial success increased his feelings of self-worth. Douglas was unusual in his climb from his blue-collar job in a skilled trade to a white-collar position managing his own thriving business. He went so far as to tell his social worker at the end of an interview that he needed to go make a phone call to his tailor. He planned to "pick up a suit at [the] tailor's, [and] wear it right out to the meeting that night"—something he had wanted to do since childhood. He explained with a grin that "at last [he was] going to have [the] opportunity of wearing new clothes 'right out of the store.'"[67]

African American wives, who also often worked to help support the family, applauded their husbands' efforts to earn a stable income in the face of adversity. They embraced a definition of domestic masculinity that prized perseverance. During one interview, as welder Frederick Richardson described the varieties of odd jobs he had done since leaving school to work at age eleven, his wife Agnes "interjected . . . with a great deal of praise for her husband because of his resourcefulness in finding work and never being without a job even when other people couldn't find it. She point[ed] out that 'no job was beneath him.'" Consequently, she boasted, the family had "never really wanted for anything they needed." Their social worker elaborated in 1958 that "since 1951 [Frederick] . . . has been working with the same firm as a welder and he thinks it gives him an excellent living, pays much better than the average job."[68] For both of the Richardsons, their pride resided primarily in Frederick's skill at breadwinning rather than in the job itself.

African American men also carefully strategized in order to maximize their incomes—often at the cost of having time to spend with their families. Charles Clark, a railroad employee, had a long work history, starting when he was a child in the South. His social worker wrote, "Even today he finds his greatest recreation in work much preferring to be busy than attending sports, picture shows and social gatherings." His commitment to work was not simply recreational, however. In addition to supporting his wife and three children, Clark also lived next door to his parents and, as the oldest of twelve children, helped support his parents and younger siblings who still lived at home. According to his social worker, "He realizes that by working as hard as he does he deprives his wife and his family of so much of his companionship." However, "now that they have their own home and their financial circumstances are not so strained, he will devote more of his time to his home as he will not feel so obligated to work."[69]

Although black men's obligations as breadwinners in discriminatory labor markets frequently limited their ability to be involved in the day-to-day affairs of their families, their families still gave meaning and purpose to their labors. In particular, men described their efforts as a way to redress their families' unequal racial status and as a means to provide better circumstances for the next generation. Elmer Arnold, a black postal clerk, worked long hours at two jobs in order to support his family. He worked nights at the post office, leaving each day between 4:00 and 5:30 p.m. and getting home at 3:30 a.m. at the earliest. He slept for a few hours and then got up to do another part-time job in the neighborhood. His social worker recorded his explanation of his schedule in 1955: "When Mr. A was growing up he did not have much. . . . They did not starve and yet they did not have much." Consequently, "he wants to work hard and provide comfort and opportunities for his own family."[70]

Elmer Arnold's wife, Beatrice, supported his work schedule and his hopes for his family. She told her social worker, "He is one who likes to make big plans, like building a house within the next year or two or buying another car very soon." He tended "to think . . . grandly and expansively without the means" to carry out his plans, but she was not bothered by his impracticality, because she had "discovered that he likes to have those dreams and it is part of his being a family man responsible for his family." When it came to their everyday choices, he "usually simmers down and goes right along with what is realistic."[71] As described by both men and women, black masculinity revolved around men's ambitions to provide adequately for their families in the face of discrimination— even if it meant long hours at work and unachievable goals.

Black men's busy work schedules and obligations as breadwinners also meant that they did not necessarily anticipate being deeply engaged with their children. Like most white men in my sample, they mostly envisioned their time with their children as recreational. For instance, a social worker described Melvin Walker's beliefs "that it is commonly accepted that the woman should be charged with the responsibility of rearing a child, but that he feels the father had a responsibility to give some physical care and attention to a child, too." He thought his participation, however, would mostly consist of playing with his child each evening in addition to providing for it financially. He felt that he probably would not want to wake up if the child cried in the middle of the night and would leave nighttime duties to his wife.[72] Another social worker recorded Benjamin and Nellie Williams's discussion of what would happen if their foster child cried in the middle of the night: "She was saying that she would get up and look after the baby and that he wouldn't even wake up. And he remarked that after all he goes out and works. They were joking about the fact that her work is never done and he is able to come home and sit down and relax." Benjamin felt that he would be involved with the child, but he said that "most of the job of infant care will be up to his wife" and that he would only "help out where needed." The Williamses already had several young children of their own, with whom their father participated in playtime when he could—but "he help[ed] with feeding and bathing . . . only if he ha[d] to." Although he was one of the only black men in the records who mentioned having any time to "sit down and relax," Benjamin's assumption, like that of many others, was that his breadwinning exempted him from extensive childrearing duties at home.[73]

African American fathers, like their white counterparts, also left most of the discipline to their wives, although information in the records on discipline is sparse. For example, Nelson Sutton, a painter, mostly teased and played with his foster daughters, doing little to punish or train them. His social worker wrote that "his role was one of the jolly parent who exercised little discipline, leaving most of this to the F[oster] M[other] since all of the children were girls."[74] Other men stepped in as needed to enact more serious discipline but left the bulk of the work to their wives. Ervin Harris, a cobbler, settled accounts weekly with his three sons on what he called "strap day," when he would exact punishment for each child's misdeeds for the week. His wife Della kept track of the children's infractions, and the number and severity of whippings on "strap day" depended on their gravity.[75]

Black fathers' recreational activities with their children, meanwhile, often focused on providing their sons with the masculine strength and courage to persevere in a world where the odds were stacked against them. While they often doted on their daughters, these men, like their social workers, believed that boys needed masculine role models and strove to instill a sense of masculine self-worth in their sons. Joe Bates, a prospective foster father, hoped that he and his wife could care for adolescent boys because he felt he could provide "adult guidance, and encouragement." Although Bates was busy at his post office job, he wanted "a boy old enough to take with him to ball games, 'father and son' dinners at the Y., and who could share his interest to a greater extent than could a smaller child." The pre-adoptive foster care program did not work with adolescents, so the Bateses eventually took in and later adopted a preschooler, who was younger than Joe had anticipated, but he did his best to spend time with the child. He encouraged the boy to help him wash the car, go on shopping errands and trips to the barbershop, and to talk "man-to-man with him." But he was doing more than simply enjoying quality time with his son. Like several other involved African American fathers in my records, he was also trying to prevent the boy from becoming effeminate from too much time spent with his mother. Joe "want[ed] the child to grow up as what he calls a normal healthy boy which means getting into fights, getting dirty and tearing his clothing." As the social worker put it, "he feels foster mother wants a 'Little Lord Fontleroy' (foster father's terms) and he does not agree that this will make for good development."[76]

Similarly, Vincent Jackson played roughly with his toddler foster son and began teaching him how to box. Although the social worker worried that his style of play was aggressive and frightening for the child, Jackson explained that "he wanted to be sure that F[oster] M[other] 'doesn't make a sissy out of him.'"[77]

These men also hoped to provide their sons with more schooling than they themselves had had because, as Curtis Sanders's social worker wrote, "he felt that nowadays there was very little future for a man without some formal education."[78] Likewise, the men who had had the worst experiences in their jobs most wanted their sons to reach the upper echelons of education and success. For instance, Kenneth Hanks, who tended a furnace at a factory, told his social worker that he worked very hard and "would be sorry if [a] youngster wanted to go into the same kind of work." Instead, he hoped his child would be a "preacher, lawyer, or doctor."[79]

As we will see, many black families put more resources into educating girls than boys. It was presumed that boys would be able to find some kind of work even if they did not have much training or education—and many black men's experiences with racism suggested that being highly skilled or educated was not a surefire way to get a better job in any case. Families hoped their sons would find meaningful careers but believed black boys would be able to find some way to make a living as long as they were willing to work hard. They instead focused on instilling in their sons masculine courage and pride, which were deemed the more necessary traits for black male advancement. As Floyd Rivers put it, when it came to their future prospects, "girls can be made, boys make themselves."[80]

More than anything, African American families assessed the limits on their own social and class mobility, and they hoped that their children, regardless of gender, would be able to safely navigate the future and eventually break through the barriers of racial discrimination. Historically, there were a number of ways black parents tried to accomplish this task. Historian Jennifer Ritterhouse, in her study of children in the Jim Crow South, suggests that southern black parents in the first decades of the twentieth century faced a particularly challenging parental duty: they had to provide their children with enough information about the unwritten rules of racism to help them survive, while also instilling in them a sense of racial and personal pride. Black parents taught their children about the injustice of racism and the importance of personal respectability, while also making sure that they understood the importance to their personal safety of obeying Jim Crow.[81] Likewise, sociologist Ralph LaRossa argues in his study of fatherhood after World War II that teaching one's children about race and racism remained among the most difficult tasks for black parents in later decades. LaRossa suggests that some chose to ignore or evade their children's questions about race, in the hopes of shielding them from the realities of racism, which they feared might have diminished their children's hopes and ambitions.

Others actively discouraged civil rights activism among their children in an effort to protect their safety and welfare, while others still chose to encourage their offspring, both young and old, to challenge racism by joining the civil rights movement.[82]

In the case records, black applicants maintained that providing their children with the means to overcome the limitations of racism was integral to their parental responsibilities. Those applicants who had migrated from the South to the North were pleased that they had been able to offer their children the greater opportunities available to them in the North, despite the racism they continued to encounter. Sidney Humphreys, who spoke with his social worker at length about "the situation of the Negro people as far as housing and jobs were concerned," said that "he enjoyed Chicago so much more than the South for the acceptance which he has been receiving on his job and in the community." Moreover, "He was happy he was able to bring his children here to enjoy the advantages which he never had."[83] By coming north, many black couples felt that they had already made crucial strides toward providing the next generation with greater opportunity.[84]

Besides working to make sure that their children would be both personally and financially more successful than they themselves had been, applicants also hoped that their children would help uplift their race. A number of black parents expressed the sentiment that they wished their children to "lift as they climbed," and help out others as they advanced themselves. For example, Earl and Gladys Bond had taken on the role of community leaders in their deteriorating West Side neighborhood. Seeing themselves as models of success, they hoped that their children would take advantage of what they provided and go further. Earl Bond, wrote the social worker, "thoroughly enjoyed hearing success stories of people who have risen from humble beginnings and 'made something of themselves.'" The worker continued, "Both Mr. and Mrs. B . . . [cited] examples of famous people such as George Washington Carver and also acquaintances of theirs." The social worker noted that the Bonds believed that individual character was crucial to both personal success and community uplift: "Both Mr. and Mrs. B decided that they admired people who bettered themselves and at the same time did not lose sight of the fact that they had a duty to society to help others. In contrast they knew young people who had come from fairly prosperous families and to have been given much by those families who had turned out quite the opposite." The couple held "that something was in the individual, each person having a varying capacity for achievement and constructive living both as an individual and a member of the community. . . . Mrs. B thought it was just a matter of being given opportunities and making the most of them with a determination to be a worthwhile member of society. Mr. B concurred in this." Although they focused on personal attributes rather than structural inequality, this couple firmly hoped that their children would make good use of the advantages they had been given to be personally successful as well as helpful to the community.[85]

Overall, black couples pointed to the inequity of pervasive racial discrimination, which profoundly shaped their work and family lives. They emphasized the strength and determination required for black men to support their families against the odds. They also noted the frequent sacrifices their families had to make in terms of quality time spent together. As black couples coped with men's difficulty providing for their families in the face of discrimination, they saw in their children the potential to contest and combat racial inequality. During the decade that black Chicago mourned the death of Emmett Till and eagerly followed the emerging southern civil rights movement, African American men also assessed their racial status through their efforts to provide for their families and saw the family as one avenue for pursuing racial uplift.

∽

In conclusion, domestic masculinity encompassed a range of expectations and obligations. Workers and diverse applicants agreed that men's primary responsibility to their families was breadwinning, and that men should otherwise do their best to be involved in the everyday affairs of their wives and children, but they offered differing pictures of how these two aspects of a man's role in his family were related. Workers' psychodynamic orientation encouraged them to understand men's personalities and emotional lives primarily through the lens of psychology rather than in relation to the social and structural conditions of their lives. Applicants, meanwhile, made the case that a man's emotional role in the family was inextricable from his role as breadwinner. Men and women described the significant impact of work on a man's family and his own self-esteem. Workplace accomplishments and disappointments shaped a husband's mood and informed his sense of purpose and pride as a provider. Likewise, his job made demands on his time and energy that frequently limited his ability to engage in the everyday life of the family.

Applicants' accounts of the obligations of husbands and fathers highlight the fact that breadwinning did not happen in a vacuum. The workplace was where many men encountered both the privileges and deep inequalities of race, education, and class background. These social and structural inequalities carried extra weight because they were inextricable from men's emotional and financial commitments to their families.

The very centrality and importance of the family in men's daily lives made it a particularly emotionally charged site, where experiences of both inequality and privilege were acutely felt. For some, being family providers fed their sense of confidence, affluence, and faith in future prosperity. For others, the task of supporting the family created at best a sense of cautious optimism, or at worst a pervasive anxiety about their ability to adequately provide for their children's futures. Consequently, family ideals that were largely shared across lines of race and class also informed divergent worldviews among diverse men: they created very different family patterns and expectations, and they inspired opposing interpretations about the promise that America held for its citizens.

Nurturing Frustration and Entitlement
Domestic Femininity

In her 1963 critique of postwar domesticity, *The Feminine Mystique*, Betty Friedan memorably described the era's idealized portrayal of the ordinary housewife in magazines and on television: "Millions of women lived their lives in the image of those pretty pictures of the American suburban housewife, kissing their husbands goodbye in front of the picture window, depositing their stationwagonsful of children at school, and smiling as they ran the new electric waxer over the spotless kitchen floor. . . . Their only dream was to be perfect wives and mothers; their highest ambition to have fine children and a beautiful house, their only fight to get and keep their husbands. They had no thought for the unfeminine problems of the world outside the home; they wanted the men to make the major decisions. They gloried in their role as women, and wrote proudly on the census blank: 'Occupation: housewife.'"[1] Friedan argued, however, that reality often failed to live up to this romanticized depiction. She suggested that many housewives felt empty, unfulfilled, dissatisfied, and even desperate. Experiencing "the problem that has no name," these women blamed themselves and believed that there was something psychologically wrong with any woman who felt unhappy with what was supposed to be every woman's dream and destiny. Friedan blamed instead the unattainable fantasy of domestic bliss, positing more stimulating work for women and truer equality between the sexes—in both the workplace and the home—as the solution to women's malaise.

Friedan's analysis resonated with many at the time. On the one hand, she captured the pronatalism of postwar America, with its promises of happiness to women who became wives and mothers. As we have already seen, ordinary men and women from diverse backgrounds did indeed embrace the nuclear family as a key source of fulfillment and meaning in their lives. They ascribed many personal and social benefits to family living at the time, and they reiterated the importance of the family as they moved through their daily lives. On the other hand, Friedan also drew attention to many women's underlying dissatisfactions with housewifery. Rather than domestic bliss, many women encountered boredom, isolation, and a persistent feeling that their hard work went unnoticed. By naming the "feminine mystique" and highlighting the many shortcomings of housewifery, Friedan made sense of the negative feelings many women experienced while seeking happiness through marriage and motherhood.[2]

Yet, as a number of scholars have pointed out, Friedan's text failed to recognize some of the important changes already occurring in American society. Although Friedan described the 1950s as a particularly stifling and repressive era for American women, significant shifts in gender relations within marriage were already well underway prior to the publication of *The Feminine Mystique*. Jessica Weiss, in her study of middle-class white families during this period, emphasizes the innovations this generation of couples brought to their married lives. Through their youthful marriages and large families, they often made marriage and parenthood more egalitarian as they struggled with the demands of supporting and raising children while still so young themselves. The growing importance of family "togetherness" and, as the last chapter demonstrated, many men's efforts to combine breadwinning with at least some participation in the daily lives of their families also changed the gender dynamics of marriage—though the contours of this change depended greatly on the family's race and class.[3]

There were also important shifts already occurring in women's paid employment. Though many women had been pushed out of the labor force at the end of World War II, the 1950s witnessed a growing number of women returning to paid jobs. The rates of white married women's labor force participation rose particularly significantly during these years, going from 12.5 percent in 1940 to 20.7 percent in 1950 and to 29.8 percent in 1960. More women worked outside the home before having children and were more likely to return to the workplace at some point later in their marriages once their children were older.[4]

Friedan also overlooked mixed messages in the media about women's options at the time. Historian Joanne Meyerowitz has demonstrated in her study of postwar journalism about women that, in contrast to Friedan's claims, there were in fact a range of portrayals of women's lives and labors in the popular press during the postwar period. Motherhood and housewifery were not the only acceptable options for women presented in the media.[5] Similarly, Eva Moskowitz shows in her study of postwar women's magazines that women's discontent with domesticity was a frequent topic, expanded upon with an array of quizzes, articles, and images that asked readers to consider their own feelings about caring for the home and family. Readers were well aware of the problems of being a full-time housewife, and many even expressed fatigue with the subject.[6]

Noting these trends, historians have suggested that *The Feminine Mystique* garnered so much attention not because its call for women's employment and equality were so groundbreaking, but because, as Meyerowitz puts it, "it reworked themes already rooted in the mass culture."[7] The benefits of women's paid work and the inadequacies of housewifery were already familiar issues for many women before Friedan's identification of the "feminine mystique." Friedan's work was popular not, as she claimed, because she had named heretofore-unknown problems with domesticity. Instead, her work resonated with women because she managed to succinctly capture and explicate ideas that many women had considered but had not necessarily assembled into a cohesive critique.[8]

The case records of the Illinois Children's Home and Aid Society reveal that diverse women were indeed well aware of a variety of options for paid and unpaid work, and they ascribed benefits and drawbacks to each option. Social workers, as working women themselves, understood the joys of paid work and the occasional monotony of housework, particularly for women without the joyful distraction of a child in the home. But they believed that successful motherhood required that a woman put her family's needs first by devoting her full time and energy to the household. While paid work outside the home could be satisfying—perhaps more satisfying than housewifery—it had a circumscribed time and place in a woman's life: it was to be done prior to having children or after those children were grown. Working while mothering young children was acceptable only if it was necessary to the family's financial survival and was therefore part of a woman's caretaking duties.

Applicants, meanwhile, largely agreed with social workers' ideas about femininity and women's work. They remained committed to the feminine mystique's promises and felt obligated to serve as the family's primary caretaker and nurturer. But many also noted the many shortcomings of domesticity in their daily lives, emphasizing the deprivations of full-time housewifery and the benefits of paid employment or other meaningful work. Even as they sought to best serve their families' needs, applicants described self-consciously crafting a space for personal autonomy and fulfillment through jobs and other activities. These diverse women were not consumed by an all-encompassing domestic ideology. Instead, they used the resources available to them to pursue pleasure and purpose from their domestic labor, and to circumvent some of the difficulties they faced when that labor was not so rewarding.

Further, race and class proved central to their efforts. The case records reveal that there was not one model of postwar domesticity, nor one model of contentment or discontentment with paid and unpaid work. Instead, there were many, and they were intimately tied to women's material circumstances and to shifting expectations about women's labor. Friedan's "problem that has no name" in fact had many names—and many solutions—in the 1940s and 1950s. Women's family labor, and women's assessments of their family lives, were not simply a response to restrictive postwar gender roles but were instead inextricable from larger social and structural inequalities outside the household.

᷍

Social workers were strongly committed to a very conventional definition of femininity when evaluating applicants. Influenced by their psychodynamic training, workers looked for applicants who were, in their eyes, maturely adjusted to their feminine role. Although they recognized that many women, themselves included, worked for pay outside the home and saw a number of potentially healthy satisfactions to paid work, they believed that the best mothers desired motherhood above all else and completely devoted themselves to housewifery. Workers therefore scrutinized applicants to be sure they would have the dedication and temperament to persevere in their nurturing responsibilities. They looked for female applicants who would be willing to take on the bulk of nurturing and care work within the family without complaint, which required both toleration for domestic tasks and a genuinely warm—and perhaps a bit selfless—personality.[9]

Workers used a series of measures to judge female applicants' potential for motherliness. A woman's physical appearance was among workers' first clues as to her proper femininity. Workers took pains to describe each woman's dress, gestures, and physical features. Women were often described as feminine, dainty, attractive, soft-spoken, and pleasant. But appearances could be misleading. Jennie Westin welcomed the social worker to her home wearing no makeup, "blue denim overalls, a white crew-neck sweater, heavy wool socks, and heavy shoes." Though the worker was initially put off by her sense of style, Jennie's wholesomeness eventually won the social worker over to the femininity beneath her unconventional dress: "Although she is dressed in masculine attire, she seems to be a feminine person and has warmth."[10] For social workers, kindness, generosity, and warmth signaled authentic femininity, and were the most desirable traits for future mothers.

Among applicants who were unable to have children, a woman's attitude toward her own or her husband's infertility was also a common litmus test for workers seeking to evaluate an applicant's true inclination for nurturing. Assuming that adoption was always the second choice for couples wanting children, workers routinely asked applicants to describe their feelings about their infertility in order to ascertain their psychological readiness to accept an adopted child.[11] This line of questioning was also useful for workers seeking to understand a woman's inherent motherliness. Ideally, a woman who was infertile had accepted the situation with grace, expressing a strong desire to nurture those around her rather than anger or grief. A woman's overall inclination to take care of those around her was to be the driving force behind her application to adopt.

A proper affection for housework also inspired the approval of social workers. They wrote very favorably about women who were good at and enjoyed domestic tasks. When evaluating the Holts for a second child, a social worker noted, "Mrs. H is quite domestic and apparently bakes and sews a great deal and takes pride in these feminine pursuits. She said she had made the curtains and I was impressed with the number of plants and the cooking regimen and she seemed quite content and happy in the home."[12] Likewise, after interviewing Margaret Wilson, the worker decided that "Mrs. W has accepted her feminine role in terms of an interest in cooking and sewing, takes a great deal of pride in her home."[13] Homes themselves were often described as "feminine" because they reflected the taste and handiwork—including homemade curtains, doilies, and bedspreads—of diligent housewives. Workers also hoped women would pass these traits on to the girls in their care. When evaluating the placement of a child with the Jacobs family, the worker recorded that the little girl "is beginning to make feminine identification with her M[other]. She likes to putter in the kitchen, wants to help her M[other] with the dishes, asks to help make the beds and dust."[14] As the family's primary caregiver, a woman was to enjoy putting her energy into her home and to teach her daughter(s) to do likewise.

Women's paid work outside the home, however, created considerable anxiety for social workers. Reflecting rising rates of women's paid employment during this period, many female applicants had worked or were currently working outside the home for pay when they applied. Social workers' greatest challenge when evaluating these women was to make sense of their attitudes toward paid work. Women who had long given up their jobs, perhaps when they married or when they became interested in trying to have a baby, easily impressed social workers with their commitment to their appropriate feminine role in the family. It was women who worked outside the home even while pursuing motherhood that raised red flags. Were these women more fulfilled by working than by domestic duties, making them undesirable adoptive or foster mothers? Were they simply working to help pass the time until they were able to fulfill their true calling and become mothers? Or were they providing important financial assistance to their families, making their work an appropriately selfless, feminine act? Teasing out the real meaning that paid work played in a woman's life was crucial to workers' assessment of her suitability for adoptive or foster motherhood.

Workers generally encouraged working women to quit their jobs during the home study, before a child was placed. Believing infants and young children needed the full-time care and attention of a mother, they were reluctant to place children in households where both spouses had paid jobs outside the home. Further, workers considered women's attitudes toward quitting work as evidence of their readiness for motherhood. A willingness to give up a paid job served as proof that a woman was indeed psychologically ready to commit herself to full-time nurturing, while any signs of reluctance suggested to social workers that a woman was perhaps ambivalent about devoting herself to the welfare of a child over her own enjoyment. Quitting one's job demonstrated one's sincere commitment to being a mother by acknowledging that a child would be more fulfilling than a job.

Of course, workers' concern about whether or not a woman would be willing to quit her job tacitly acknowledged that many women enjoyed paid work more than they enjoyed being housewives. Social workers were themselves working women, and they easily understood the joys and benefits of a job.[15] Although they presumed that well-adjusted women would take pride in "feminine pursuits" like cleaning and cooking, workers admitted to the potential loneliness and monotony of housewifery, especially for childless women. They accepted a woman's paid work as a particularly appropriate response to childlessness—as long as she worked only to fill the time she would otherwise be stuck at home alone and as long as she eagerly quit work at the first prospect of motherhood.

Social workers' interest in women quitting their jobs prior to the placement of a child also tacitly acknowledged that staying home all day would require a period of adjustment for working women. As historian Barbara Melosh points out, workers admitted not only the potential attractions of work for women (and the potential dissatisfactions of staying home all day), but also the possible discomforts of being financially dependent on one's husband.[16] Workers sought to evaluate how formerly working women coped with leaving their jobs in order to better ascertain their mothering potential: did they become restless and unhappy, or did they adapt to their new circumstances with ease? That a woman might quit her job only to find staying home unpalatable was a real possibility for social workers. They wanted applicants to take a trial run at housewifery prior to placing a child in the home in order to make sure they would be able to handle it.

Further, even though social workers urged women to stay home full time, many families relied on the incomes of working wives, and workers accepted that some women simply could not quit their jobs. Although social workers worried about these women's true intentions, they also recognized that some working-class women and most African American women provided crucial financial assistance to their families. As long as these families made arrangements for adequate child care, and as long as they could demonstrate the financial need for two incomes, these applicants would be approved if they met the agency's other requirements.

Social workers encountered daily the changing landscape of women's familial obligations during the postwar period. Workers believed that, whenever possible, young children were best served by mothers who devoted themselves to caring full time for the household. Yet, even as authorities committed to conventional gender roles in the family, social workers recognized the many pleasures of paid employment and the potential difficulties of housewifery. They struggled in their evaluations to make sense of applicants' growing commitment to paid employment alongside their deep interest in becoming adoptive or foster mothers, and they discovered that it was not always easy to extrapolate the implications of a woman's paid work for her femininity or family life.

〜

Among white women, class was a crucial axis of difference in terms of their attitudes toward and experiences of domesticity, just as it was for their husbands. Women's expectations for and feelings about their domestic duties depended largely on the material circumstances that shaped their daily lives and labors. White middle-class women described in the records a sense of satisfaction and optimism about the work they did on behalf of their families. They embraced the promises of the feminine mystique, and they expected to find fulfillment and pleasure in caring for and nurturing their families.

Middle-class affluence facilitated the contentment these women found in their domestic pursuits. They enjoyed comfortable homes, labor-saving consumer appliances, and, in contrast to families with fewer resources, time to focus on themselves and their children rather than making ends meet. At the same time, however, a number also described some benefits to paid employment, such as social contacts and a sense of professional competence. Though they generally chose homemaking over paid jobs, white middle-class women enjoyed class and race privileges that allowed them greater choices and opportunities about their daily lives and labors than women with fewer means at their disposal.[17]

White working-class women faced a very different set of circumstances than did their middle-class counterparts. Although these women expressed a similarly strong dedication to caring for their families, they expressed considerably more discontent about their lives. The records depict working-class wives who defined themselves by their many efforts to nurture and sustain the family even when finances were tight, a task which often required taking on unrewarding low-status jobs in addition to managing a number of cost-saving measures within the household. Rather than choice and opportunity, these women encountered much more limited options for pursuing personal happiness and satisfaction in both their paid and unpaid labor. They often lacked autonomy and felt hemmed in by poor housing, meager family budgets, and unfulfilling work. Stifled as much by the material circumstances of their lives as by the feminine mystique, these women critiqued the limitations they faced as women and as members of the working class.

In the records, many middle-class white women articulated a similar commitment to personal fulfillment and happiness by caring for and nurturing the family as that described by Friedan. Embracing the family ideals of the time, they turned to motherhood as the best outlet for their energies. Marian Cross explained in 1958 that she was sad because her sons had all started school, and they were less interested in being affectionate and sitting on her lap. She wanted more children because she felt "it's too soon in her life to have given up this sort of thing. It's a lost and empty feeling when the boys are in school all day and she can't imagine why some people look forward to the age when the children will go to school. If she had been able to she would have had lots of children." Although, as Friedan had predicted, Marian did find motherhood less fulfilling than she hoped (for her children's inevitable growth left her feeling lonely and "empty"), she remained committed to the sense of purpose and meaning she had felt while mothering small children. She continued to look to motherhood for fulfillment rather than turning to pastimes outside her family: she had applied to adopt, or to at least provide foster care for an infant, so that she would have another young child to whom she could devote her energies.[18]

Yet despite middle-class women's overwhelming ideological commitment to full-time housewifery and motherhood in the records, many had worked outside the home in the past, and several women still held jobs when they applied to ICH&A. White middle-class women and married women were the fastest-growing segments of the labor force during this period, and those pursuing foster and adoptive parenthood were not exempt from this trend.[19] Many of these women had started working while their husbands were either overseas during the war or in college finishing their degrees. They worked to pass the time and support themselves while their husbands served in the military, or to help support the couple until the husband finished school and became the primary breadwinner.[20] Female applicants did not describe working outside of the home as necessarily a path toward fulfillment or happiness in a career, but instead considered it a way to help out financially and stay busy until they became mothers. The few who continued to work years into their marriages did not have children.

Women who had worked in the past described an array of subtle pressures that had shaped their decisions to leave work in order to devote themselves to full-time homemaking. For instance, Doris Thomas discussed her choice to give up her work as a hospital laboratory technician soon after her husband returned from service in World War II. She had always loved chemistry as a girl and had thought she might go on to train as a doctor, but she told her social worker that she had decided "for a woman the expense involved and the long preparatory time seemed a little too demanding."[21] She had enjoyed her work in the lab, and the social worker noted that her husband, Edward, a lawyer, seemed even more proud of her accomplishments than she did. Despite Edward's support for her career, she told the worker that she preferred being a housewife: "She doesn't think that she misses her work too much and in thinking it over she doesn't really think that she would have made a good career woman." Instead, "She enjoys her home and working in the garden, she is a member of the . . . Infant Welfare group and she is active on the board. Her husband gave her a sewing machine for Christmas and she likes to sew her own clothes. She thinks that it brings out whatever creative abilities she has and she said that she had made the skirt which she had on." Along with her hobbies, there was also always housework to do: "She has a Bendix Washing Machine and is able to do all of her own laundry. She does not find that taking care of her house is drudgery."[22] It is impossible to know whether Doris felt as fulfilled by sewing, gardening, housecleaning, and volunteer work as she did by chemistry—or if she was simply saying what she thought was most likely to bring her a child. Regardless, her account of her decisions about work exemplifies the mix of social pressures and personal aspirations that encouraged middle-class women to define themselves as primarily housewives and caregivers during this period.

Doris also articulated the ways in which she, as an educated, middle-class woman, had a variety of resources at her disposal to make her work at home easier and more fulfilling. She could express her creativity through sewing and gardening, she had appliances to make her housework less taxing, and she had the skills and knowledge to be of real value as a volunteer. White middle-class wives had more access to labor-saving appliances, the time and supplies for self-expression, and the skills to help out their communities than did their white working-class and African American counterparts. Although commentators at the time argued that middle-class women felt especially trapped at home because their skills, talents, and intellects were mostly developed prior to marriage and mostly neglected once they became housewives, these women actually had the most resources to make their work as housewives comfortable and even interesting.[23]

Despite the pressures to quit their jobs and look for fulfillment at home instead, these women also described pleasure and a sense of accomplishment from working. Ann Robbins had done research work at a laboratory before her marriage, but she had quit because "she thought that the research type of work was more strenuous and hard on her emotionally and physically." While her husband was serving overseas, Ann had trained as a Comptometer operator. She had felt that skilled office work would keep her busy while her husband was away, and that it would be better suited than research work to her responsibilities to her home and husband after he returned. She continued to work after the war because she enjoyed her relationships with the other women at work and appreciated that her employer wanted to teach her to use a more complicated bookkeeping machine so she could advance further. Ann also admitted to her social worker that if giving birth or adopting was simply not in the cards for her, she would like to pursue more education to study chemistry and return to work as a researcher.[24] She put her obligations to her husband and her hopes for motherhood above her work, but she also found a sense of purpose and pride through her job and would look to a career for happiness if she could not find it through family life.

Even though middle-class women generally agreed with social workers that paid work outside the home and motherhood should not overlap, both activities were viewed as potentially meaningful and rewarding ways to spend one's time and energies. In fact, middle-class women expressed an entitlement to fulfilling work—whether it was inside or outside the home. From Marian, who wanted more children so as to avoid the "empty" feeling of being home alone, to Doris, who involved herself in housework and community affairs after leaving her job, to Ann, who considered a professional research career if she could not be a mother, these women all expected to spend their days engaged in useful, enjoyable work. Not quite the selfless, nurturing mothers their social workers desired, these women prioritized their families, but they expected personal happiness and interesting activities as well.

For one unusual middle-class woman in my sample, Carol Freeman, that quest for personal happiness ultimately inspired her to abandon the feminine mystique altogether. Carol had been employed for many years before she married. After marrying, she left her job to help out with her husband's family business. She enjoyed her work but felt she could only be truly fulfilled as a mother. Carol and her husband, Jesse, applied to ICH&A, and they eagerly took in a foster child whom they planned to eventually adopt. After a great deal of indecision, however, the couple eventually requested that the agency remove the child because Carol did not enjoy motherhood as much as she had expected. Carol questioned this choice for months afterward, repeatedly changing her mind about whether she wanted the child back. Finally, she told her social worker that while she felt extremely guilty for giving the child up, "she had come to the conclusion that she was the business type and not the motherly type and that she just hated to do cooking and to take care of children when she was missing so much socializing with business executives connected with her husband's firm."[25]

This was a difficult choice for a middle-class white woman to make, and this was the only couple in my sample to return an adoptive child. It was one thing to choose a career over motherhood because one was infertile and unable to adopt; everyone knew there were far more couples that wanted to adopt than there were children available and there was only so much one could do if parenthood proved impossible to achieve. It was quite another thing to have a child to adopt and to return it to the agency—particularly after the months of interviews and scrutiny this couple had undergone prior to the child's placement. On the one hand, Carol's sense of anxiety when she discovered that she did not enjoy motherhood as much as she had expected and her ongoing feelings of guilt about giving up a child illustrate the intense pressure and desire middle-class white women felt to fulfill the proper mold of motherhood. On the other hand, her decision to give up the child because she found more personal fulfillment by devoting herself to her husband's business than through motherhood highlights the underlying premise of family ideology itself: that women could and should find personal happiness and meaning by pursuing a particular life path. It was family ideology that inspired Carol to pursue personal fulfillment through motherhood; when motherhood did not fulfill her expectations for happiness, she instead chose to prioritize her marriage and her work with her husband as a more desirable option for her. She was likely able to make the choice she did, in part, because she was helping out Jesse's business, rather than working independently of him, so family concerns remained central to her overall identity. But her decision to focus on herself, rather than devoting her energies to her potential daughter, was enabled by the very same expectations that led so many other women to embrace the feminine mystique.[26]

Working-class women, meanwhile, also ascribed to the consensus view that their primary wifely obligation was to care for and nurture the family—perhaps even more strongly than their middle-class counterparts. In her 1962 study *Blue-Collar Marriage*, sociologist Mirra Komarovsky suggested that working-class women felt that their jobs as housewives were important and respectable, and they did not look down on the work or feel it was beneath them in the way some college-educated women did.[27] Likewise, in their 1959 marketing study of working-class wives, sociologists Lee Rainwater, Richard Coleman, and Gerald Handel suggested that these women embraced housewifery particularly ardently because it was the primary evidence of their devotion to their husbands. Their concern for keeping the home running smoothly was partly practical given the many strains of blue-collar work: "a happy, unworried husband will do the best job of bringing home the bacon." But they also accepted primary responsibility for caring for the household and children because these were central to maintaining a meaningful marital relationship. Working-class wives "believe that their efforts at keeping his clothes clean, at rearing the children properly, at remaining respectable women, are the very best proof of their interest in their husbands."[28]

Among adoptive and foster care applicants, white working-class women similarly endorsed the notion that, once married, and particularly after having children, their primary obligation was to be the family caregiver. Although they readily acknowledged that many women worked for pay outside the home, and perhaps they simply hoped to please their social workers, they suggested that once a woman had a family she should devote herself to housewifery full time, if possible. For example, Joan Ford explained that her twin sister had never married and that she had had a successful career because she did not "feel that it would be satisfying to care for children." Joan thought that her sister had made a fine choice for herself, but she preferred "being a housewife to working" and boasted to her social worker that she had "never worked since her marriage."[29] Peggy Yates similarly offered her belief that "if a woman gets married and has children the thing to do is to stay home."[30]

This commitment to housewifery, however, could create tensions in a marriage. Komarovsky found that even though many blue-collar wives believed that their work as housewives was important both personally and for their families, they did not believe it was always pleasant. Many women felt "tied down" by caring for young children. Komarovsky noted, "the homemaker herself attributes her major problem to the lack of sufficient money for necessities of life, for pleasanter living arrangements, for baby-sitters and fun." In Komarovsky's opinion, women's dissatisfactions with their work as housewives was caused by a lack of funds, but it was magnified by "the sharp segregation of the roles of the sexes, [which,] despite her acceptance of it, adds to her sense of restriction and isolation." While men had greater freedom to come and go at will, working-class women's responsibilities as wives and mothers, as well as their limited access to child care, nicer homes, and other resources that would ease their burden, often kept them confined to the household. These circumstances created marriages that lacked emotional closeness, and women who felt resentful of their husbands.[31]

Blue-collar adoptive and foster care applicants tended, in contrast, to emphasize the companionship they found with their spouses—but beneath their assurances of happiness lurked a great deal of discontent with their domestic routines. For example, when applying to care for infants awaiting adoption, Bonnie Phillips told her social worker that she particularly disliked cleaning, and she thought her husband Hubert was much more "fussy" about housework than she was. She told her social worker in an early interview that she "wonders sometimes if she shouldn't have been the man and F[oster] F[ather] the woman, so that she could go out and earn the living while F[oster] F[ather] stayed at home and kept house to suit himself." Bonnie then realized she had let her temper get the best of her, her social worker noted: "At this point F[oster] M[other] seemed to become somewhat self-conscious, remarking with a little laugh, 'there's nothing like airing all the family problems, is there?'"[32]

Bonnie was not the only working-class woman to express dissatisfaction with her work in the home. Despite working-class women's overwhelming profession of commitment to housewifery as married women's chief obligation, they also described a great deal of frustration with the limitations placed on them as both women and members of the working class. Unlike their optimistic and empowered middle-class counterparts, many working-class women were depicted in the records as exhausted, overworked, and dissatisfied with their duties as housewives.

Susan Porter Benson argues in her work on the survival strategies of poor and working-class families in the 1920s and 1930s that many working-class wives were busily making ends meet as "good managers." These women spent wisely and carefully, stretching the family's few resources.[33] The poorest white families in my sample, like the African American families I will discuss below, continued to rely on the careful economizing of housewives well into the postwar period—and these women generally described their efforts as stressful and unrewarding. Vera Fulton, for instance, slept only five hours a night because she was so busy with child care and household labor. Vera's family appeared to be financially stable: her husband Harvey earned a moderate income of around $3,000 a year at the factory of a printing company, which was just below the median income for white men in Chicago at the time.[34] But the Fultons faced ongoing economic hardship because Harvey's job was insecure, and he often worked nights in order to make a little extra money. Consequently, the family relied heavily on Vera's labor to help make ends meet. She sewed most of her family's clothes, and she did sewing for the neighbors in exchange for old children's clothes to remake into items for her family. She also took in a foster child as a way to earn a modest boarding stipend (which might be stretched to cover additional family expenses). Harvey's night shift meant that after working and sleeping he had little time or energy to help with the children and the housework. Vera cooked him a hot meal before he left for work each night, and she had another one ready for him when he came home each morning.

Vera resented her hard work for her family, and she expressed her hostility about it to the social worker after Harvey was injured at work and unemployed for several months. She "was quite frank in telling W[orker] that she was dissatisfied with her position as a housewife. She resented being confined to the home and not being able to have nicer clothing because she needed to spend so much money on the children." She also admitted that she envied the mother of the foster child for whom she was caring, who worked in a tavern in the Loop in downtown Chicago. Vera believed that this woman "worked in a glamorous place and was able to meet people there," and she would go visit this woman at the bar whenever she was downtown.[35] She recognized and did her best to cope with the overwhelming demands placed on her to make ends meet for her family, but she also resisted the classed and gendered limitations placed on her by playing hooky some days to visit the bar and to dream of a more exciting and interesting life for herself. The very centrality of her family in her life forced her to confront the ways in which gender and class inequality limited her options and opportunities as a working-class woman and mother.

Although some working-class wives described feeling frustrated with their gender and class status because they had too much to do at home, others based their discontent on having too little to do there. For example, Wesley Epson, a steel worker, and his wife, Rosemary, lived in a dank basement apartment in an area full of transient hotels. The couple struggled to earn enough money to get by. Rosemary longed to work outside the home to earn extra money so they could move and boost their standard of living, but Wesley insisted that she stay home. The social worker explained, "Her husband does not want her to take a job, although she is perfectly capable and has had many offered to her." But Rosemary agreed with her husband that her primary responsibility was to care for her home and family. As the social worker put it, "He works 12 hours a day and she feels that she should be home preparing his meals and keeping the household running smoothly. She said that tempers often become frayed if both parties worked and were tired."[36] Like middle-class women, working-class women faced many pressures to devote themselves to full-time homemaking, even when their families could use additional income.

Rosemary was frustrated not only by their poverty, however, but also by the boredom of spending most of her time in a small, uncomfortable apartment in an unpleasant neighborhood. She "said that she had nothing to do all day and she became quite restless." Unlike some middle-class women, who looked to local groups and volunteer work to fill the time, her bad neighborhood meant that there were not many social groups for her to join, and she had few skills to offer as a volunteer. She also had no washing machine to make the housework easier, nor a sewing machine to help with mending or provide creative expression. Rosemary tried to fill her time by reading novels, listening to the radio, and crocheting, but she ended up spending most of her time at a nearby diner, drinking coffee and helping out the staff for free. She finally applied to take in foster children in hopes that the extra income would ease their financial situation and that the children would give her something to do. As she put it, "she really felt she needed a child more than the child needed a home."[37] Looking to motherhood as a way to make her otherwise unfulfilling role as a housewife more bearable, Rosemary and others like her reiterated the importance of the family and caregiving to working-class women's sense of themselves during this period. At the same time, however, her dissatisfaction with being a housewife shaped her assessment of both her gender and class status: she felt obligated to devote her attention to her home because she was a woman, and she lacked more fulfilling activities and more comfortable housing because she was working-class.

Despite their many frustrations, working-class women, like their middle-class counterparts, did their best to find fulfillment. They particularly looked to paid work as a way to help out their families while also keeping occupied and feeling useful. Regardless of the pressures they faced to stay home as housewives, many working-class women did work outside the home during their marriages—even when they had children.

In the records, working-class women tended to explain their decision to take paid work as an extension rather than a violation of their gendered obligation to help care for their families, and they were careful not to tread on their husbands' breadwinner status. In particular, women boasted about the luxuries—rather than the necessities—that their incomes provided for the family. For instance, Norma Carter, a printer's wife who had worked for years in a low-level secretarial job, explained, in her social worker's words, that she "[f]eels wife's place is in the home, and was planning on quitting work at any time, as husband would prefer this." She believed that it was "bad for a man's morale to have wife's earning power the same as his." But Norma continued working because her income provided a useful—but supposedly not essential—supplement to their household finances: "They purchased [the] car with her money and have been able to get a few little luxuries, but have at all times lived on his income alone for the bare necessities. She felt that this made the husband feel more pride in providing for his home and his wife."[38]

Norma rationalized her gender transgression by framing her work in terms of the supposedly temporary, inessential assistance it provided her family. Yet, regardless of her claims to the contrary, Norma's income clearly went to purchases that greatly improved the Carters' standard of living. In discussing her job with her social worker, Norma simultaneously disavowed the importance of her labor and pointed out the obvious: her job had a real impact on her family's quality of life and economic stability. In her work on baby boom families, historian Jessica Weiss suggests that middle-class women who worked outside the home similarly justified the gender transgression of working for wages by explaining it as a means of helping the family. Weiss points out, however, that these women's income was also crucial to shoring up the family's middle-class status. Weiss contends that the income of middle-class working wives became increasingly important to the family's financial well-being during the 1960s and 1970s, as men's incomes began to stagnate while growing children's needs became more costly. The experiences of Norma and other employed working-class wives suggest that the financial pressures of childrearing took a toll on working-class families even earlier, making wives' income an important tool for improving the family's standard of living throughout the 1940s and 1950s.[39]

A number of women also expressed a desire to work for reasons other than simply meeting their families' clear financial needs, and here they echoed the experiences of middle-class women. Komarovsky found that even women's economic motive for taking a job was "not one but a cluster of motives." She noted that blue-collar wives worked because they desired "what money can buy," but they also found that "the sheer pride of earning . . . [was] itself another reward." Money was "a source of self-esteem and of power" for these women. Further, "working wives mentioned other rewards of working: the enjoyment of social life on the job, the pleasures of workmanship, the bracing effect of having to get dressed up in the morning, some relief from constant associations with young children, and 'having something interesting to tell my husband.'"[40] Like middle-class women who expected to be busy and fulfilled during the day, working-class women also worked for the pleasures work offered, beyond its financial benefits.

When it came to their hopes for their daughters' futures, white applicants unanimously suggested that their girls would find purpose and meaning as wives and mothers, but they admitted that girls might also need or desire additional skills and interests. Middle-class couples particularly focused on the personal happiness of their daughters. They generally assumed that daughters' future fulfillment would rest primarily on their marriages and families, and that paid employment and a college education would be more important to boys than to girls. But for girls who expressed interest in higher education or a profession, these couples at least wanted social workers to believe that they would be supportive. For instance, when thinking about whether he would prefer to adopt a boy or a girl, Stephen Echols, a middle manager at an airline, explained that "he thought a major difference in sex might be in educational planning. He thinks college would be more important for a boy than for a girl . . . unless the girl wished some career where this would be required." His wife, Carolyn, agreed "that college is not important for a girl, unless planning a career that would require this or a strong desire for it, but she feels that college . . . is more important for a boy."[41]

Even if it was less important to a girl's future, a college education was sometimes described by potential parents as an enriching, enjoyable life experience that their daughters deserved to have. Maxine West, who was married to an executive, had gone to a year of college herself before marrying. She explained that she would want her daughter to also go to college "because of the fun they had and the things they learned there, mixing with people and having good times."[42] Further, even a girl who did not desire a career could still use her college education as a mother. Alfred Roberts, a retail executive, explained that he would send a daughter to college if she wanted it, but he did not feel college fulfilled the same role in a woman's life as a man's: "He explained this by saying that a girl might go to college and then turn around and get married, whereas a boy would probably go on and make some further use of his college education. Mr. R said that he did not mean by this that he thought a girl should not have a college education, as she could probably use it later on in passing on her own knowledge to her children; nevertheless he thought a boy would probably use his education in more obvious ways—ways, Mr. R admitted, which would give him an opportunity as a father to be 'puffed up' over his son's achievements."[43] Not only did college have a different place in the lives of men and women, the perceived satisfactions of raising boys could also relate to the greater stakes of their academic and professional achievement. While girls' futures in the marriage market generally seemed more important to parents than their futures in the job market, middle-class men and women still acknowledged that girls might want a variety of options in their lives.

Working-class couples, on the other hand, were less focused on their daughters' educational and career options. Despite working-class wives' frequent participation in the job market, these women tended when considering their daughters' futures to focus on their marriage prospects rather than their work prospects. Even Margie Sparrow, who said that she would like to adopt a daughter who was as active and outgoing as her son, still felt she would not need a girl to be as academically successful as her son. The worker summed up her feelings by writing that "more than anything else this woman is looking for . . . a little girl that will grow up and eventually marry."[44] Laura Rushing had worried when, at age twelve, her daughter was found to have a curvature of the spine. Apparently, "Mrs. R was quite worried about her getting married, not knowing how things would work out." However, this girl had gone on to marry, and was happily settled with her husband in another state.[45]

Working-class women held their daughters to many of the same expectations they held for themselves: their lives and labors would revolve around their families rather than paid work. In contrast to their sons, whom they hoped to offer more education and better life chances, education and training for working-class daughters was never mentioned. It is, of course, difficult to account for this absence. Perhaps social workers simply ignored or overlooked white working-class couples' mentions of higher education for their daughters. But this is unlikely given their careful attention to these discussions in the records of all other applicants, and when they pertained to working-class boys. It is also possible that working-class couples were afraid of transgressing perceived gender norms by suggesting that their daughters might go to college or want a career. But even this possibility is not entirely persuasive, as working-class wives in particular expressed a number of other transgressive ideas in their applications. Instead, it is entirely possible that this group of white working-class parents simply did not see extra training and education as important to their daughters' futures. Even though it was highly probable that their daughters would at some point have paid jobs, their parents perhaps believed that they were unlikely to work their entire adult lives or believed that their work would not require special education or training. Even as many working-class wives seethed over the restrictions on their lives, these women did not describe any attempts to save their daughters from a similar fate.

Overall, then, white middle-class women looked to nurturing and caring for their families for fulfillment—but they also felt so entitled to happiness that they occasionally looked for it in other areas of life as well. They expected their daughters to enjoy the same choices and opportunities. Although these women described significant pressure to find fulfillment through homemaking and motherhood, their middle-class affluence gave them access to labor-saving appliances, well-appointed homes, and stimulating volunteer and job prospects. Their very access to these comforts and opportunities encouraged their sense of entitlement to fulfillment and happiness both inside and outside the family.

Scholars tend to think of the 1950s as a time when women—and particularly middle-class white women—were confined by the feminine mystique, only to rebel in later decades. But the adoption and foster care records articulate a different set of values about women's options for fulfilling work. Middle-class women's choices were certainly circumscribed by the gender conventions of the time, and many doors and opportunities were closed to them: they faced pressure to focus their energies on caring for their homes and families, and several gave up interesting careers in research for less-stimulating jobs in order to have more time and energy for their husbands. But these women's racial and class status made them uniquely positioned—and increasingly entitled—to choose a path in life that would make them happiest. For most, that path was still supposed to be marriage, motherhood, and housework. But the very focus on those activities as bringing meaning and happiness to a woman raised the prospect of other options: if it was happiness that mattered, then perhaps full-time housewifery could be taken out of the equation and a full-time job substituted instead.

In contrast, working-class women's material circumstances magnified some of the shortcomings of the feminine mystique. Working-class women pointed out a number of ways that their household labor was boring, difficult, or otherwise unfulfilling due to their class status. They frequently looked instead to paid work to help lift the family's standard of living and to provide a more rewarding outlet for their energies. But despite their many frustrations with their situation, these women continued to define themselves primarily in relation to their obligations as caretakers and nurturers and envisioned similar futures for their daughters. They described feeling that they deserved to be happier and more fulfilled, but they had limited options for doing so.

Although scholars generally associate disillusionment with the feminine mystique with the suburban middle-class women Friedan described, it was—at least among adoptive and foster care applicants—in fact the straitened circumstances of many working-class women that inspired more stringent critiques of postwar gender ideals. Middle-class applicants expressed some discontent with aspects of their domestic lives, but they were often able to use their many financial, educational, and personal resources to work around these issues in order to fill their days with relatively interesting tasks. Working-class applicants, in contrast, faced far fewer choices. They had fewer resources to pursue careers or stimulating jobs, while their cost-saving labor within the household was often more demanding and necessary to the family's well-being. Although many looked to work to relieve their own dissatisfactions while also earning some much-needed family income, their pressing domestic obligations frequently took precedence over their own happiness.

⚭

Like their white counterparts, African American women presented themselves to social workers as the natural nurturers and caretakers of the family. Yet their race and class background profoundly shaped black women's gendered obligations to their families. Black women encountered many of the same frustrations and limitations that white working-class women did, such as cramped and uncomfortable homes and strapped family budgets. Alongside those challenges, black women also confronted the infuriating impact of racial discrimination on their own lives and those of their families. African American wives and mothers were often compelled to work for pay because many black men could not earn enough to support the family alone—a problem made worse by exploitatively high rents in Chicago's segregated Black Belt and their limited access to affordable credit. But these women also generally wanted to work because they viewed earning income as integral to their obligations to their families, even though their husbands did not always agree. To resolve this conflict with their husbands, as well as to avoid a racially discriminatory labor market, many earned income by caring for foster children and starting their own small businesses from home. These women frequently struggled with competing pressures to be both providers and nurturers at the same time, but many also described a sense of pride in their innovative efforts to care for and provide for their families in light of the many forces stacked against them.

African American women have historically had a very different relationship with paid labor than their white counterparts: from slavery onward, black women have long juggled a range of obligations to masters, employers, husbands, and children. Historian Jacqueline Jones suggests that "to most black women, regardless of class, work seemed to form an integral part of the female role." Indeed, "black married women have always worked in proportionately greater numbers than white wives," with rates of labor force participation converging for black and white wives only in the last quarter of the twentieth century.[46] Similarly, sociologist Bart Landry argues that, beginning in the second half of the nineteenth century, many black middle-class women combined a commitment to marriage and family with a dedication to a career and social movements. These women and their husbands were practically and ideologically committed to a greater equality among spouses than their white counterparts, and their beliefs influenced later generations of both black and white couples.[47]

But black women's significant history of working outside the home did not completely liberate them from ideals of domestic femininity that prized caretaking over income earning in the postwar years. Instead, African American women found themselves struggling with competing demands to both nurture and provide for their families—and at the same time not usurp their husbands' authority as breadwinners. Black feminist theorist Patricia Hill Collins argues that the historical linkage between black women and domestic labor trapped black women in an "untenable position" during the postwar period. Black women were idealized as mammies who provided nurturing succor for the white families who employed them, while at the same time they were vilified by white policy makers for leaving their own children in order to work. Further, among white policy makers and within the black community—and even in their own families—black working women were left open "to the charge that Black women emasculate Black men by failing to be submissive, dependent, 'feminine' women."[48] Collins's analysis suggests that black women were stuck between two equally urgent demands: they needed to earn income to survive in a society that frequently did not pay black men enough to support a family, while at the same time they were expected to nurture their families and take on a passive, feminine role so as not to compromise their husbands' authority within the family.

Likewise, black popular culture in the postwar period wrestled with the competing demands made on black wives and mothers. In March 1947, *Ebony* ran a photo editorial entitled "Goodbye Mammy, Hello Mom," which celebrated the impact of wartime incomes and postwar job opportunities on black family structures. The article contended that dual-income black families had managed to save up while doing lucrative war work, and that at war's end a growing number of black men were able to earn enough that their wives no longer needed to earn income to help support the family. Charting a chronology of African American women's work, the editorial suggested that "World War II caused a kitchen revolution. It took Negro mothers out of white kitchens, put them in factories and shipyards. When it was all over, they went back to kitchens—but this time their own."[49]

Despite the article's resounding call for black women to focus their time and energies on nurturing their families, it also conceded that this ideal family arrangement was not likely to last forever given racial inequality. As the author put it: "Much as the Negro mother loves her home, she can't live on love. In the more than three million Negro households in the nation, the economic barometer seems to have its most drastic effects on the colored mother. She is the last resort, the ever-important reserve to hold the family together when unemployment strikes." In short, "Mom will have to earn some money again." The article celebrated black women for their ability to serve as both nurturers and providers, and both responsibilities were depicted as crucial to the well-being of their families. Although staying home was clearly the more desirable option for black wives and mothers—the ideal to which black families should aspire—the reality of women's financial contribution to the family through their work outside the home was still valued.[50]

African American applicants describe similarly conflicting pressures in the case records. Like their white working-class counterparts, African American women recognized their families' financial need and their real ability to be of assistance by taking a paid job, but at the same time they worried (or at least wanted their social workers to believe that they worried) about the gender implications of their work. Florence Reed, for instance, described some unease about the larger implications of her job for her marriage, confiding that "she had always firmly believed that a man should 'head the house'" and saying that she "had some feeling that she has been making him dependent on her salary."[51]

Many of these women's husbands also expressed concern about the implications of their wives' salaries on their status within the family. Harriet Johnson, who had been a housekeeper at a hotel for many years, finally quit because her husband Jerome, also a hotel employee, "had often told her that 'a wife's place is in the home.'" He had wanted her to quit so badly that when she resisted by explaining "that she became lonesome sitting around the house all day and had frequently cried because of it," he "proposed that he would try to leave his work during irregular periods in the day to come home and see her in order to offset her lonesomeness." Jerome found he could not come home to see her very often, however, and finally allowed her to work a little longer to make her happy.[52]

It is certainly possible that these and the many other couples that expressed similar sentiments were simply trying to impress their social workers with their commitment to conventionally white gender roles. But their comments also point to the many pressures on both men and women of color at the time. First, despite the long history of black women's paid employment, in the postwar years black women were clearly aware of the potential of their labor to upset the era's prescribed gender roles, even if they did not sincerely believe that there was a real danger to a wife earning a sizable income. Second, while men might have intended to demonstrate their authority in the household and their skills as breadwinners by describing to social workers their efforts to keep their wives out of the labor force, it is equally likely that black men sincerely wished that their long hours—in what were often unpleasant jobs—would be enough to support the entire family. African American men often struggled to keep their families afloat financially, and they frequently lacked the time and energy to spend quality time with their wives and children. Husbands' busy schedules and low wages made their wives all the more eager to find interesting activities, companionship, and needed income through paid employment, and it likely made husbands all the more dedicated to being the sole breadwinner in the family.

Men's long hours at work also meant many women, particularly those with children, took complete responsibility for the family's emotional and physical care alongside their paid employment. Most women assured their husbands that they could juggle both household and job responsibilities. Emphasizing her unhappiness at home alone, Harriett also made her case to keep working by reminding Jerome that she had managed to take good care of household needs even while working: "She stated that it had been somewhat difficult for her to keep house and do the service outside of the home but that she managed fairly well. She would usually arise early and make his breakfast and give him his lunch to take on his job before she left for her work." She also noted that she "was earning a little money toward the purchase of her clothing that he would not have to be 'out of.'" Like many other women, black and white, whose families struggled to get by financially, Harriett contended that she could be of the greatest use to the couple by both caring for the house *and* earning a little extra income. She accepted her primary responsibility as family caretaker, but she thought that she could provide financial assistance as well. She also admitted that she was simply happier with a paid job than she was as a fulltime housewife. She eventually gave in to her husband's wishes that she quit her job, but the decision spurred her to apply to ICH&A to care for foster children instead. She saw caring for foster children as a way to fill her time and continue earning a little money.[53]

Harriett's plan to earn money and stay busy at home by taking in foster children was particularly common among black families in my sample, though this strategy was employed by white women as well because it offered the fulfillment promised by motherhood while still providing the family financial assistance. Taking in foster children for income also resolved the tension between men's discomfort with having wives and mothers work outside the home and the family's need for extra income. For black families, caring for foster children was just one strategy among several for earning income from home. Many African American women secured additional funds by taking in roomers and renters, and by starting small home businesses. For example, Tom Hicks managed apartment buildings for a living and had done so for over thirty years. He was so busy with his work that he left the management of a building that he and his wife, Opal, owned in Opal's capable hands. The social worker wrote that "she is the manager. He works with his buildings and she manages their building they own, and makes the finances go around, and he thinks she does a good job at this." Opal did more than simply manage finances, though. From her past work as a domestic for white families, she had learned a number of valuable skills for running their building, including how to fire a furnace. She also did all of the plastering and redecorating. Both her husband and the social worker were impressed with her skills: "Mr. H remarked that his wife didn't do badly on her building at all. Mrs. H laughingly responded to my surprise at this (the plastering) and told me that she had learned much in service which had really served her well in her own life situation."[54]

Other African American women supplemented their family incomes from home by taking beauty training courses and then opening small beauty shops on their back porches or in their basements.[55] Muriel Gregory earned extra income giving piano lessons to neighborhood children. She also did occasional dressmaking for her friends.[56] Hattie Hill coped with her husband's unemployment during a strike by running a numbers game from her apartment.[57] Further, just as the white working-class "good manager" helped make scarce ends meet, poorer black wives—even those who did not earn income—also performed a lot of labor designed to save the family money, and they were crucial to the family's financial stability. These women mended, gardened, raised chickens, baked bread, and canned extensively to help save money.

Working from home did more than just resolve the gender tensions created by black women's conflicting obligations to both provide for and nurture their families. It also proved an effective method for coping with racialized labor markets and avoiding racism at the workplace.[58] As the last chapter demonstrated, these women's husbands repeatedly encountered racist employers and limited job options, with detrimental effects on the family's overall well-being. Women also found themselves restricted to menial jobs, often working as domestics for whites, and frequently encountered racism in the workplace.

Women's experiences in the labor force heightened their racial consciousness, and many black women linked the financial assistance they provided for their families with a sense of racial pride. Agnes Richardson was devoted to her job as a cashier even though her husband Frederick, a welder, wanted her to quit working. Her social worker wrote, "She was the first Negro in the Halsted shopping district to be given office work. Currently though a cashier she is managing the floor, does all of the inventory reports."[59] Likewise, Eleanor Brown had worked for five years at the beauty salon of a downtown department store. She loved her job and told the social worker that she worked on both white and black customers, including "many prominent Negro Chicagoans from the South side." She had hoped to keep working even after adopting an infant, but she ended up quitting suddenly because her boss decided to no longer serve black clients in the shop after a white patron refused to accept curlers that had been used on black customers. Her boss's decision infuriated Eleanor, but the final straw was the boss's plan for implementing the change: when black patrons called in the future she was to tell them that there were no appointments available and "after two or three calls—she felt they would get the idea." Sick of her own encounters with this kind of oblique racism, Eleanor told her boss that she should at least tell her clients that she no longer served black customers, and then she quit that day.[60] For these women the workplace was not just a location in which to earn income, it was also a place to advance the cause of racial equality.

Although black women faced a range of conflicting pressures regarding their caretaking and income-earning labor, black families across the board recognized the value of black women's labor for coping with inequality and helping the family survive hard times. The real value that black families placed on women's work was especially apparent in their hopes for their daughters. While white families focused on their daughters' marriage prospects, black families instead hoped to provide their daughters, even more than their sons, higher educations. College was a common aspiration for daughters, and many families expressed their wish that their daughter would become a social worker or teacher. This dedication to girls' education stemmed in part from a belief that black women were particularly disadvantaged in the labor market, facing extreme difficulty if they hoped to do anything beyond low-paid service work for white families. However, black families also knew that if a woman was well educated, she had access to professional jobs that held quite a bit of status in the black community—and often paid better than the jobs open to men. For instance, in the early section of the Young family's record, the worker recounted a 1936 interview with the wife, Delores: "For a number of years, she had held a good paying stenographic position which opened her eyes to the difficulties confronting a young colored girl in the business world. Mrs. Y spoke, 'Colored girls, even well-educated ones, could hardly get jobs before the depression, now it is even harder, I can understand how a refined girl would be made to stoop to almost anything. That's why I have made so many plans for [our foster daughter]. If I ever have a child of my own, I shall want it not only to be educated, but Mr. Y and I hope to lay by enough money so that if we are taken away the child will have something to fall back on.'" This family, like others, put its resources into educating the foster daughter the couple later adopted. They continued to emphasize her education even after the crisis of the Depression had ended. In 1943, the husband, Bernard, "remarked that he and his wife plan to make either a teacher or social worker out of [her]. He didn't care which one she decided to be." He went on to say that he would send her to school for as long as she wanted to go, hoping she would eventually have some sort of professional job.[61] Similarly, Myrtle Parson, who had long felt that her husband did not fully appreciate her hard work at home, told her foster daughter "'not to be foolish like her' and do menial work around the house and in the yard, as husbands do not appreciate this." She instead helped put the girl through college in the hopes that she could pursue a career.[62] In fact, several families were disappointed when their daughters married young because they had hoped they would have had more education first.

Further, when daughters did not desire much education, families still wanted them to have some skills to fall back on in case of emergencies. The Websters had adopted a very bright boy in the late 1940s, and they very much expected him to go to college eventually. When they applied to adopt a little girl for whom they had been caring and who was not considered to be as bright as their son, Sylvia Webster was fine with the child's prospects. She would be satisfied if her daughter got a vocational education rather than college training—as long as she had some employable skills: "She said that she feels a girl should be prepared to earn a living if she has to. She said that sometimes something might happen to her husband or to her parents and that she should be prepared."[63] While white families entrusted their daughters to the marriage market, assuming that if they needed to they would be able to support themselves, black families instead trusted neither the marriage nor labor markets to provide a safety net for their daughters, and instead sought to provide them with enough education to improve their prospects.

Overall, black women's work inside and outside the home played a crucial role in facilitating family survival in the face of racial discrimination. Black women combined caretaking and income-earning obligations, and they believed that their daughters would play a similar role in their own families. At the same time, however, working women faced resistance from husbands who wanted their wives to stay home full time even as they also relied on their incomes. They further encountered racial discrimination from employers who failed to appreciate black women's skills and abilities. Many women pursued creative strategies for earning extra income from home as a way to combine their income-earning and caretaking responsibilities while also placating their husbands and avoiding racism in the job market.

One might assume that black women's long history of employment outside the home would make their efforts to combine paid employment with family caretaking a nonissue, even during the height of the feminine mystique. But African American women did struggle with competing ideals. Historian Sharon Harley argues that during the Progressive Era and the Depression, black working women "more readily embraced their status as mothers, wives, aunts, and sisters than their more embattled status as wage earners" in jobs that were often racialized and demeaning.[64] During the postwar years, many women continued to emphasize their role as family nurturers by subsuming paid work in (often unfulfilling) jobs into their caretaking duties. But despite their encounters with menial work and racism in the workplace, they also expressed a degree of pride and pleasure in their paid work—particularly when it broke racial barriers. Their husbands, meanwhile, worked very long hours in what were frequently undesirable conditions in order to be successful breadwinners, and they hoped to be able to support their wives and families without assistance. Many women chose to resolve these conflicting ideals by earning income within the household so that they could devote their labors to caring for their families while still providing the extra economic support on which many black households relied. Black women worked to craft a feminine domestic ideal that combined full-time homemaking with paid labor in order to accommodate a fierce devotion to family well-being to the unique challenges of racial inequality.

〜

In conclusion, all of these women, regardless of their racial and class status, defined themselves through their obligation to care for and nurture their families. They strongly embraced the promises of the feminine mystique by seeking purpose and meaning in their lives as the primary caretakers and nurturers within the household. But the case records reveal that both applicants and social workers also recognized the falsehoods that lurked beneath the feminine mystique. They endorsed its premise—that women should be the family caretakers and that this work would provide them great joy—but they also noted the many ways daily household labor could be unfulfilling and lonely. Domesticity was far from all-encompassing in people's day-to-day lives, and it instead intersected with other aspects of women's identities.

The case records also underscore the important influence a woman's material circumstances had on her relationship with the feminine mystique. Women brought different resources to homemaking and experienced different struggles and satisfactions depending on their race and class. Domestic femininity was diverse, and its contours depended on a woman's circumstances. Wrestling with the demands of the feminine mystique highlighted not only the gendered restrictions on women's choices, but also inequalities of race and class. Postwar family ideals structured daily life within the household, but they were also intimately tied to the world outside the household.

These connections between the family and the world outside the household also shaped ordinary people's interactions with the wider public. As the next two chapters suggest, family ideals shaped people's priorities for where and how to live, and affected people's involvement with their communities. Adoptive and foster applicants inscribed family significance onto domestic and residential space, giving powerful emotional and symbolic meaning to their homes and neighborhoods. They also looked to their communities to support their families' well-being, and they participated in civic and political affairs to advance their families' interests. Rather than diverting applicants' attention toward a privatized domestic sphere and away from social and political controversies, family ideals instead mediated their interactions with the world around them.

PART III

Family inside and outside the Household

Constructing Domesticity
Family Ideals and Residential Space in Postwar Chicago

In Lorraine Hansberry's 1959 play *A Raisin in the Sun*, three generations of the Youngers, a black family living in a cramped kitchenette apartment on Chicago's South Side, struggle to improve their lives. The family is composed of matriarch Lena Younger, her eldest son—Walter, Jr.—with his wife and young son, and Lena's twenty-year-old daughter, Beneatha. Anticipating the substantial life insurance check of the recently deceased elder Mr. Younger, the family dreams about what to do with the money. Walter, feeling frustrated by his servile status as a chauffeur for a wealthy white man, pleads with his mother to help him open a liquor store in the neighborhood. He feels that owning his own business will rescue him from his emasculating dead-end job, while also eventually providing increased income for the entire family. But Lena is uneasy with the idea of owning a liquor store and hopes instead to invest her husband's legacy in a home outside of the Black Belt so that the family will finally have the space and security they need to thrive.

Hansberry's play provides a memorable portrayal of the many inequalities facing African Americans in the urban North at the time, including employment discrimination, housing segregation, and ongoing poverty despite one's best efforts to get ahead. The Youngers' plight movingly captures the texture of black life at a moment when, even as the civil rights movement was beginning to escalate in the South, the cultural, economic, and racial lines around northern urban ghettos were increasingly impermeable. While the play ends on a hopeful note, with the family purchasing a single-family house in a white neighborhood, the closing scene suggests the persistent threat of racial violence and leaves the audience with a sense of uncertainty about the family's future in their new home.[1]

Housing integration was, without question, one of the most volatile issues in Chicago in the 1940s and 1950s. As historian Adam Green notes, "Between 1946 and 1953 six episodes of rioting—involving anywhere from 1,000 to 10,000 whites—followed attempts by African Americans to move into communities such as Cicero, Englewood, and Park Manor."[2] Further, as *A Raisin in the Sun* suggests, family was never far from the minds of those who pursued integrated housing or those who resisted it.

This chapter interrogates the relationship between home and family. How did postwar families relate to diverse domestic and residential spaces? What kinds of family meaning did they inscribe on those spaces, and how did Chicago's racially discriminatory and economically stratified housing market shape that meaning? Most importantly, how did these factors influence the many violent racial conflicts over housing at the time?

Other scholars have sought to understand the relationship between family and housing, but ICH&A's case records offer a unique lens into the problem. On the one hand, the rich historiography on the elaborate ideological framework of postwar domesticity relies on the space of the single-family suburban home to reinforce its claims about the primacy of nuclear family privacy and the containment of women within the family. While this literature gives us excellent insight into the ways in which the home as both a space and an idea were important to people's understanding of the domestic sphere, it loses its traction if the location and domestic space are changed. On the other hand, there is a growing and impressive body of scholarship on suburbanization and the rapid changes in the racial geography of American cities that assumes a domestic motivation to protect the family's personal and financial safety. While this work helps us understand the racial and ideological implications of policies such as highway construction, loan programs, and metropolitan development strategies for ordinary people, it is unable to fully access the intimate symbolic and emotional meanings people placed on their homes. These areas of scholarship reference one another, but they are answering such different questions that they have not addressed each other directly. Analyzing the intersection of these literatures—the place where ideas about family and ideas about housing met in people's daily lives—broadens not only our analysis of postwar family life by exploring family locations and practices beyond white middle-class suburbs. It also broadens our understanding of the intimate, deeply held meanings people placed on housing and their motivations for where, and in what kind of dwelling, to live.[3]

Before we can understand the intersection between domesticity and housing, however, we first need to know a bit about the major racial and structural transformations occurring around housing during this period. The tremendous expansion of the suburbs in the postwar years changed many Americans' options about where and how to live. As historian Kenneth Jackson has argued, the growth of suburbia in the second half of the twentieth century was so overwhelming that "Americans tend to regard a move to the suburbs as natural— even inevitable—when people are given choices about where to live."[4] Jackson and others have rightly pointed out, however, that the tremendous expansion of America's suburbs was not inevitable at all, but was instead primarily due to public policy decisions that promoted suburban growth over other alternatives. The expansion of the suburbs in the postwar era was particularly due to federal loan policies and tax codes that favored single-family home ownership over other housing options. Government-subsidized highway construction also facilitated the commute between suburban home and work in the city center, making large-scale suburbanization possible. Further, developments in home building technology allowed for cheap mass construction of single-family housing, thereby making suburban homes more readily available and affordable than ever before, as builders were able to purchase land and then develop entire subdivisions and communities at once.[5]

Postwar mass suburbanization was, from the outset, linked with housing segregation and racial inequality. Although the huge expansion of postwar suburbs allowed many white Americans access to the benefits of home ownership, it also exacerbated economic and racial inequality and often had tragic consequences for city centers. As whites took advantage of a range of new segregated housing options in the suburbs, African Americans were left struggling to improve crumbling urban neighborhoods and fighting for access to the communities white suburbanites were leaving behind. Likewise, as suburban locations became more accessible to more workers, industry followed white home owners. Industrial parks sprang up in areas with few transportation connections from the city center, leaving black workers further isolated.[6]

These problems were particularly acute in Chicago. The large influx of black southerners during the Great Migration put significant strains on housing in black neighborhoods as new residents were forced to settle into Chicago's segregated residential geography. The city had a long-standing Black Belt on its South Side, as well as a smaller and generally more poverty-stricken black ghetto on the near West Side. Described most famously as "Black Metropolis" by sociologists St. Clair Drake and Horace Cayton, Chicago's Black Belt in the mid-twentieth century loomed large not only in the daily lives of the city's black residents, but also in black popular culture across the nation.[7] But Black Metropolis left much to be desired in its housing stock. Even in the earliest years of the migration, Chicago's African Americans faced inflated rents, small quarters, overcrowding, and fierce resistance to the expansion of black neighborhoods.

These pressures only increased in the postwar period as Chicago, like many cities, experienced a severe citywide housing shortage, which was particularly serious in the Black Belt.[8] Historian Arnold Hirsch documents the significant crowding facing Chicago's families: "The 1950 census uncovered 79,300 married couples without their own households; 64,860 'subfamilies' (groups related to and living with the enumerated primary family) and 32,334 'secondary families' (groups unrelated to but living with the enumerated primary family) were also discovered." In the Black Belt the shortage was much worse. According to Hirsch, "the percentage of nonwhites living in overcrowded accommodations rose from 19% in 1940 to 24% in 1950."[9] The number of "crowded" nonwhite households (households with 1.51 or more persons per room) had slightly more than doubled during that decade.[10] Even African American families who had managed to earn competitive salaries and accumulate significant savings after the war were often unable to find decent housing for purchase or rent.[11] Racist selling practices such as restrictive covenants effectively excluded African Americans from the housing markets in many areas, and targeted violence on the part of white home owners against blacks picked up where the covenants left off.

As new building in the suburbs and on the urban periphery added to the city's housing stock, Chicago's housing shortage—at least among white families—eased.[12] But housing segregation had led to the emergence of a dual housing market in the city—where blacks would pay a premium to rent or buy even the worst housing because the demand was so great and the supply so limited. Consequently, when new units opened up as whites left the city for the suburbs, it became more profitable to sell or rent those units to blacks at higher prices.

This practice eroded some of the rigid boundaries of the Black Belt, but the change was not without its repercussions. As blacks moved to previously white areas, they sparked two different (but often simultaneous) reactions on the part of white home owners: targeted violence designed to scare new black residents into leaving, and a flurry of rushed sales (encouraged by blockbusting real estate agents) as whites fled in fear that their property values would drop if they did not sell soon.[13] As white flight to the suburbs left inner-city areas with residents who were least able to provide a municipal tax base and yet most in need of social services, the very poverty of African Americans both encouraged whites to leave and served as evidence that if blacks were allowed to move into white suburbs, they would depress property values by bringing with them urban ills such as overcrowding and crime.[14] (Observe the demographic transitions apparent in the racial distribution maps for Chicago's neighborhoods and suburbs of 1940, 1950, and 1960 on pages 131, 132, and 133.)

The city's political leadership did little to address the problem. In the late 1940s, Mayor Ed Kelly was forced out of office after announcing his support for open housing for African Americans, and later administrations saw little to gain by supporting neighborhood integration. As Adam Cohen and Elizabeth Taylor suggest in their history of Mayor Richard J. Daley, who entered office in 1955, "Daley's modern city was built . . . on an unstated foundation: commitment to racial segregation. He preserved the city's white neighborhoods and business district by building racial separation in the very concrete of the city."[15]

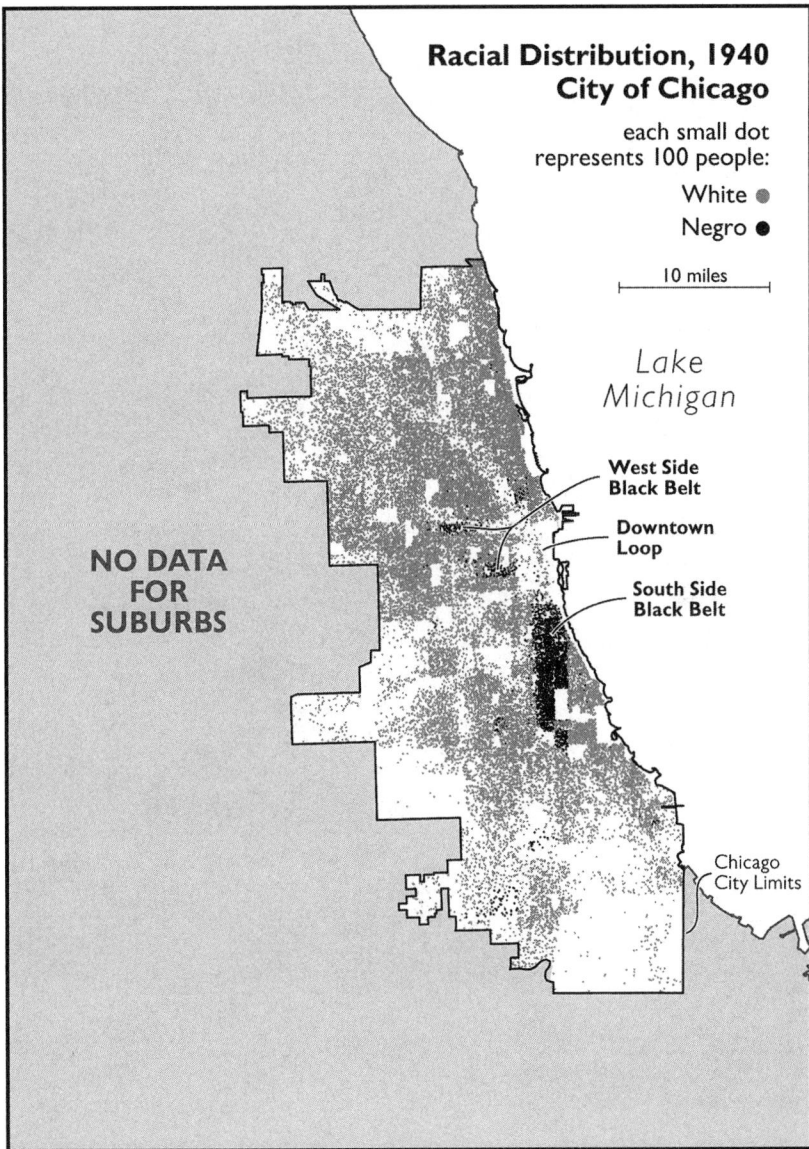

Racial Distribution, 1940
City of Chicago

each small dot
represents 100 people:

White ●
Negro ●

10 miles

*Lake
Michigan*

West Side
Black Belt

Downtown
Loop

South Side
Black Belt

NO DATA
FOR
SUBURBS

Chicago
City Limits

Tract-level census data from the National Historical GIS. This map does not include the
U.S. Census category of "other non-white," which totals less than 0.2 percent of the city
population. Map by William Rankin, Yale University.

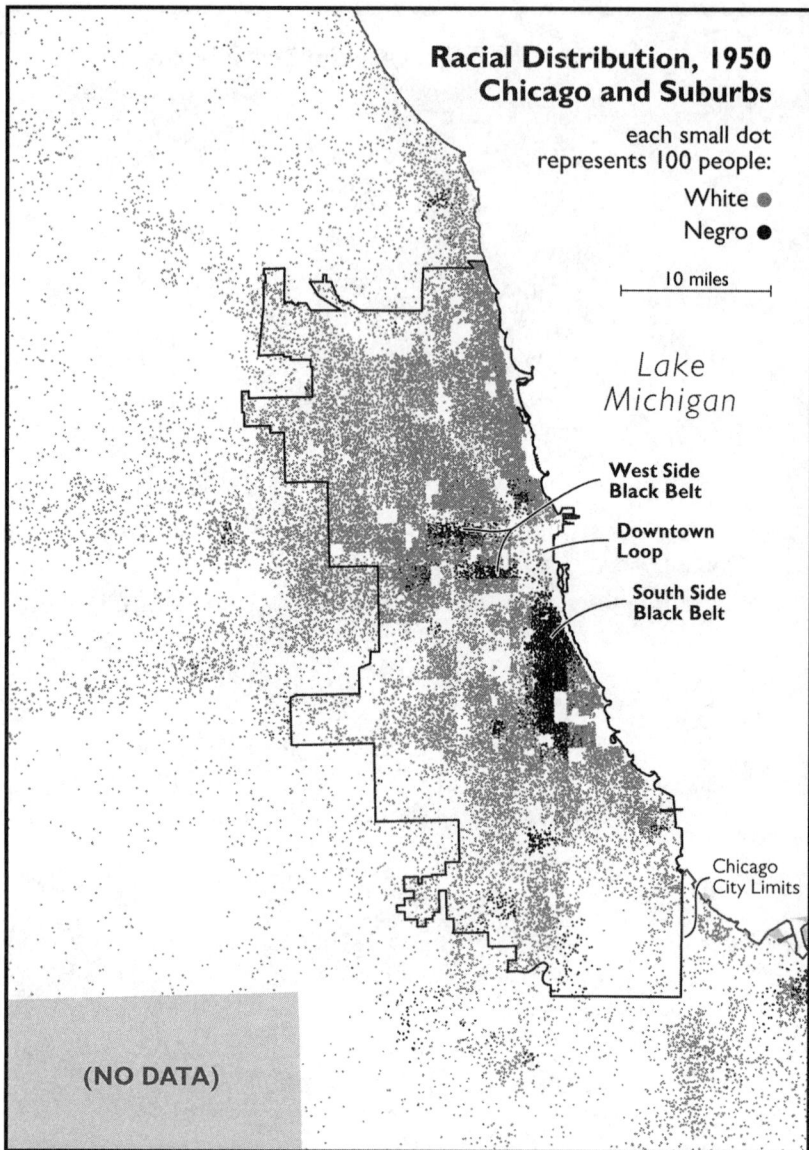

Racial Distribution, 1950
Chicago and Suburbs

each small dot
represents 100 people:

White ●
Negro ●

|——— 10 miles ———|

Lake Michigan

West Side
Black Belt

Downtown
Loop

South Side
Black Belt

Chicago
City Limits

(NO DATA)

Tract-level census data from the National Historical GIS. This map does not include the U.S. Census category of "other non-white," which totals less than 0.4 percent of the metropolitan area population. Map by William Rankin, Yale University.

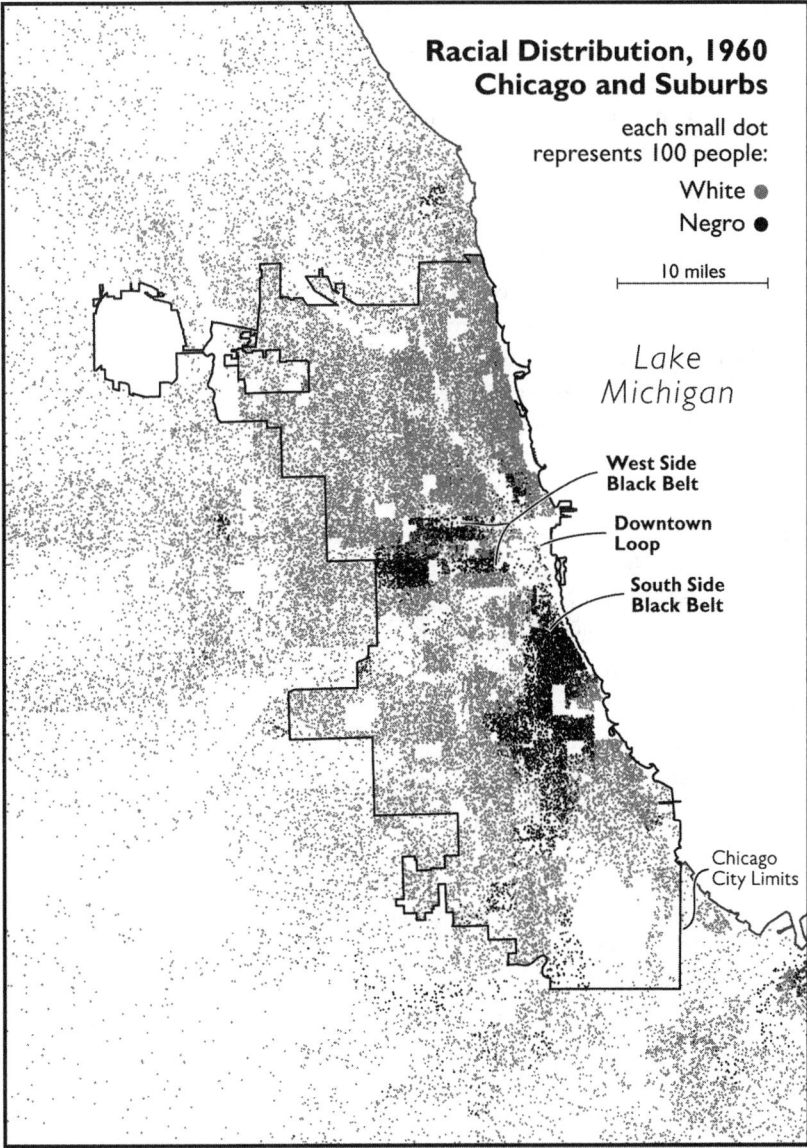

Racial Distribution, 1960
Chicago and Suburbs

each small dot
represents 100 people:

White ●
Negro ●

|————— 10 miles —————|

Lake Michigan

West Side Black Belt

Downtown Loop

South Side Black Belt

Chicago City Limits

Tract-level census data from the National Historical GIS. This map does not include the U.S. Census category of "other races," which totals less than 0.5 percent of the metropolitan area population. Map by William Rankin, Yale University.

Returning to the ICH&A case records, then, we begin to see what the stark segregation and deep inequities in the city's housing markets meant in the day-to-day lives of ordinary families. The records reveal that, regardless of the kind of home one occupied or where it was located, diverse applicants and social workers drew quite similar ideological connections between housing and the quality of its residents' family life. They contended that the home embodied the emotional bonds of the family and was rich with meaning about the family's character. Although popular culture celebrated postwar family-oriented consumerism, the case records instead emphasize people's personal attachment to their homes, where the family spent much of its time and energy.

But there was a material reality to housing as well. Applicants had access to different kinds of domestic spaces, and they used those spaces differently depending on their circumstances. Consequently, everyday family life varied tremendously depending on one's housing and neighborhood. While some applicants enjoyed ownership of a single-family home with a yard for family cookouts, others found themselves confined to renting a crowded kitchenette apartment where the domestic lives of their neighbors were intimately tied to their own. These distinctions were not lost on applicants, or to other Chicagoans. Instead, many evaluated their own family lives—and judged those of others—in relation to how they used and occupied domestic space: some families simply used housing in better ways than others. These diverse domestic patterns and expectations, when coupled with the strong emotional connection between housing and family, made for a potentially volatile combination.[16]

⌒

The case records reveal that housing was ideologically tied to the family in ways that reinforced the significant emotional connection people felt toward their homes. Both social workers and applicants attached emotional and symbolic meaning to purchasing a home and arranging domestic space. Social workers saw housing as reflective of applicants' personalities, priorities, and capabilities for childrearing. They read into applicants' domestic space a range of meanings about their potential attitudes toward the children in their care. Likewise, applicants described housing as inextricable from their sense of closeness and intimacy as a family: the domestic space of the home served as both the physical embodiment of a family's life together and a shared project that further strengthened family bonds. Because domestic space was so essential to building and maintaining family relationships, people organized much of their daily lives around obtaining desirable housing and then improving their domestic spaces.

When evaluating applicants, social workers paid particularly close attention to their housing, visiting every home at least once prior to placing a child. Workers described in the record the decor of the house, the style of the furnishings, and upkeep. Their concerns were partly practical. They sought to ensure that the children in their care would be placed in homes that had adequate indoor and outdoor space for a child to be comfortable, and that homes and apartment buildings were safe. They examined bedrooms, living rooms, apartment hallways and lobbies, and backyards to make sure each child would have privacy, ventilation, security, and space to play.

While one might assume that workers were also interested in examining the home to assess a family's relative affluence, in fact they already had extensive financial information on applicants. Instead, their interest was in the couple's character. Workers believed that homes offered a wealth of concrete and symbolic information about the kind of life applicants could offer their children. They looked for clues as to the kind of culture and interests a family might share with a child. They noted the types of books or magazines lying about, whether there was a phonograph, radio, television, or piano, or if the family had any collections or hobbies evidenced such as stamp collecting, sewing, or woodworking.

Social workers also praised homes with a lot of sunlight and bright colors, for these qualities signaled that the home was warm, tasteful, and welcoming. A clean, well-maintained house suggested that the family took pride in making their home a comfortable, orderly, and friendly place to live. Presumably, they would convey a similar warmth and care to the children placed in their charge. For instance, one worker remarked that the "simple but excellent taste" of the white middle-class Winters' home suggested that it was "obviously the home of two people who enjoy each other and it very much."[17] Another worker reported that the home of an older white working-class couple, the Brookses, appeared "to be very much lived in and it is apparent that there is no over emphasis on the home but more on the activities within the home."[18] Likewise, an African American social worker found the black Tomkins family's home to be rather "cluttered and gaudy," but concluded that "the atmosphere of the home is so cheerful and warm, that one overlooks the fact that it is somewhat overdone, and notes the fact that this is a very comfortable home where people seem to be happy."[19] These were the kinds of homes—and parents—that would provide young children the security, attention, and loving care they required.

Like social workers, applicants also contended that their homes were rich with personal family meaning and represented their goals and values. They frequently told stories about the deep significance their homes had for them. For instance, Gene and Mattie Duncan, a young white couple, had rented their first apartment together shortly after their marriage in 1940. Gene was soon sent overseas to fight in World War II, but the couple decided to keep the apartment during his absence, even though Mattie planned to live with her parents while he was away. During the war, she did not sublet it or even move the furniture.

She recalled in 1947 that she had gone over to clean it once a week because spending time there made her think of her husband and their life together. They both spoke of their joy the day Gene came back from service and Mattie was there waiting for him, with everything just as he remembered it. He told the social worker, "when he went in the door and found her there and found all their furniture in exactly the same spot as when he left, he said that he knew that he was home. The fact that she had been thoughtful enough to leave the furniture as they had had it when they lived there together seemed to mean a great deal to him, and he said many times when he was overseas he visualized their apartment, and recalled their life there together."[20] During the war, the space of the home served for this couple as a vivid reminder of the comforts of their life together, and it continued to be for years afterward an important symbol of their love for each other.

Many couples also suggested that purchasing a home together was an important step in a couple's marital life, which increased its emotional and symbolic significance. Although some families preferred to rent, a number of applicants had spent years saving up to buy a house, scrimping, sacrificing, and sometimes living with relatives to achieve their goal. For example, Johnnie and Eileen Saunders, a young white couple, moved into an apartment above Eileen's family's small business just after they married in the early 1950s. Her family owned the apartment, and they referred to it as the "honeymoon apartment" because all of Eileen's siblings had lived there right after getting married. It was taken for granted in this family that young couples would use this apartment and rely on the support of extended family until they could afford a home of their own, and that the purchase of a home was a crucial accomplishment for a young family.[21]

Home ownership was especially emotionally important for African American families who had moved to Chicago from the South. A number of applicants reported saving up for years upon arriving in the city in order to purchase a home of their own. Several black families explicitly likened purchasing their homes in Chicago to putting down "roots." Curtis Sanders "summed up his feeling about his home when he said that when he found a home, he wanted to stay in it; he wanted roots; he now feels he has them."[22]

Applicants also described spending a great deal of time fixing up and improving their homes, which both reflected and increased their emotional investment in their housing. A number of families engaged in home improvement due to their limited financial resources. These families had purchased homes that were rundown and needed repair, or they had invested in less expensive suburban homes in new developments that had unfinished second stories and basements. A few had bought only the shell of a house and done the rest of the work themselves. These families had only been able to purchase a home because they were willing to finish or repair their homes with their own labor.[23]

Working on one's home preserved or increased its value, which was a crucial consideration for young families at the time. Historian Lizabeth Cohen, in her work on the policies and ideologies that shaped the twentieth-century consumer economy, argues that postwar mass suburban housing became a consumer good much like any other, "to be appraised and traded up like a car rather than a longstanding emotional investment in a particular neighborhood, ethnic community, or church parish."[24] Although Cohen underestimates people's emotional commitment to their suburban homes and communities, she points to the importance of property values to people's relationship with their housing during this period. By putting their own labor into their homes, families were able not only to purchase homes they might not have been able to afford otherwise, but also to boost the value of their investment.

Many applicants sought to personalize and improve their spaces even when they had little to gain financially from their efforts. Instead, their interest was in creating a domestic space that would best serve their family and express their personality. Even renters in well-maintained apartments occupied themselves with extensive redecorating projects, sometimes becoming so emotionally invested in their apartments that they were in no rush to leave them even as other options opened up. Many put in significant time and energy redecorating and fixing the place up, doing everything from scraping paint and putting up new wallpaper to building bookcases and installing a shower. Though couples did not gain financially from their efforts in terms of increasing the value of their home, they enjoyed the projects as a shared activity and saw them as a means of improving the quality of their life together.[25]

Likewise, middle-class home owners who had access to higher quality housing also engaged in home improvement. Many of their projects were relatively minor and were designed to simply make the home more comfortable and personal. Middle-class applicants frequently engaged in projects such as building a small bar for the kitchen or other minor improvement. Many also repainted or repapered the walls with some frequency. In addition, many wives made their own drapes and coordinating slipcovers for the furniture.[26]

The yard was also a favorite improvement project. Many couples gardened together on evenings and weekends. Wallace Smith and his wife, wrote their social worker, have "a fairly sizable garden and one of his chief sources of recreation is to come home to work on it. He spoke of the fact that last Sunday he had gotten up at around 6:30 and had done a lot of weeding in the garden because they have plants and were going out in the afternoon. He commented that a lot of men like to get out and play golf, and maybe it seems silly but he gets the same kind of relaxation and rest out of his garden and in keeping things up around the house."[27] Likewise, Maxine West talked about how she and her husband were learning how to garden together now that they had their first yard. She told jokingly of the wagers they had made that year about whether the squirrels and birds would eat the corn and strawberries they had finally managed to grow.[28] Energy spent gardening and working on the house gave couples a shared hobby, made their home feel like an expression of themselves, and encouraged a deeper investment in their lives together.

Home improvement was also appealing to couples that bought in newly developing suburbs because these neighborhoods tended to have very similar housing and few distinguishing landmarks, so couples sought to make their homes more noticeable and personal. For instance, as one social worker found when visiting Pauline Winter, unfinished suburbs could be confusing and alienating places. The worker got lost trying to find the right house, and when she told Pauline, she laughed and said that "none of their friends were able to find them unless they stood out on the porch and waved whenever they saw an auto coming." The worker noted in the record: "Actually had I not seen Mrs. Winter on the steps, I would have gone right by as the house seems to be in the middle of nowhere and none of the streets are marked."[29] Many families in the records who lived in new suburbs described painting the exterior of their homes noticeable colors, putting in patios and shrubbery, and otherwise trying to make their houses look more distinctly their own.[30]

The case records repeatedly describe home improvement as family-centered recreation, giving the family a shared project and set of goals. For instance, the Smiths, who had bought their first home in the northwestern suburb of Arlington Heights in 1951, saw the house as a new adventure they shared together. Wallace Smith "spoke of the way in which they work together fixing things up saying that each of them can do certain things and they seem to fit in well together. He illustrated this by saying that he laid the linoleum in the kitchen, and . . . [his wife] from her knowledge of sewing was able to lay up a pattern for the irregular shaped pieces and then he could do the work of cementing it down. They still have a great deal of work to do on their house and these are things they are looking forward to doing as the years go by."[31] This couple built their commitment to their marriage into the very floors of their home, enjoying it as a joint hobby while also seeing it as a symbol of their unfolding life together. Although it is certainly possible that these and other applicants overstated their interest in home improvement in order to impress their social workers, their emphasis on working on their homes nonetheless suggests that this activity was widely understood as an important indicator of one's devotion to family living.

Families with children also used home improvement as a way to spend time together and to make their domestic space more meaningful and comfortable. The Campbells, who moved in the early 1950s to suburban Oak Lawn, on the southwest side of the city, all worked together on their house. Steve Campbell, a truck driver, had built the home himself, and made it "to meet their needs and 'whims.'" Although he had done most of the construction work, his wife Ella and their five children had also pitched in. Ella "said that she had even mixed concrete."[32] The picture of togetherness, this family was pulled closer through their home improvement projects—enjoying family-focused recreation and saving money for the family's future.[33]

African American families also built and improved their housing as a means of achieving family dreams and cementing family relationships. A number of black applicants hoped to eventually move with their children to a country farm. Several of them had even bought small plots of land well outside of the city in order to begin building a country home themselves. These families kept their homes in the city while doing their best to improve their rural property so they could enjoy it during weekends and vacations, but they all planned to eventually move permanently to the country and to support their families through light farming. The Jenkins family particularly enjoyed roughing it and camping with their children while they built their farmhouse, while the Websters kept chickens and raised vegetables on a distant truck farm with their foster sons. These families saw their rural land as a project for the whole family to work on and enjoy. It also represented the family's commitment to building their future together in the North. Drawing on their memories of the rural South, they dreamed of returning to the countryside under circumstances that were a far cry from their sharecropper roots.[34]

All of these families were literally constructing domesticity themselves, in the very foundations and yards of their homes. This aspect of daily domestic life shifts scholars' focus away from the home as a shell waiting to be outfitted with the latest consumer gadgets or as a commodity that was important only for the status value of its location and size—and instead highlights the concrete everyday interactions between families and their living spaces, and the impact they had on each other. Home improvement encouraged families to view their domestic spaces as a realm for self-expression and provided them with a shared project even as it also facilitated the family's upward mobility.[35]

But despite the importance of home improvement projects for reinforcing the close relationship between family ideals and domestic space, home improvement also had its drawbacks. It was time consuming, it was expensive, and—as anyone who has ever tried a home improvement project themselves knows—it could be tiring and frustrating work. An unfinished home could be a continual disruption of family life and could frequently upset the very domesticity it also instilled. The Lawrence family illustrates the tangle of benefits and sacrifices of home improvement particularly well, suggesting that ultimately the tensions and stresses created by home improvement projects could also serve to solidify a couple's commitment to each other and to the life together that their home represented. Irene and Ronald Lawrence, a welder and his wife, had purchased their first home together in the working-class suburb of Cicero, which was just outside the city's western boundary, in the late 1940s. They had spent their first year of marriage living with Irene's parents, and although the family members all got along, Irene and Ronald felt it was not the same as having a house of their own and were eager to purchase for themselves. After they bought their own home, they first painted it and built their own kitchen cabinets. They then spent the better part of a summer building their own garage, relying on Irene's brother-in-law, a cement layer, to help them pour the foundation and plan the structure. This was a particularly time-consuming project and the couple, with the help of their in-laws, worked for three months "on Saturdays and Sundays and in the evenings, putting up two-by-fours and then the roof" to finish it.[36]

All of their work on their home was also quite expensive, and it used up most of their financial resources. Their large investment of both money and energy certainly increased their stake in the community and its property values. But the Lawrences saw the project as more than just a financial investment—it had real personal and psychological benefits for them. Ronald "said that he didn't mind putting money into it because it was his own, and that it gave him kind of a sense of security to be in his own home. They could have spent the money on paying rent or just going out and spending it on movies and clothes, but he thinks that both he and his wife have gotten much more out of their house than they would have if they were renting an apt [sic]."[37] Although home ownership required significant sacrifices of time, energy, and money, and it certainly curtailed engaging in other forms of recreation, it was an investment in both the family's financial future and the "much more" to which Ronald referred—the sense of pride, security, and social adulthood that made both home ownership and family membership so compelling in the postwar period.

⌒

Homes were not just symbols of a family's life together. They were also physical structures that were located in different kinds of residential spaces. Chicago and its suburbs offered a wide variety of neighborhoods that were quite different in feel and housing stock. There were the small single-family homes of Chicago's white working-class Bungalow Belt, the crowded confines of the Black Belt, city neighborhoods with apartment buildings and multifamily dwellings, and areas with larger lots and more single-family homes that were both well within the city limits and in its suburbs. The case records reveal that, in addition to viewing applicants' houses in terms of their family lives, applicants and social workers also read a great deal of family significance into their neighborhoods. Regardless of where they lived in the city or its suburbs, they sought out neighborhoods that they deemed friendly and well maintained, which would provide them with the emotional, social, and material resources to best rear their children.[38] (See the racial distribution maps on pages 131, 132, and 133 for more information on the demography of the regions of the city described below.)

Although we might expect social workers to be particularly picky about where adoptive and foster parents lived, they in fact saw a variety of family costs and benefits to different neighborhoods. They tended to prefer quiet residential neighborhoods, which they believed would offer children more safe space to play and a community of supportive neighbors. But they also recognized that some applicants found these areas lonely and isolating while bustling city streets felt warm and welcoming. For instance, George and Mary Branch, a white couple, sold their home in suburban Oak Lawn to move to an apartment in the all-white Chicago Lawn neighborhood on the city's southwest side in the mid-1940s. The Branches felt that their suburban home had been time consuming and expensive to maintain, and while living there they had "had difficulty getting into the city to enjoy their social contacts." They were "very pleased with their [new city] apartment," and for her part the social worker also thought the home would be a good place for children, noting with particular approval that there was a large lot next door where children played and dug foxholes.[39]

Social workers were also well aware of the real financial and racial restrictions on applicants' choice of neighborhood. Most social workers who worked with African American applicants were also African American themselves, making housing discrimination no secret to them. Similarly, because ICH&A often relied on low-income families to provide foster care in return for a modest boarding payment, workers recognized that some applicants simply could not afford better housing. Workers' priority was to provide the children in their care the best homes possible. To do so, they worked to identify supportive, loving families who would offer adequate nurture and care for a child. Workers carefully considered a range of qualities of applicants' communities and houses, and they found suitable families in suburbs and city, in apartment buildings and single-family homes alike.

Many white applicants, however, idealized suburbia and imagined communities on the city's fringes to offer a friendlier, more child-centered living experience than the city could offer. White couples' belief in the potential for close, stable relationships in the suburbs likely rested on the assumed racial and class homogeneity of many suburban areas, but none explicitly mentioned race or class when recounting their desire to raise their children in a suburban community. Instead, these applicants tried to impress social workers by repeatedly describing the suburbs as like a "small town," associating suburban living with friendly, closely knit neighborhoods. They echoed the language in subdivision advertisements promising communities "where small-town friendships grow."[40]

Morris and Christine Jones described their home in Palatine, in the far north-west suburbs, as particularly pleasant because it had "a small hometown atmosphere."[41] Similarly, Lloyd Robbins, an urban dweller, explained that he "would really prefer living in a suburban area, partly because he misses the friendship he used to have as a child, living in a small town. He said as a child, he knew everybody within a mile radius, but now he knows only the people who live on either side of him." Hoping to re-create this pastoral experience, the Robbinses eventually purchased a home on the outskirts of the city in which to raise their adopted children.[42]

Like the Branches, who left Oak Lawn in order to live in a city apartment, some white applicants did not pursue suburban home ownership and instead chose to live in neighborhoods within the city limits. They chose to stay in city neighborhoods because, like suburbanites, they wanted to live in a close, family-centered community and found that kind of life possible in racially homogeneous Chicago neighborhoods. For instance, Lucille Henry described her fondness for the urban neighborhood of Portage Park in 1951. This area on the city's Northwest Side was almost entirely white, offering a mix of rental apartments and single-family homes along with a popular park that attracted neighborhood residents. Portage Park was more densely populated than most of the city's suburbs, but it was less crowded than areas closer to the lakefront and downtown Loop. The Henrys had rented a small one-bedroom apartment and then bought a single-family home in the neighborhood, explaining that "on Sundays it was just like a small town, and the men get out and wash and polish their cars, and there is a great deal of chatting back and forth."[43] Suburbs were not the only location where ample play space and "small town" sociability could be found.

A supportive community could also be found in the city's Bungalow Belt, which was a series of white working-class neighborhoods with small, single-family bungalow-style homes that had been built just inside the city limits in the first decades of the twentieth century. As Alan Ehrenhalt points out in his study of postwar Chicago, the Bungalow Belt's housing was often cramped, with little living space inside and even less space between dwellings. But for some families, this was a mark in its favor. In Ehrenhalt's view, the city's blue-collar residents expected to be close to neighbors and embedded in a web of community relationships. These individuals saw city neighborhoods in the Bungalow Belt, with their denser housing stock and small single-family homes, as more beneficial to their personal and family interests than other options.[44]

Among ICH&A applicants, white working-class families also often purchased two- or three-flats, with the expectation that these homes would allow them to stay in city neighborhoods where they had many social and familial connections, and many hoped to share their homes with relatives. A number of these applicants shared multifamily dwellings with their parents or adult children, and they planned to live together for the foreseeable future.[45] Others shared multifamily homes with siblings or other relatives. These families shored up their class status by relying on each other for unpaid help with housework and child care, and they generally looked out for one another. Sam and Marilyn Lewis bought their three-flat on the far Northwest Side with the understanding that Marilyn's two sisters would be their initial tenants. As their social worker put it in 1952, "When the Lewises decided to buy their present home, it was a family affair." Marilyn's older sister, whose children were grown, lived with her husband upstairs, and her younger unmarried sister lived in a small basement unit, while Marilyn lived with her husband and two daughters on the first floor. Marilyn explained that the three sisters had always tried to live near each other, and they were very happy to share a home.[46]

Black applicants, meanwhile, were often confined to predominantly black neighborhoods, with fewer available choices about where they could purchase or rent a home. Yet many black applicants expressed similar desires as their white counterparts in terms of seeking family amenities. Although their options were much more limited than those of white applicants, they looked both within and beyond the Black Belt—and within and beyond the city limits—in order to find communities that best served their families' material and social needs. For instance, Earnest and Hattie Hill, after riding out the Depression as renters, sought to buy a home so that they would have greater financial security in case of future economic instability. They purchased a two-flat in the South Side neighborhood of Fuller Park during World War II, where there were a number of crumbling buildings that home owners were slowly improving. Because of the area's poor housing stock, they told their social worker "that this was the last neighborhood which they considered when they were contemplating the purchase of a home. However, their financial circumstances were such that they were unable to buy in what they then considered a more desirable neighborhood."[47]

The Hills, like many white applicants, had hoped for a friendly, supportive community in which to raise children, and they feared that Fuller Park would not live up to their expectations. But they were surprised by what they found there. They emphasized that, despite the neighborhood's poor physical condition, it was actually quite family friendly. Although they might have simply been trying to impress their social worker, their comments provide a glimpse into what they believed a "good" neighborhood should be like, even if their particular neighborhood did not actually fit this description. Their social worker noted, "They have never enjoyed living in a community in Chicago as much as they have enjoyed this one. The people are neighborly and yet not meddlesome, quiet and orderly. With the exception of the voices of the children playing in the afternoon they are surrounded by quiet. Parents are interested in their children, seeing that they go to bed at a reasonable hour after which quiet descends such as they had never expected to find in the city."[48]

Black families with greater financial resources pursued better-maintained housing, less-crowded neighborhoods, and more space for children's play. They generally found homes in more expensive areas on the borders of Chicago's Black Belt. Oliver and Mae Rickert, a middle-class family, began to contemplate leaving their home in the Grand Boulevard area in the early 1950s because the area was becoming overcrowded. The neighborhood had been central to the community life of Bronzeville in the 1930s and 1940s, but in 1956 the couple believed it was "changing in terms of fewer stable home owning people." Mae's mother, who lived with the family, contemplated a move "with reluctance," but appreciated "the advantages to her grandchildren in being in a community where there is more freedom, playmates of comparable standards." In 1958, the family relocated to, as the social worker described it, "a quiet, newly integrated substantial neighborhood" in the Chatham area. Chatham went from over-whelmingly white in 1950 to over 63 percent black in 1960, becoming home to a large number of black middle-class families like the Rickerts. It offered high-quality housing, space for recreation, and like-minded neighbors. The community also organized to avoid racial violence as it integrated, and the Rickerts claimed that they were "well received in the neighborhood."[49]

Although it was rare, some black families also moved into integrating sub-urban communities in order to find family-friendly amenities. Otis and Erma Stanton had lived in both the small West Side Black Belt and on the South Side during the 1950s, and they had moved to the integrating neighborhood of North Lawndale on the city's far West Side in the mid-1950s, when it "was just begin-ning to change and property was well maintained." Although "their particular building had been quite impressive," the area quickly fell on hard times, and "the entrance and stair hall . . . [became] very deteriorated." Erma began urging Otis to move the family to a better neighborhood, and when they purchased a home in an almost entirely white community in suburban Broadview in 1960 she called her social worker to say that it was "the kind [of home] that she had dreamed of but never actually felt she would be able to afford." The Stantons had saved carefully for years, and the house was modern, with wall-to-wall carpeting. Erma was "very well pleased with the fact that [her son] can get out-doors daily and that there are a number of small children with whom [he] can play. Since the community is small, [he] can go outdoors by himself with[out] their keeping on eye on him and the usual traffic hazards are not as great as they would be in a more urban community."[50] Most black families—just like most white families—looked for communities that would contribute to their family's comfort and well-being through quality housing and supportive social networks.

⟜

As we have seen, houses were both emotional and material resources, and applicants viewed them through the lens of their families' needs and desires. Applicants imbued their homes with intense emotional significance, while also noting their financial importance to their family's future. Likewise, they judged neighborhoods in terms of both the perceived personal benefits of different communities, such as "small town" friendliness, and the more practical benefits they could offer their families, such as living near friends and relatives.

Despite the strong family attachments to housing and neighborhood, applicants did not suggest that these spaces could or should be occupied and used in the same way. Instead, both houses and families came in a variety of shapes and sizes, and homes could be put to a variety of uses. Although scholars usually associate single-family households, home ownership, and nuclear family privacy with postwar domesticity, the case records reveal that even as applicants desired to convince social workers that their homes were the best available for adopted and foster children, they related to and utilized their homes differently. Applicants chose a diversity of living situations depending on their financial resources and priorities, their beliefs about who could and should comfortably share a home or household, and, most importantly, the ongoing impact of racial discrimination on the city's black residents.

White Chicagoans had many options when choosing a home and how to live in it. White applicants who could afford to purchase single-family homes often did so, and this was clearly the model to which most of these families aspired. Whether in the city or the suburbs, on a large lot or in a cramped bungalow, single-family home ownership was described as fostering family intimacy through greater domestic privacy and control over one's living space. The case records depict owning a home of one's own as offering both parents and children space that was truly their own, making it easier to play, relax, and spend time together as a family. For instance, the Kerns, a white middle-class family who lived in suburban Melrose Park, admitted to their social worker that they kept "a library in the bathroom for the whole family to enjoy." Dora Kern "said that this is a family idiosyncrasy that only close friends know about, and W[orker] remarked that she had heard of other family libraries in the same location, and Mrs. K laughed and conceded that the Ks thought it wasn't a bad idea."[51] Although reading material in the bathroom is certainly a trivial comfort, it was part of this family's shared private space, linking its members, and it would have been a domestic impossibility (or at least impossible to keep secret) for families living in Black Belt kitchenette apartments who shared a hall bathroom.

But there were a number of exceptions to this rule. Some very well-off white applicants, who could have easily afforded to purchase a home in a wealthy suburb, chose to rent in urban neighborhoods instead. For these couples, ownership was less of a priority: their wealth meant that they did not need a home as an investment in their future financial well-being, and they could afford to rent desirable housing. Consequently, they chose to enjoy the quality of life of a desirable urban neighborhood without being tied there through home ownership. In the case records, couples with particularly upwardly mobile husbands— executives, medical residents anticipating the start of their own practices, and lawyers—tended to rent either single-family homes or apartments in luxury high-rises, with the expectation that they might soon relocate. Their rental status did not affect their emotional investment in their housing, for these families looked carefully for desirable communities and ample space, and they remained attached to their homes, but it did help protect their financial stability. They could leave if the husband's job required it or if the neighborhood changed, and it would not affect their class status for they had no economic stake in the area's property values. For these families, financial and geographic flexibility, alongside pleasant surroundings, mattered the most.[52]

Likewise, a number of working-class whites who could have afforded to purchase a single-family home in the Bungalow Belt or in a less-expensive suburb chose instead to buy a multifamily home in a city neighborhood. They prioritized home ownership but not the domestic privacy of a single-family home or the supposed family benefits of a suburban location. Instead, for many of these families, a two- or three-flat in a city neighborhood allowed them to stay in a desirable community (one typically not yet integrating) near family and friends. These couples also often shared their two- or three-flat homes with their relatives, so even though the nuclear family unit had less privacy, their homes were still occupied by family members.

Applicants who took this path usually described their living arrangements as durable and desirable because they offered the ongoing support and assistance of loved ones very nearby. But this also required frequent negotiations with relatives. Keith Hahn's parents, who lived downstairs in a house they owned together, bothered him with intrusive questions as to when his wife Emily would become pregnant.[53] Meanwhile, when Carolyn Echols's parents provided a home for her and her husband in their two-flat, they expected to dine every evening with the whole family together—an expectation that Carolyn and her husband did not share.[54] When problems arose, they were usually resolved so as to maintain the comfort and convenience of living so close to extended family members. The Hahns put up with intrusive questions because they appreciated having Keith's mother there to nurse them through a bad cold, and Carolyn's parents accepted that the younger generation would commit to eat with them once or twice a week rather than every night.

Renting to strangers changed the equation a bit. Most two- and three-flats were simply multistory houses with separate entrances for each floor, which did not allow for a great deal of anonymity. Nor did it shelter a spouse's daily comings and goings, a couple's domestic squabbles, or a father's overly strict child-rearing practices. Renting units in a multifamily dwelling also brought market transactions into the domestic space for daily living, for it required landlord owners to handle emergencies, keep rental units in good repair, monitor the tenants' treatment of the space, and collect the rent. Yet many families did not mind these intrusions. For the families who took this route, the private autonomy enabled by financial stability and the benefits of living in a neighborhood they knew and liked mattered more than the physical privacy of a single-family household.[55]

Poorer white applicants did not have as many options. Those who could not afford to purchase a home tended to rent in more dilapidated and crowded neighborhoods. For instance, in the final months of World War II, when housing was in short supply—as were foster homes—ICH&A began investigating Rosa Pierce's home in a rundown section of the city's North Side. Rosa's husband Patrick was away at war, and Rosa and her mother were sharing a small apartment to help make ends meet. Having recently given birth to a stillborn child, Rosa saw foster motherhood as way to cope with her grief and desired only to care for very young infants. Even though infants were unlikely to need a lot of space to play, the social worker was concerned about Rosa's living situation. The home was small, in poor condition, and in a very crowded area right on a noisy streetcar line. As the worker put it in the record, "We do not require that families own their homes, but we do want to know that the children will grow up in surroundings where they will have good opportunities for play." Rosa, on the other hand, did not share the worker's concerns. "It became evident that Mrs. P could see nothing wrong with the neighborhood where she lived," the worker wrote. She even "pointed out that her nephews grew up all right in this neighborhood and she doesn't see why another child couldn't."[56] Rosa rebuffed the worker's assessment of her community as deleterious to the health and character of children, and instead contended that it was as suitable for children from the agency as it was for those from her own family. The agency ended up using this home for several years after the war, but social workers were never happy with its conditions.

Rosa's case file reveals the very different expectations ordinary people brought to organizing their day-to-day domestic lives within their homes. While applicants agreed that homes were loaded with family significance, and they sought out neighborhoods they believed would be beneficial to their children, they did not necessarily agree about exactly what kind of dwelling one should choose, in what kind of neighborhood it should be located, or how families should structure their daily activities within those homes and neighborhoods. Despite Rosa's belief in the suitability of her home and neighborhood, social workers had reservations that many better-off white applicants would likely have shared. As we will see, these disagreements could lead to tension and even violence, particularly when race was involved. But it is first important to understand the diversity of acceptable options. Whether to own or rent, share a two-flat with relatives or a one-bedroom apartment with one's mother, live in a fancy high-rise or a modest bungalow: the case records reveal a variety of living situations that applicants themselves deemed good for their families and potential children. When we imagine white baby boom families as living—or aspiring to live—in primarily suburban single-family homes, we are missing a tremendous amount of domestic diversity.

African Americans, meanwhile, shared white families' acceptance of diverse living situations, but they faced many more challenges when trying to provide shelter for their loved ones, which limited their options. While many white families had an array of alternatives about where to live, and in what kind of dwelling, with what kind of tenants or relatives, the case files depict black families' decisions about their housing as much more constrained by both financial hardship and the city's racially discriminatory housing market. Even black applicants with ample financial resources often struggled to find and hold on to adequate housing.

Among black families, housing was often a symbol of discrimination, for they were well aware of the many ways their race made it much more difficult to obtain reasonably priced, well-maintained homes. Housing was also for black Chicagoans a particularly important material resource that could be used to help improve the family's financial stability and to assist friends and relatives in times of need. Yet families' reliance on housing to both secure their own financial stability and help others had consequences. Their homes were frequently crowded and busy with an array of relatives, friends, roomers, and renters, whom they had to accommodate into their daily domestic lives.

Race proved a crucial factor in shaping how families occupied and related to their homes. We can see the important impact of race on the contours of families' daily lives within their homes and neighborhoods through the example of the Cashes, a white couple, and the Millers, a black couple, who both purchased multifamily houses in the South Side neighborhood of Englewood in the postwar decades. Their experiences reveal that even black and white families who owned homes that were similar in type—and even in the same neighborhood—faced very different day-to-day living conditions because of their race.

Englewood had been annexed by Chicago in 1889, and it had become a mature residential neighborhood by the early twentieth century. It had some large, stately homes from its early years as an outlying settlement, but by the turn of the century it also had many multifamily dwellings and small homes belonging to immigrants, working-class families, and stockyard workers. By the time the Cashes and Millers moved in, Englewood was undergoing a racial transition. There had been a small population of African Americans in Englewood since the late nineteenth century, but the racial makeup of the neighborhood began to change dramatically after 1940. The area went from 97.8 percent white and 2.2 percent black in 1940 to 89.4 percent white and 10.5 percent black in 1950. The trend accelerated in the following decade, and in 1960 the area was 30.8 percent white and 68.9 percent black.[57]

William and Anna Cash, who were white and Protestant, had grown up in Chicago. They had dated in high school and married in 1944 at the age of twenty. They moved into Englewood in 1949, when they bought their first house together there. The house had three separate apartments. There was the first floor, where William and Anna lived, and two more apartments upstairs, which they used for rental income. Jokingly naming the house Tottering Towers because it was so old, they spent their early years there fixing it up just the way they wanted it. They redecorated their own apartment, built a garage out back with the help of their neighbors, and even furnished the rental units so that they could charge higher rents.

The couple was also very involved in local community activities, with Anna playing the lead in several plays in the nearby park's drama club, and William leading a local Boy Scout troop. Meanwhile William worked as a driver and salesman for a bakery, and Anna, after working earlier in their marriage to help pay for and furnish the house, quit her job two years after they had settled into their home. Anna felt that their neighborhood had an exceptionally rich community life, and the social worker wrote that "there are over 100 children in the square block where they live." It was "a very tight neighborhood with much visiting, block parties, etc."[58] The couple particularly appreciated the area's social life and the extra income from their rental apartments after they adopted two children during the early 1950s.

While the Cashes were adjusting to parenthood and raising their children within the vibrant community life of the neighborhood, Englewood was going through significant changes of its own in terms of its racial makeup. As in many places across the city and the nation at the time, these changes created anxiety and even violence. Despite their fondness for the area's social life and the close friends they had made, the couple was not oblivious to the changes happening around them. In the summer of 1958, William offhandedly mentioned to his adoption social worker that he was worried about his property value because more African Americans were moving in nearby, and he said that the family had been thinking about leaving the area. He was reluctant to go, however, saying that "his family had always lived around this part of Chicago and that he would be hesitant about moving to the suburbs but that they had been looking at some houses."[59] He felt tied to the neighborhood and he and his wife had invested a tremendous amount of time, energy, and money into their home. A combination of racism, fear, and a concern for the financial future of his family prompted him to consider leaving the area, but he was not eager for a suburban life and hated to give up the life (and lucrative rental property) his family had built in Englewood. This record closed in late 1960 with the family still living in Tottering Towers, and there is no way to know how much longer they stayed. Chances are that they took off sometime in the following decade, for Englewood was only 4 percent white in 1970.[60]

Meanwhile, Archie and Rosie Miller, a black couple, moved into Englewood in late 1958. They lived just a few blocks from the Cashes and their Tottering Towers. The Millers had met and married in rural Louisiana in 1949, when both were in their late twenties. They moved to New Orleans and built a small home for themselves there in the early 1950s, but after watching relatives earn more money in Chicago, they soon decided to move there. Once in Chicago, Archie and Rosie organized their lives around purchasing a home. Archie was a skilled construction worker who eventually became a foreman. He worked long hours and took a job that was physically dangerous because it paid more. Rosie also worked regularly as a nurse's aide to help save up for a house. To economize, the couple lived very cheaply in a one-room kitchenette apartment in the community of Douglas, at the northern end of the Black Belt. The area was at the cultural and commercial heart of Bronzeville but was increasingly dominated by public housing projects during the 1940s and 1950s.[61]

By 1958, the Millers had enough money saved to purchase a home, but they were slow and careful in their home search. Rosie's sister, who also lived in Chicago, had recently bought a three-flat, and, based on her experience, Rosie thought this was a wise investment because the building basically paid for itself and covered their housing costs. Archie, however, "commented that buildings entailed a 'headache'; he felt that he would be better satisfied with a cottage and Rosie said that if that's what he wanted that's what he would get." Despite her assurances to her husband, Rosie prevailed and the family purchased a two-flat in Englewood. The family decided that a multifamily home had "more advantages in terms of their future security. They have both learned . . . from her sister's experience what to look for in a building in terms of predicted future income."[62]

Home ownership, however, did not translate into greater security for the Miller family in the same way it had for the Cashes. Although they lived in an area that was generally quite well maintained, their house was old and required more work than they had anticipated, including expensive plumbing and electrical repairs. Further, their upstairs tenant quickly became behind in rent, and both Archie and Rosie had to scramble for extra work to cover their mortgage payments. There had also been a racially motivated bombing nearby a few months before, and the area had twenty-four-hour police protection. The Millers brushed this off, probably hoping not to alarm the social workers and jeopardize the placement of an adoptive child with them, and said they felt safe and that more black families were moving in all the time.

The Millers' and Cashes' stories reveal the vastly different circumstances of black and white Chicagoans at the time, as well as the ways the city's deep racial tensions shaped black and white families' relationship with housing. These two families occupied quite similar structures within a few blocks of one another, both hoped to use their homes to make a little extra income, and both had put tremendous emotional and physical labor into their homes. But the similarities end there. While the Cashes emphasized Englewood's friendliness, with its block parties and wide array of community activities, the Millers instead faced potential violence. Although they appreciated the neighborhood's good housing and were determined to stay in their home, they did not express in the record any indication that they felt particularly welcome there. In fact, it was just as the Millers were moving into the neighborhood that William Cash began to discuss with his social worker the prospect of leaving the area. The neighborhood had much to offer a white middle-class family, but it was living near families like the Millers that began to tip the scale in favor of other options.

Likewise, each couple's housing profoundly affected their financial stability, but in opposite directions. While the Cashes boasted of the generous income they made by renting apartments in their home and described their many leisure activities, the Millers housed tenants who were, like themselves, financially unstable due to the ongoing hardships endemic to black life in the city. Although the Millers had tried to increase their financial security by purchasing a multifamily building, they instead became tied to both their own economic and employment marginalization and that of their tenants. Rather than finally having the resources for Rosie to quit her job and for Archie to relax, the couple instead found themselves working even harder just to hold on to their home.

The Millers were not the sole black couple to purchase a multifamily dwelling. In the case records, black applicants like the Millers, far more often than white working-class applicants, regularly purchased two- and three-flat buildings. Single-family homes were expensive and hard to come by in the Black Belt, and multifamily houses made particular economic sense. The racism of Chicago's dual housing market kept African Americans mostly confined to the limited housing of black neighborhoods and assured that they would pay premium rents, which could be an asset to those families who could afford to become landlords themselves. Even fairly well-off African Americans always faced insecurity in their incomes because of employment and wage discrimination, so black families were far more careful about ensuring multiple sources of income for the family unit. Although owners of rental units were, like the Millers, often subject to the economic hardships of their tenants, multifamily dwellings could provide some financial and emotional security because they were a source of income that was under the family's control. The full benefits of owning rental units would not be realized until the mortgage or contract had been paid off, which took years, but many black families were eager to begin investing in their future security—and in the meantime enjoy housing that helped pay for itself.

Beside investing in multifamily homes, many residents of Chicago's Black Belt also took in strangers to board as a way to make extra income for their families. Although a handful of white families did this too, it was by far more common among African Americans and was generally much more important to the family's financial survival. Roomers were always in ample supply because housing in the Black Belt was so often scarce. Their payments helped cover the inflated rent of a small apartment or the mortgage and daily expenses of home owners facing tough times. For example, in the late 1940s and early 1950s, the Clay family relied on taking in roomers as a way to support themselves. Dennis Clay had lost his hand in an accident at work. Although he had been promised a lifetime job at the company as compensation for his accident, the company soon reneged and fired him, leaving him with few ways to support his family. So the family first converted the top floor of their two-story home into a separate rental unit as a way to make income, but they could not earn enough to survive with just the one unit. Instead, they increasingly relied on taking roomers into their half of the home as well.[63]

African Americans were also more likely to use property productively as a way to earn income than any other group in the case records. Beside renting space to tenants and roomers, they also frequently engaged in extensive gardening and canning, took in mending work, or ran a small beauty parlor on the back porch. On the one hand, as the last chapter demonstrated, using the space of one's home to earn income proved an innovative way for black women to help boost household finances without challenging husbands' status as breadwinners or facing racist and sexist employers. On the other hand, African Americans' productive use of housing also made the home an especially important resource for family and community stability.

In a community where many found themselves in precarious financial circumstances even when trying their hardest to get ahead, providing shelter to friends and relatives in need was a given for many black families. There were a variety of arrangements, from temporarily housing a niece or nephew who was new to the city for a month, to long-term arrangements where friends or relatives paid board and expected to live there until their circumstances changed. For example, Duane and Fannie Butler, who lived in West Englewood, began in the late 1940s to convert their two-flat into a single-family home. This was an unusual decision, for most other families were likely to be adding rather than eliminating rental units. But the Butlers were soon glad they had so much space at their disposal. Just as they had begun working on the plumbing and plastering in the downstairs unit, Duane's parents found themselves stranded and needed to move in because their home was in an area that was being demolished as part of a slum clearance project. The parents had already purchased a new home but the tenants of that house had nowhere to go so they were not moving out on schedule. The elder Butlers pitched in with the renovation work and provided a lot of free child care to their grandchildren, so they were easily assimilated into the family's daily life.

Meanwhile, Duane had a close friend who had been evicted from his apartment because his wife was pregnant and the landlord did not allow children. This couple had nowhere to go, and they were having trouble finding a rental that would permit children. They moved into the upstairs apartment with the Butlers, and took over the children's bedroom. The Butler children started sleeping downstairs with their grandparents, and most of the Butler clan would spend their time downstairs to give their friends more privacy upstairs. Fannie, however, was gracious about the arrangement, and had "assured the couple that they need have no anxiety over having to move until they find an acceptable place even if it takes as long as a year."[64]

Like the Butlers' family members and friends, many black Chicagoans experienced ongoing precarious housing arrangements, and the records from black adoptive and foster care applicants were filled with similar stories of people with no place else to go. Black men and women, by necessity, envisioned their family lives within the context of their community, and they found themselves frequently juggling the needs of their immediate families alongside the needs of relatives and friends. For many black families, housing was both a burden and a resource, which had a profound impact on how they occupied and used it. It could be difficult to obtain decent housing and to keep up payments once one did obtain it, but it could also provide financial benefits to the family and to their loved ones. African Americans' homes were rich with intimate familial meaning, but they were also sites where people coped with the very public problem of racial inequality.

The practice of using housing as a resource for not just the nuclear family unit, but also friends, renters, and relatives, also shaped black applicants' approaches to domestic privacy. Many black families had both loved ones and strangers sharing everything from a hall bathroom to the household itself. These families accepted—or were forced to accept—close proximity of others as part of the daily course of family life. They developed a variety of strategies and attitudes to accommodate these conditions of structural inequality while still prioritizing the needs and interests of their families.

Taking in roomers made strangers part of the daily patterns and routines of family living. In some families a roomer might stay for years and become almost a member of the family, who ate meals with the family and helped out with child care. In others the relationships were a struggle, but financial desperation made them a necessary part of family life. Miriam Clay, the wife of Dennis Clay, who relied on roomers after he was injured at work and lost his job, complained about this. Her social worker wrote, "She told us that after the last woman roomer had left, she took 16 of her sheets with her. She also pointed out that at one time she had felt that if she secured a person who was a good friend of hers that she would have more assurance that that would work out. She found, however, that it was more difficult to get along with people she knew well than it was with . . . strangers."[65]

Miriam's frustration with taking in roomers had led her to ICH&A, for she had decided to try foster children as a way to make income from the available rooms in her home. Her social worker wrote, "One of her church members suggested this to her as a means of securing additional finances without the usual headaches that go along with having strangers in the home." Despite their advantages, foster children were not as lucrative as adult roomers, and, still struggling for money, the Clay family eventually broke the upstairs unit into very small bedrooms, thereby making most of the home available for both individual roomers and foster children. In 1952, the social worker described the scene: "During this period F[oster] M[other] was very concerned with making money; she was permitting the roomers upstairs to use her kitchen which made her home less private. In each visit I would see a new face using the kitchen, or moving through the house." These conditions forced the agency to close this home for foster care, only keeping it on file in the case of emergencies. The social worker later noted that the agency "would not want girls in the home, as the [family] had turned their home into a boarding arrangement for single men, and most of the roomers were transient type."[66]

Some black applicants also sought to live near or with extended family, viewing relatives as more desirable housemates and neighbors than friends or strangers. Living in close proximity allowed extended family members to maintain meaningful relationships and to stay involved in each other's daily lives. Further, staying near kin was a source of emotional comfort and a way to secure help with everyday problems and needs. Kenneth and Edna Hanks had welcomed Kenneth's brother into their small rented apartment when he had returned from serving in the army. When the brother got married, he and his wife moved into the apartment next door, and the families shared the bathroom on their floor. Edna enjoyed having her in-laws so nearby, and the social worker noted in a 1949 interview her pleasure when she mentioned that her brother-in-law sometimes called her "mom." She had been helping her in-laws fix up their apartment in preparation for the baby they expected, and had recently made them new curtains. She had snuck into their apartment to hang them up as a surprise, and she told the worker with pride that her sister-in-law had liked them so much that she had invited other people in the building to come see them.[67]

Other families made their own form of extended kinship among friends and neighbors as a way to cope with crowded conditions and little money. Melvin and Hazel Walker lived in the mid-1940s in an unusually nice building with a lot of community spirit among its residents. The tenants on each floor had worked out a plan to comfortably share the common kitchen and bathroom and keep the place clean, and Hazel mentioned that everyone left their drying laundry in the bathrooms, never fearing it would be stolen or misplaced. The Walkers were especially close to another couple in the building—they had even applied at the same time to become foster parents—and the wives were nearly inseparable. At the start of the record, Hazel's sister was dying in the hospital, and Hazel and her friend put in long hours together at her bedside. The intimacy of sharing kitchen and bathroom meant that building residents were well informed about each other's lives, and when a social worker stopped by when both women were at the hospital, their neighbors figured out who the worker was and informed her of the ill relative. These two couples soon decided to leave the building and to rent an apartment together. They shared the tasks of providing for the foster children in their care, and children from each family shared a bedroom. In the late 1940s, the Walkers' friends moved to a nearby apartment to relieve crowding, but the couples stayed very close and continued to look after each other's foster children.[68]

Overall, the case records reveal an array of living arrangements of postwar families. Rather than a single neat model of nuclear family living, diverse families occupied their homes in starkly different ways depending on their resources and priorities. Moreover, race proved the most crucial factor in shaping how ordinary men and women related to and used their housing. White applicants chose from an array of housing options that would best serve their needs, ranging from the ownership of single-family homes, to rental apartments and multifamily houses. They sought a variety of family benefits in their choices, each demonstrating different priorities: some sought financial stability, some wanted to live near relatives and friends, and others preferred domestic privacy or economic autonomy. Black applicants, meanwhile, faced constricted options and often used housing to both provide financial security to their families and offer assistance to friends and family who needed shelter. They coped with cramped spaces, shared living quarters, low wages, and overpriced dwellings with creativity and flexibility.

↶

The strong ideological and material relationship between family and housing, when combined with diverse domestic practices, made for a potentially combustible mix. Even though applicants and social workers were generally accepting of diverse domestic arrangements, many Chicagoans at the time in fact judged their neighbors by their use of domestic space. Chicago experienced a number of violent conflicts around neighborhood integration during the 1940s and 1950s, and domesticity could help fan the fires of anger and prejudice. Many whites associated African Americans with decrepit housing, overcrowding, neighborhood decline, and depressed property values. But much of what was at stake was how black families occupied their homes: whom they allowed to live there, how they conducted their daily family lives, and how they minded their children.

The activities of the Hyde Park–Kenwood Community Conference (HPKCC) illustrate the importance of these factors in shaping Chicagoans' reactions to neighborhood integration. The HPKCC was created in 1949 to protect, through peaceful measures, the Chicago neighborhoods of Hyde Park and Kenwood from the physical and social deterioration that plagued the nearby Black Belt. It was, as one of its founders described it, an organization "of people of all races and creeds who believed in their community and worked together to save it" by reversing "the patterns of blight and flight that threatened to destroy their neighborhood."[69] The group sought to maintain the area as an interracial middle-class enclave, or, as the header of their newsletter put it beginning in 1956, "to maintain and improve a stable interracial community of standards."[70] Although in practice the HPKCC was mostly white, members encouraged their black middle-class neighbors to join their efforts to preserve the area's middle-class character.

The HPKCC had several strategies for preserving the neighborhood. Its most important tactic was organizing residents into block clubs and committees dedicated to making physical improvements such as replacing sidewalks, installing playgrounds in empty lots, and urging property owners to maintain their yards and buildings. The HPKCC was also committed to preventing property owners from converting the area's single-family homes and stately apartment buildings into crowded kitchenettes that were marketed to the poor and working-class African Americans who sought to escape the confines of the black neighborhoods nearby. The group also eventually became an influential supporter of urban renewal in the neighborhood, and it spent much of the second half of the 1950s promoting renewal plans to area residents.[71]

The HPKCC's response to integration was not a typical one for Chicago. Unfortunately, in many neighborhoods that bordered the Black Belt, integration was met with fierce, angry resistance. As Hyde Park and Kenwood were home to the University of Chicago and other institutions of higher education, their communities were generally wealthier, better educated, and more politically progressive than many of the surrounding areas. The HPKCC, therefore, sought to respond to the challenges of neighborhood change in a less violent and more organized manner than most.[72] To achieve this goal, the organization spent considerable energy discerning the key reasons that middle-class residents abandoned a neighborhood. Consequently, even though the HPKCC's response to integration was somewhat atypical, it offers us a lens into some of the concerns ordinary Chicagoans had about neighborhood change at the time. As the organization's members worked with area residents to fight middle-class flight, they encountered a range of beliefs about the dangers of residential integration.

One of the chief concerns that the HPKCC encountered in the neighborhood was the belief that poor and working-class black families did not occupy their homes in desirable ways—their willingness to share their homes with others was itself seen as undesirable. Incoming black families' willingness to live in the cramped conditions of converted apartments in Hyde Park and Kenwood signaled to their new neighbors that they did not adequately respect the importance of nuclear family privacy. Older residents believed that crowding had a negative impact on a home's occupants, but also, more importantly, that it dragged down the character of the entire surrounding area. Newcomers were thereby morally deficient on two counts: they were willing to live in overcrowded homes, and they were carelessly bringing down the rest of the neighborhood with them.[73]

The HPKCC found that these beliefs about black families usually circulated through the community as rumors. A published report on the group's activities from the mid-1950s described one of the most common of the rumors the group addressed: "The fear that purchase of a house by Negroes would ruin the block." But the real anxiety that lurked beneath the rumor was the concern that new black neighbors would start bringing others into their home. This fear could only be "allayed when a call provided that the family was neat, orderly, educated, and planned to use the house as a single-family home."[74] The leadership of the HPKCC also created a series of "socio-dramas" that depicted the most common concerns of their neighbors about integrated housing. These dramas were enacted in front of various local groups in order to elicit discussion of proactive ways to address the problems facing the neighborhood. In one, a white woman was shown telling her neighbors that the "neighborhood was definitely on the skids. . . . The new Negro family was going to start a rooming house. That was the beginning of the end."[75] The HPKCC's task was to combat such rumors.

To do so, the HPKCC sought to replace rumor with fact. In response to the powerful role of rumor in leading to "panic and flight," members saw it as their mission to find information that would put a stop to the local rumor mill.[76] They thereby gave themselves license to monitor the domestic activities of their neighbors in the name of preserving neighborhood integrity. Often, in order to dispel or confirm a rumor, they visited new neighbors to evaluate their character and family lives, as well as their plans for their new home. For instance, on one block "a panic was in the making" in 1950 after "rumors had spread up and down the block that a speculator was planning to sell one of the houses on the street to Negroes who would then crowd a family into every room." In response, several homes on the block had already been put up for sale by their white owners, and other home owners "were anxious and worried and not sure what to do."[77] A call on the new neighbors, however, revealed that they "were sensitive people" who did not plan to house multiple families in their home. They were also willing to work with their neighbors to preserve the block's character. "Anxiety was relieved" and home owners decided not to sell their homes after all.[78]

The group also sought to promote its own depiction of desirable neighbors. An HPKCC publicity pamphlet entitled "Are You Getting Good Neighbors?" outlined the criteria by which one should judge new neighbors. The pamphlet posed a series of questions about how good neighbors maintained their homes: "Do they get a fresh coat of paint every so often, or are they drab and neglected? Is the lawn well tended, or is it allowed to run to seed? Is the yard a garden or a garbage dump?" Equally important, however, were the moral fiber and family practices of new neighbors. One should ask: "Are they of good character? Are they quiet and considerate? Do they pass you with a friendly smile and a cheerful how-d'ya-do? Are their children learning the same good manners and moral values that we teach our own children? Will they keep the neighborhood standards high?" The pamphlet pointed out that people of all races made good and bad neighbors, and urged readers to judge their neighbors by how they kept their homes and how they reared their children rather than by race.

To drive the point home, the pamphlet chastised whites who fled when black neighbors moved into the neighborhood, noting that "good homes and good investments were sacrificed to prejudice" when this happened. The pamphlet used photographic evidence to help make its argument. Rather than selling at the first sign of black neighbors, "wiser people are happy to see a well kept home like this"—and here followed a photograph of a tidy two-story home with a well-kept yard. That well-kept home was "occupied by an admirable family like this"—and here followed a picture of a photogenic black family consisting of a mother, father, and two preschool-aged children playing together in a very nicely furnished and clean living room.[79]

The HPKCC also sought to counter anxieties about new neighbors' childrearing practices by becoming increasingly involved in the activities of local children and families. One block club chairman created a Rangers Club for his block's children. Although he initially planned the group as a way to deal with "the so called 'bad' boys of the block, those who were creating special problems," the group eventually involved many of the block's boys. They wore western costumes as uniforms, and "each of the boys was given a badge and impressed with his responsibility for keeping up standards on the block." The children were "involved with picking up trash, keeping streets clean, and in trying to regulate their own conduct and the conduct of other children."[80] Another club looked into starting a clothing exchange for area parents in 1953, and several organized supervised play areas for young children, with mothers on duty.[81]

As the 1950s wore on and juvenile delinquency gained wider public attention, activities for older children and teenagers also became quite important. The organization's December 1958 newsletter surveyed block groups about their activities. "Youth Recreation" was third on the list, with twenty-one groups having met to plan some sort of youth activity in the prior three years. Discussions of "Urban Renewal" and "Building and Zoning" were the only items on the list that outranked it.[82] The HPKCC also took over the Hyde Park Youth Project in 1958, which worked with young people and their parents to help troubled youth avoid "an anti-social life adjustment."[83] The quality of local elementary and high schools, as well as teen job programs, were also discussed with some regularity in the organization's newsletter.[84]

The residents of Hyde Park and Kenwood confronted the real diversity of domestic practices as they weighed the impact of integration on their neighborhood: poor and working-class black neighbors were frightening, in part, because they might not occupy their homes or rear their children in the proper manner. The deep linkage between family ideals and housing made domestic diversity seem particularly threatening—especially when coupled with race and class difference. Some residents even admitted that they had overlooked the crowded homes and poor parenting of some of their longtime white neighbors and had only noticed them and sought to change them when they began to worry about the possible problems of their new black neighbors.[85]

༄

Housing was intimately connected to the era's intense domestic ideals. Diverse applicants and social workers alike read profound family significance into people's homes and neighborhoods. They believed that carefully tended domestic and residential spaces indicated the love, care, and warmth of the family unit. These spaces also facilitated a good family life because they provided desirable amenities such as space to play and friendly neighbors, which enhanced family bonding. But despite the shared embrace of the importance of domestic and residential space to domesticity, diverse applicants did not inhabit their housing in identical ways. Instead, families used their homes differently, depending on their access to certain kinds of houses and neighborhoods, as well as their family's particular needs and desires. These differences were inextricable from Chicago's deeply stratified and racist housing market, for issues of costs and, for black families, the many limitations of the Black Belt profoundly shaped how people occupied their homes.

When combined, the intense family meaning inscribed onto housing and the real diversity of how families occupied that housing could fan the fire of racialized housing conflicts. As the HPKCC discovered, part of what was so frightening about housing integration was the belief that black families did not use their housing or raise their children in appropriate ways. While some Chicagoans took to violence to combat this perceived threat to neighborhood stability, the HPKCC organized to create controlled, peaceful integration and to avoid neighborhood deterioration. Yet the members of the HPKCC were not the only Chicagoans to organize around community problems that they deemed potentially detrimental to their family lives. The case records also document applicants' extensive efforts to improve their communities on behalf of their families in arenas that went far beyond housing. As the next chapter will argue, applicants and social workers linked civic participation with being good parents, and applicants became involved in their communities in a variety of ways as they sought to protect and advance their families' well-being.

SEVEN

To Take Some Responsibility for Community Problems

Domesticity and Good Citizenship

Earl and Gladys Bond, an African American couple, applied to board infants in 1951. They were quickly approved, and they ended up adopting the only child ever placed in their care: a daughter who joined their family when she was just one week old. Earl Bond was a janitor, and his wife worked occasionally as a domestic. The couple was particularly proud of the home they owned in a deteriorating West Side neighborhood. They were very involved in their local community center and had helped to found a neighborhood improvement council to address the poverty and blight in the area. They hoped to convince the home owners around them to plant gardens, clean up the streets, and generally make the area more attractive. During the home study, Gladys "was quite frank in stating that the new arrivals in the community represented a very different class, usually recent arrivals from rural sections of the South, who had quite different educational and cultural standards. Without creating antagonism they hoped to assimilate these new arrivals into their community and create a pride in it."[1]

The Bonds were not the only African American applicants to ICH&A who belonged to local neighborhood improvement clubs that sought to inspire (or perhaps force) neighbors to take better care of the neighborhood. For instance, Cora Lane, the wife of a railroad cook, was involved in a local women's civic and improvement club in her black suburban community of Phoenix. During each meeting, the club spent part of the time discussing the "good training and care of their children" and the rest of the time making "suggestions and recommendations relative to improvements of the neighborhood."[2] Others joined neighborhood groups because they were confronted daily with the marginalization of their communities by the city and sought better for their families. Earnest and Hattie Hill, a laborer and his wife, had formed a club with their neighbors that was devoted to "the building up and maintenance of their neighborhood." At the time of the interview, Hattie was "working closely with the precinct captain to get action on the part of the city department of streets and sewers, to clean the streets and remove the garbage regularly."[3]

These applicants had multiple motivations for their activities. By participating in civic activity that would improve the neighborhood and raise property values, they could provide a more respectable and safer neighborhood for their children, become engaged members of the race, and protect the value of their families' largest asset. Black home owners in Chicago invested much in the way of money, time, and emotion in their homes, yet they continued to face substandard conditions. Even those with adequate financial resources were often forced to purchase housing that had been poorly maintained by its previous owners. They also frequently had to buy on contract rather than using a conventional mortgage, and the Black Belt's inflated prices made it impossible for many to buy a home at all, given many black workers' low wages. These men and women had as much stake in their neighborhoods as those in the relatively privileged neighborhoods of Hyde Park and Kenwood, and they too organized to protect their investments and improve the behavior of their neighbors.

But civic participation had other benefits as well. Even though Earl and Gladys Bond did not hold particularly high-status jobs in the black community, their participation in community affairs raised their own and others' sense of their status among their neighbors. Not only did they believe that they were "of a very different class" than newly arriving southerners, several of their adoption references hoped to impress the social worker by pointing to the couple's activities in the community, and their particular interest in children and youth, as evidence of their virtuous character and solid potential for parenthood. For instance, the recreation director of the community center described them as very "'high class' people with considerable community spirit." She gave as evidence Gladys's volunteer work at the center's nursery and Earl's donation of craft supplies for the children. Similarly, the wife of a local funeral director, who was herself a quite active black clubwoman, praised this couple's efforts to "protect the youths by providing good recreation and also improving their community in general."[4] The couple themselves hoped to pass their work ethic and upward mobility on to their daughter, noting that "they admired people who bettered themselves and at the same time did not lose sight of the fact that they had a duty to society to help others."[5]

African Americans were not the only ones who associated civic activism with increased respectability and suitability for adoptive or foster parenthood. A number of applicants, both black and white, boasted to their social workers of their involvement with their communities. On the surface, this seems an unsurprising tactic for proving one's worthiness for parenthood: voluntary community participation suggested one's kindness, goodwill, generosity, and concern for the well-being of others. From the present-day perspective, these seem like obvious ploys to win over a social worker. But applicants' and workers' emphasis during the postwar period on applicants' involvement with their communities actually represented a shift in the history of adoption and foster care. Earlier adoptive and foster care applicants emphasized their morality and their ability to provide for a child as their reasons for deserving children. In the case records, applicants continued to emphasize these qualifications, but they added to the mix a strong dedication to civic participation and good citizenship.

Applicants explained to social workers that their commitment to their families motivated and justified their civic activism. Rather than diverting attention away from community and public activities, the case records instead reveal that the family was intimately tied in people's minds with their civic, and even political, participation. Community and family welfare were linked, and being a good parent required being a good citizen as well. But there was not a straight line between family well-being and any specific civic activity. Instead, diverse families lived in and considered themselves a part of quite different communities, each with its own needs. The Bonds' neighborhood improvement club was but one strategy for addressing community well-being. Others joined PTAS, worked with local churches, or considered running for office. Applicants' assessments of how to best participate in their communities therefore also depended greatly on how they understood their community's shortcomings and how they believed their community could best be improved to support their families' welfare.

⌒

The practices of adoption and foster care have a complicated historical relationship with civic duty. In the first decades of the twentieth century, taking in a child to care for as one's own—through either formal legal adoption or through foster care—was culturally posited as a civic act. Adoption and foster care were depicted as extensions of women's civic housekeeping duties, with potential mothers portrayed as rescuers of needy children. Foster and adoptive mothers were particularly valued for their ability to Americanize homeless and dependent immigrant children into productive members of society.[6]

In the 1920s and 1930s, ideologies of motherhood and adoption changed significantly, and the practice of adoption and foster care moved outside of the civic realm. As sexual fulfillment within marriage, birth control, and family planning became more prevalent in the 1920s, and adoption itself became more widely accepted, cultural depictions of white middle-class adoptive mothers no longer emphasized these women's civic contribution but instead portrayed adoption as epitomizing contemporary family ideals. The adoptive family was the carefully chosen, planned-for family, where every child was a wanted child.[7] By the 1930s, as the Depression created widespread family distress, couples desiring adoptive or foster children explained their desire and deservingness to raise a child in terms of their sincere longing for a child and their ability to be competent caretakers and providers. Couples did not boast of their good citizenship; they boasted of the financial security and nurturing care they could provide a child.[8]

In the 1940s and 1950s, however, the cultural ideals around childhood shifted to emphasize both the emotional rewards of parenting and the physical and emotional vulnerability of children, which in turn changed the practice of adoption and foster care. Children, who were so ardently desired during the baby boom, seemed all the more precious and rare to both the adoptive applicants who desperately wanted to be parents and the social workers who decided where to place the small number of available children. As we have seen, prospective parents did all they could to obtain a child, while adoption agencies tightened their screening procedures in order to make the best possible placements.

There were also broader changes in the history of childhood that made children seem all the more vulnerable and valuable to both potential parents and their social workers during the postwar years. The first decades of the century had witnessed the widespread emergence of modern childhood as it would be recognized today. By 1940, children across class were no longer viewed primarily as potential laborers, even if they still helped out inside and outside the household. Children's value was increasingly embedded in the emotional and sentimental rewards they provided to their parents, rather than in the potential family labor they could provide or caretaking duties they could assume as their parents aged. Further, children as a group more often interacted and identified with each other, creating a peer-based children's culture. By the end of the Depression more children than ever before were enrolled in and attending school, and taking part in youth groups and government programs that reinforced generational divides between parents and children. As a distinct group with its own unique emotional and developmental needs, children were increasingly viewed as delicate and precious, requiring greater attention and more resources than ever before.[9]

The rise in popularity of childrearing advice books in the first half of the century, from Watson to Gesell to Spock, likewise encouraged parents and society as a whole to increasingly view childhood as a series of life stages, each with its own particular demands and needs that had to be met. Historian Peter Stearns has suggested that the twentieth-century growth of advice literature for parents made children seem all the more helpless and vulnerable, requiring constant vigilance and proper handling, which only served to increase parents' anxiety in their attempt to achieve the best outcomes for their children.[10] Similarly, as teen culture became more visible in the 1950s, parents and society at large also worried much more about the causes and consequences of juvenile delinquency, which further delineated youth from adulthood and increased the stakes of proper parenting.[11]

The events of the era also increased the visibility—and perceived vulnerability—of the nation's young people. World War II raised a variety of concerns about how children would cope with the emotional and psychological stresses of war. Because so many men—including fathers, brothers, uncles, and sons—were absent from the home front, psychologists worried about the proper gender and sexual identification of a generation of young boys and girls left at home. Parents and experts also worried about their children's ability to deal with grief and the possible loss of a loved one, and the impact of living with the constant threat of an attack on the home front. In addition, as wives and mothers went to work to support the family and help the war effort while their husbands served overseas, the nation reckoned with how to care for children who were without their usual caregivers. Some extended families pooled their resources to help care for young children, but many school-aged children were left to fend for themselves while their mothers worked, which raised the specter of the potential dangers of—and for—"latchkey children" who had little adult supervision.[12]

The war was not the only event to focus greater attention on the needs of the nation's children. As the polio epidemic roared through communities in the late 1940s and early 1950s prior to the introduction of the Salk vaccine, children's physical vulnerability was ever present in the minds of parents, physicians, and policy makers struggling to curb outbreaks of the disease. For African American families, the murder of Emmett Till reiterated the constant danger and inequality their children faced as they moved through the world. The *Brown* decision, struggles to integrate southern schools, and diverging opinions about black and white children's rights to education further raised the centrality of children's needs and desires among the American public.[13] These personal and public anxieties about children's vulnerability shaped adoptive applicants' and social workers' ideas about protecting and nurturing children both within the household and in their neighborhoods and communities.

Social workers, who had largely abandoned the linkage between adoption and good citizenship in the 1920s, began to again highlight applicants' community mindedness throughout the application process in the 1940s and 1950s. While social workers rarely wrote formally about civic participation as a qualification for adoptive or foster parenthood, case records from the period repeatedly emphasize the importance of community activities in workers' assessments of applicants. Workers did not believe that adopting a child itself should be posited as a civic act, since they sought applicants with a sincere personal commitment to parenthood, not people who sought a child for public recognition or a sense of civic virtue.[14] Rather, they valued community activity because it demonstrated a giving, sociable personality.

Workers recorded extensive descriptions of applicants' civic activities, and their comments in the records suggest that community engagement, particularly activities on behalf of children, served as favorable evidence of applicants' kindness, warmth, and sincere interest in the welfare of others. For instance, in her positive evaluation of the Emersons, a white couple who adopted a son in 1946, a social worker noted the couple's extensive involvement with the community. In the adoption decree that finalized the adoption, she described Glenn Emerson's success as an "understanding, capable and interested" adoptive father, noting, "He is a community minded person, and an active Boy Scout leader." His wife Ida, meanwhile, "is a person of many interests, having assisted in the community nursery school, sewing classes for older girls, and other community activities." She was, therefore, "an intelligent, mature person who manages her home well and handles the children with warmth and understanding." Based on their many activities, the social worker believed that "they both have shown themselves to be very homeloving and community-minded persons without being stuffy or too settled for their years."[15]

Social workers also endorsed community participation because it demonstrated applicants' willingness to work hard for the betterment of themselves and others. Mildred Clark, an African American woman, described her frequent involvement with the "PTA, YWCA group meeting and other educational and civic activities." The worker noted that she did not seem like "a person who would enjoy visiting ordinary social gatherings as she seems to have a drive to extend her educational and intellectual development, which she admits she feels [are] somewhat inadequate." For both Mildred and her social worker, Mildred's involvement in intellectual and civic pursuits was a mark in her favor because it revealed her intellectual curiosity and determination, and her commitment to the community, despite her limited formal education.[16]

Social workers, however, were not the only ones who linked community activities with being good adoptive and foster parents. Applicants likewise emphasized the importance of social participation to their qualifications for parenthood. From supervising parties for local teenagers, to challenging Chicago's Democratic machine, to simply being good neighbors, applicants participated in a variety of activities that they hoped would strengthen their communities, help their families, and prove their worthiness for parenthood.

⌒

Applicants to ICH&A presented themselves as good people—and good potential parents—to their social workers by emphasizing their community mindedness. Black and white couples alike stressed their commitment to programs and organizations that benefited area children, arguing that such activities played a meaningful role in improving their own and their children's lives while also bolstering their applications for adoptive and foster parenthood. Their case records reveal that they believed not only that social workers would see their community mindedness as an asset in their applications, but also that there was a crucial link between the family and the community, for the health and well-being of one facilitated the health and well-being of the other.

Yet not all applicants had the same idea about what kinds of community undertakings best served their families. Although many participated in a range of child-friendly activities, such as serving on the PTA, leading a scout troop, or teaching Sunday school, other activities seemed more urgent depending on one's race and class and the needs of one's family and community. While white middle-class applicants threw themselves into creating wholesome activities that would keep young people out of trouble and solidify community moral and social standards, African Americans prioritized combating racial and educational inequality. Working-class whites, meanwhile, sought to create close networks of family and friends that would provide assistance and support for themselves and their children in times of need.

The intense civic activity of the postwar years was captured most memorably by William Whyte's study of the white middle-class suburb of Park Forest, Illinois, *The Organization Man*. Whyte indelibly linked middle-class identity and civic engagement by popularizing the notion that the newly developing suburban communities of the era were, as he put it, "hotbed[s] of Participation." In Whyte's account, Park Foresters' neighborliness went beyond mere visiting, and also involved extensive personal involvement. From asking prying questions about a neighbor's visitors and activities, to sharing lawn mowers and creating babysitting pools, the suburb's residents had created "a communal way of life," Whyte believed.[17] Further, civic participation filled the time that informal socializing and lending lawn mowers did not. Whyte argued that "Park Forest probably swallows up more civic energy per hundred people than any other community in the country."[18] From church choirs to scouting groups to the League of Women Voters, community members formed social networks and provided vital community services that helped establish the necessary social infrastructure for a newly developing community. Though Whyte suggested that Park Forest was unique in its sheer energy and devotion to community participation, he also contended that Park Foresters were representative of the young, white middle-class people of their generation who more often moved away from old friends and family in pursuit of better jobs and housing. Looking to find friends and build support networks, these young people threw themselves into social and civic activity.

Whyte is not the only observer to characterize the postwar white middle class as a new and especially social character type. From David Riesman's "other-directed" personality to Sloan Wilson's gray-flannel-suited anonymity, several writers at the time blamed postwar corporate and consumer culture for encouraging young, white, upwardly mobile men and women to be particularly focused on fitting in and making connections with those around them. Historians have also noted the importance of postwar community spirit and civic participation. In her study of women's activism in Queens during this period, Sylvie Murray emphasizes middle-class white residents' belief that "'the good life' was an entitlement." But "this sense of entitlement was paired with a clear understanding of their obligations as citizens to participate in the collective life of their communities." For the women of Queens, their extensive civic engagement was an attempt to shape their communities into the version of "good life" to which they aspired.[19]

The case records support scholars' description of white middle-class individuals as particularly engaged in their communities. Applicants who lived in predominantly white, middle-class neighborhoods were especially devoted to community activities. They often expressed an obligation to be good community members and to help out the less fortunate.

Men were remarkably committed to these causes. For example, when Vernon Whitaker, a junior executive at a major retailer, showed up for his first solo interview with an adoption social worker in 1956, the worker noticed that he was wearing a small pin on his lapel. Vernon explained that it was from the Junior Chamber of Commerce and "went into a long discussion of the work that they do and the pleasure he finds in being a member of it." He "explained their activities mostly . . . [as] an attempt to take part in community life and organization and to take some responsibility as young men who are living in the community for some of the community problems." At the time of his interview he was engaged in the group's campaign to raise money to provide Christmas meals, decorations, and presents for needy families in the area.[20] Similarly, Oscar Davis, who lived in a middle-class area of suburban Northbrook, explained in his first interview to have a foster child placed in his home, that he had "decided that everyone should be interested either in politics or in some other aspect of community life." He added that "since he does not like politics because there is so much 'stepping on people' and taking advantage of every situation involved, that he decided he would be much happier in working with community events and with his church." He had "gone into church activities quite wholeheartedly and even now sings in the choir." He and his wife were also involved in the local school's PTA and organized community events like an elaborate Halloween party for the area's children.[21]

Middle-class white housewives were also involved in their communities. Several explained to their social workers that they felt committed to helping the community's young people, often drawing on skills they had developed in jobs they held before staying home full time. For instance, Daisy Norton, a former nurse living in suburban La Grange Park, felt that she should put her expertise to good use once her daughter began school, so she helped out with the local schools' vaccination programs and dental checks.[22] Esther Jacobs, who had recently moved to the suburb of River Forest, told her social worker that she used her college coursework in psychology and sociology in her volunteer work at a local nursery school, a community infant welfare group, and in her work as president-elect of her chapter of the League of Women Voters. Her social worker noted approvingly that although Esther seemed somewhat timid and self-effacing, she "had a good deal of recognition in the community because of her work in a nursery school on a volunteer basis and her participation in the Women's League of Voters [sic]."[23] Likewise, Helen Hurley, a full-time housewife in Winnetka who had been a social worker during the early years of her marriage, "spoke of the fact that she likes to have some interests outside of her home and has given a great deal of time to the planning of a mental hygiene clinic in one of the nearby communities, since she feels there is such a need for service of this kind."[24]

Because white middle-class communities were generally quite socially and economically stable to begin with, residents often focused on making them safer, friendlier, and more wholesome places to raise children. Warren and Grace Matthews, a wealthy white couple who rented a house in a well-to-do area of Chicago's Chatham neighborhood in the late 1940s, became deeply enmeshed in making their neighborhood more family friendly. Grace was an avid gardener, so she organized a community garden in a vacant lot. She talked city garbage collectors into helping her clear the lot initially, and had workers from the railroad company donate sand and oak logs and to help build terraces on the lot. The lot had been a popular play space for children in the area, so the couple designed the garden "so that the youngsters would have ample space to play and could be kept off the streets." The entire community helped cultivate the garden and used its produce, and it became a space for family barbecues and picnics among the neighbors. The Matthews couple enjoyed facilitating neighborly contact and tried to bring more neighbors and their children into the activities of the garden.[25]

Similarly, Morris Jones, an office manager living in Palatine who was also a member of the American Legion, the Veterans of Foreign Wars, and the Lions Club, told his social worker about his participation in a youth council that planned activities for area teenagers. The worker noted that, in the council, "there was much emphasis on proper chaperonage, seeing that these kids had wholesome activity and kept out of trouble, yet also much enjoyment of them."[26] In a time of widespread concern about children's welfare and juvenile delinquency among the white middle class, people worked to create communities that would promise a different outcome for their own children, which meant creating events that would let adults keep an eye on neighborhood youngsters.

Participating in activities on behalf of the community's children was not always limited to volunteering for local neighborhood groups. A number of white middle-class applicants also suggested that their activities crossed into politics. For instance, Marvin Adams began his foray into politics on a fairly small scale when he became invested in maintaining community moral standards. Having taken over ownership of his father's pharmacy in suburban Park Ridge, Marvin was active in his church as well as a member of Kiwanis International and the chamber of commerce. While applying to adopt, he was engaged in a campaign against magazine distributors who insisted he buy "pulp magazines which he feels are not even suitable to place on the shelves in order to get the other things that he wants." He was taking a loss on the pulp magazines because he refused to sell them in his store but had to purchase them. He explained his objection as primarily moral and an effort to protect the community's children from undesirable material. As he put it, "he does sell some of the cheaper kind of material of which he doesn't especially approve but it is only the really lewd material that he withholds from the shelves. [He] . . . has some concern about youngsters reading some of this material." He had started a letter campaign to editors and publishers, and had recently gotten the federal government involved. Even as Marvin worked to increase his own bottom line, he boasted to his social worker about his personal and political efforts to protect the community's children as a small business owner.[27]

Men were not the only ones who delved into politics. Pauline Winter, the wife of an engineer, explained in late 1948 that she was "one of the charter members of their small Women's Club" in her La Grange neighborhood. She explained that the group had been formed out of the women's impulse to participate in community affairs: "There are many things in the community which need doing and this is their way of going at it in an organized fashion." In the beginning their projects were quite modest, such has helping a young widow open her own home child-care business. Some women in the group also had an interest in politics, however, and Pauline believed that "as time went on her group would probably want to become interested in legislation." She elaborated that "her mother was a member of the League of Women Voters and [she is] genuinely interested in what goes on in Springfield and what women can do to help in the way of social legislation."

The group had widespread appeal in the community and grew rapidly. Within six months they had over one hundred members. They increasingly took on more ambitious and controversial community affairs—in particular a dispute between local mothers and a school principal whom the mothers felt was too harsh with their children. In addition to arranging community meetings with candidates running for school superintendent and elected officials, they had also begun talking more seriously about affiliating with a larger women's organization.[28]

The group's social and political projects emerged from its members' interests as wives and mothers—helping a widow, intervening in local school affairs, and promoting social legislation—which drew on a much longer history of middle-class women's maternalist activism. From the benevolent and religious activities of nineteenth-century women to the civic and social housekeeping of Progressive Era reformers, there is a long tradition of middle-class women carving out a space for themselves in the public lives of their communities, and even the nation as a whole, by invoking their unique ability to bring a woman's caring and maternal instincts to social problems.[29] The activism of Pauline Winter and her friends reveals that women's status as wives and mothers continued to provide the impetus and moral authority to effect change well into the postwar years. Instead of confining these women to the home and childrearing, the centrality of their families in their lives actually motivated their activities in the public sphere.[30]

The relatively privileged white middle class was not, however, the only segment of the population engaged in extensive civic activity on behalf of their families in the postwar years. Chicago's African American community was also extremely active in a variety of community affairs beyond the block groups described at the beginning of this chapter. But in order to understand their civic activism, we must first understand a bit more about the racial contours of the city's politics.

Chicago's political leadership, which was dominated by the city's Democratic political machine, did little to advance racial equality in the city. Although in its early years the Chicago machine was composed primarily of white ethnics, by the early 1930s the city's black wards had joined the machine and created a powerful black submachine, with its own infrastructure and patronage positions.[31] For many of the city's African Americans, voting for the Democratic Party was axiomatic by the 1940s and 1950s: the party provided crucial jobs and city services in exchange for loyalty. Consequently, Democratic candidates running for city offices could rely on the black submachine's votes to win elections while simultaneously disregarding the black community's interests. On issues of housing segregation and violence, equal access to quality public education, and other civil rights matters, the machine's—and thereby the city's—leadership tended to ignore black citizens' complaints in order to maintain strong white support for the Democratic Party.[32]

For African Americans, the racial inequality endorsed by city hall only heightened their alienation and racial consciousness. Sociologists St. Clair Drake and Horace Cayton, in their 1945 study of black Chicago, explained that the residents of Bronzeville "live in a state of intense and perpetual awareness that they are a black minority in a white man's world." They continued: "The Job Ceiling and the Black Ghetto are an ever-present experience. Petty discriminations (or actions that might be interpreted as such) occur daily. Unpleasant memories of the racial and individual past are a part of every Negro's personality structure. News and rumors of injustice and terror in the South and elsewhere circulate freely through Negro communities at all times." Drake and Cayton argued, "'Race consciousness' is not the work of 'agitators' or 'subversive influences'—it is forced upon Negroes by the very fact of their separate-subordinate status in American life." The situation was particularly acute in Chicago, for race consciousness was "tremendously reinforced by life in a compact community such as Black Metropolis, set within the framework of a large white community."[33]

The city's endemic racism also informed Chicago's thriving black culture industries. The city's Black Belt was increasingly—and self-consciously—a national center for black culture in the 1940s and 1950s. Chicago's writers, photographers, and musicians provided African Americans nationwide with shared cultural touchstones—from recordings of Mahalia Jackson to the shocking photographs of Emmett Till's mutilated body—that proved pivotal to the emergence of a modern black popular culture in the postwar United States. Likewise, black community engagement during this period was often explicitly focused on racial empowerment, with Black Belt community institutions such as arts centers, recording studios, social settlement houses, libraries, schools, and presses serving as vital locations for creating and promoting African American culture and history. In addition, black women from a variety of backgrounds, from elite clubwomen to poor public housing residents, were deeply involved in creating and supporting institutions that benefited their communities.[34]

Forced to confront their own and their children's exclusion from many of the rights and privileges of whites, many African American applicants also engaged in extensive community activities. Their activities took many forms but all were focused on contributing to the community and uplifting the race. Reflecting the importance of the church to many black applicants, church projects and related organizations were central to many people's civic and social lives. Many sang in the choir, served as deacons, or otherwise played an active role in the life of the church. Some also brought their church work to the community. Verna Wiley, a South Side housewife, did "not belong to any social or civic clubs" but she was "affiliated with several church clubs and participate[d] freely in their activities." Her "major interest outside of her home . . . [was] in the church and 'doing missionary work among the people of the community,'" which included "visiting the sick and administering to their needs."[35]

Black men and women were particularly committed to activities directed toward their own children and those of the community. Lola Newton, wrote her social worker, "frequently volunteered for baby sitting. Often helped out with sick children. Volunteered with the [public housing project of] Altgeld Gardens Nursery School whenever possible and mentioned instances of buying clothing and other things for children in families of limited circumstances."[36] Darrell Tate had been a Boy Scout leader for ten years through his church even though he had no children himself. He and his wife fondly recalled having the boys over for breakfast before church each Sunday during the war. They made waffles, and purchased sausage and milk for the boys, as well as a "large stack of comic books."[37] Many also taught Sunday school or assisted with church youth groups. The Chicago Urban League also sponsored a number of block clubs that spent considerable resources creating safe, supervised activities for the area's youths. They sought to provide protection, nurture, and entertainment while also giving young people constructive outlets for their energies.[38]

Black and white applicants alike described being stalwart members of the local schools' PTAS. PTA membership was extremely common across America at the time. Almost 9 percent of all American adults were PTA members in 1955, making it the second-largest membership organization at the time, after the AFL-CIO. Members participated in over forty thousand local PTAS across the country.[39] But in Chicago, PTA membership meant something very different to blacks than to whites at the time. Although no applicants mentioned it to their social workers, the city's schools had a significant history as sites of activism in the African American community and PTAS were frequently central to these efforts. Many of Chicago's neighborhood schools were primarily, if not entirely, racially segregated—an arrangement many white parents hoped to maintain even as African Americans moved into racially changing neighborhoods. Black parents, on the other hand, frequently protested black-only schools that were so severely overcrowded that they sometimes used gymnasiums and storage rooms for classroom instruction—even when nearby white schools had empty desks. Black community groups, activists, and PTAS had been fighting since the 1930s against city policies that put many black schools on a split shift, meaning that students only attended school for half-days so that all pupils could at least have some schooling each day. Education remained a heated political issue into the late 1950s and early 1960s, as Mayor Daley supported de facto segregation in the city's public schools, with black children facing overcrowding, shorter school days, and deteriorating facilities.[40]

Just as PTA membership could straddle the line between volunteer work and political activism, black applicants described a number of social and volunteer activities that ventured into politics. For example, a number of African American applicants participated in organizations that supported the civil rights movement. Several men were members of the Elks fraternal organization, which at the time was very involved in the national civil rights movement. The Elks' financial, organizational, and political support for the NAACP began in the 1920s, and only intensified into the postwar years. The organization was deeply committed to providing members with a politicized education in support of black civil rights.[41]

Some applicants also boasted to their social workers of their participation in local and electoral politics. The city's black community encompassed a range of political and strategic orientations aimed at improving life in the city's African American districts. The black submachine dominated black politics in the city and its supporters focused almost exclusively on expanding their own political power within the machine, believing that a more powerful submachine would lead to more patronage jobs and better conditions in the Black Belt. Their gains in the Democratic Party, however, often came at the expense of a broader civil rights agenda for the community as a whole. But the machine was not completely monolithic in the Black Belt, and some individuals and organizations contested its policies. For example, the Chicago Urban League and the local chapter of the NAACP (prior to its takeover by the submachine in 1957) critiqued machine politicians for failing to fight for greater racial equality in the city.[42]

The case records reveal the community's political diversity, as well as the strong linkage between family and politics for some of the city's African Americans. For example, a lawyer and his wife, Walter and Violet Bennett, became deeply involved with city politics as well as the national civil rights movement in the late 1950s and early 1960s. Both Walter and Violet were highly educated, and, as a lawyer, Walter had a prestigious job within the black community. He had not found it easy to get ahead, however, and Violet occasionally returned to work part-time to help support the family. Reflecting their high status as well as the impact of discrimination on their lives, this couple had long been interested in civil rights politics.

In the late 1950s, Walter became very involved in an organization that promoted black candidates in local elections and urged the local Democratic and Republican Parties to court the black vote more aggressively. At one point he even ran for office as a direct challenge to the machine. Over the years he was involved with a number of local and national causes, including raising funds to investigate southern lynchings and marching in support of federal civil rights legislation. He also wrote for the *Chicago Defender* and published a political tract encouraging pan-Africanism. He further argued that African Americans would be best served by unifying their votes so that they could demand equal citizenship rights from elected officials. This couple also bragged to their social worker that they had taken their adolescent daughter to hear W. E. B. Du Bois speak in Chicago "because they were of the opinion that she should have an opportunity to hear and see this wise old man of 94."[43] Embracing a vision of citizenship that was political, extremely race-conscious, and consistently involved in local, national, and international civil rights struggles, the Bennetts suggested that their extensive activity on behalf of the race was integral to their good prospects as adoptive parents.

Sometimes, however, familial and citizenship obligations could create tension with one another—particularly because of the difficulty so many black parents faced when providing financial security for their families, which limited their time and energy for civic participation. Struggling for upward social and economic mobility for one's family could be at cross-purposes to struggling for upward social and economic mobility for the race, even when people believed the two were linked. One couple, Stanley and Ruby Douglas, expressed a tremendous obligation to serve their community. Ruby, who had been a teacher before adopting her first child, was especially involved in activities on behalf of children. She did a great deal of work with her son's interracial nursery school and later served on its board. She was also an active member of the League of Women Voters. Stanley, who owned his own business, was also quite active in local organizations—and he and his wife became involved in ICH&A's volunteer activities. Stanley hoped to eventually organize a scholarship fund for children under the agency's care who were in need of financial assistance for their educations. Further, this couple had high hopes for their own son, and they did all they could to provide him with the best education, toys, and opportunities.

In 1947 the Douglases' attentions turned to electoral politics when Stanley became involved in the newly formed Americans for Democratic Action (ADA), which was founded by the nation's leading anticommunist liberal elite. By 1952, the Douglases were deeply involved in the ADA's support of Adlai Stevenson, then governor of Illinois, in his presidential election campaign against Dwight Eisenhower.[44] Their electoral interests, however, were local as well as national— and their involvement with Democratic Party politics created frustration as well as hope. Although they were inspired by progressive Democrats on the national level, they critiqued local party politics and the Democratic machine. Stanley believed that the city needed "new people in politics, people who have independent means who can be articulate on vital issues without depending on political jobs to express views." Feeling that their community was underserved in city government, his neighbors had even urged him to run for alderman himself because he was "interested in politics, [and] in a way to aid good government."

This couple's commitment to their family not only motivated civic activity, it also limited the extent of their involvement—for caring for the family ultimately had priority. Stanley was not interested in running for alderman because he did not want the responsibilities of public office for the time being, preferring instead "to help out as a citizen." He was "interested primarily in his business" and feared that public office would interfere with the family's rising class status and financial success. Concerned about his only child's future, he eventually convinced Ruby to withdraw their adoption application for a second child because he felt that they did not have the resources to provide all he wanted for two children.[45] Although their obligations to provide adequately for their families were sometimes in tension with their obligations to work on behalf of the black community, black families like the Douglases did their best to maintain a commitment to both.

Further, despite the potential conflict between aiding one's community and caring for one's family, the family could serve as a vehicle for political change in and of itself. By exposing their children to their activist politics, the Bennetts and the Douglases were certainly priming their offspring for a future of political engagement, and they were not alone. Several black applicants mentioned to their social workers that they wished to instill a racially conscious civic mindedness in their children. Just as they hoped that their children would lift as they climbed in their professional lives, they also hoped that they would help improve race relations in their other activities. For instance, Julius Cook, a janitor, and his wife, Mabel, worked particularly hard to give their son a good education and all of the love and support they could muster. They hoped, in turn, that he would work to improve conditions for other members of the race. Regarding Julius's hopes for his son, the social worker wrote: "He would certainly like for him to do something which should be of help to the Negro race. He does not care what profession or what type of work it is as long as it is for the good of his people. This feeling has arisen because of the difficulties which are arising constantly and what Mr. C. foresees as the future for the Negro race. He feels that all youngsters should be prepared to do their share and to contribute to the uplift of the race."[46] For black applicants, the family did more than just motivate political and community activity—it could also serve as a training ground to inspire future generations to serve others and to advance the cause of racial equality.

African Americans embraced an array of civic activities as a way to make a difference for themselves, their children, and the race. Motivated on behalf of their children, as well as by their own alienating experiences with racial discrimination, they sought to support community institutions and activities that would provide uplift, nurture, and care. They further urged local and national government to provide the services, citizenship rights, and honest representation they were being denied. Even the family itself could be a site of civil rights politics. Although their obligations to provide adequately for their families were sometimes in tension with their obligations to work on behalf of the black community, black families did their best to maintain a commitment to both—for the welfare of the family and community were undeniably linked.

In an era when so many men and women devoted their energy to their communities, working-class whites were notably absent from the trend. Many observers at the time believed working-class whites to be considerably less involved in civic activities than their middle-class counterparts. For example, Bennett M. Berger, in his 1960 study of a working-class suburb in Southern California, found that very few of the men and women in his sample of suburban autoworkers were members of formal groups. Seventy percent of his respondents belonged "to no clubs, organizations, or associations at all."[47] While some women were involved in groups such as the PTA, Girl Scouts, and the Christian Women's Auxiliary, men rarely belonged to organizations and were unlikely to attend the meetings of the few groups to which they did belong, such as fraternal organizations, the PTA, or even their own unions.[48]

Similarly, sociologist Lee Rainwater and his colleagues suggested in their 1959 study of blue-collar housewives that these women joined many of the same kinds of clubs as their middle-class counterparts, such as the PTA and church groups, but as a group they belonged to fewer organizations, participated less in those to which they belonged, and preferred different activities within those groups. They argued that generally working-class women prioritized their families over club work. The sociologists contended that the working-class wife believed that "her family, her husband, and her home should come first in her attentions—and that clubs should only occupy her time after these other obligations have been fulfilled."[49] Further, "half of the clubs which working class women belong to have to do with the children—either the PTA or a scouting organization."[50] In short, when they did belong to formal organizations, these women justified their activity as "an expression of their great concern for their families and children."[51]

The case records of white working-class applicants to ICH&A reveal that much as Rainwater and his colleagues suggested, these couples believed that civic activity could play an important role in their families' well-being, and a number participated in a variety of community activities. But, juggling limited financial and emotional resources, they weighed their many personal, social, and occupational obligations carefully when choosing how to spend their time. For many, the time was better spent forging solid relationships with friends, relatives, and neighbors, rather than in more formal organizations. They described simple neighborliness as the most basic form of good citizenship, and they suggested to social workers that building solid relationships with those around them proved their good character and qualification as parents.

Working-class applicants emphasized personal relationships and obligations between individuals to their social workers. For instance, Caroline Clifford, a housewife who lived with her truck driver husband in the Chicago neighborhood of Norwood Park, explained to her social worker that "she and her husband both feel that if they live a good generous life with themselves and with the people with whom they come in contact, they are doing their bit as American citizens." Her husband Larry echoed her beliefs, saying that his "motto is 'live and let live'. He likes to live a good, clean life and do right by other people. He does not expect to be repaid when he does a favor for a neighbor or friend, such as helping him repair the car, mow the lawn or otherwise do a favor. He thinks that someday he may need something and that perhaps someone would be nice enough to help him out, too."[52] The Cliffords embraced neighborly goodwill and generosity as essential to doing "their bit as American citizens." Positing clean living and "doing right by other people" as the crux of their obligation, this couple's vision of good citizenship was linked to individual qualities, it was reciprocal, and it was constituted through interpersonal relationships.[53]

Working-class white applicants also mentioned to workers their reluctance to engage in activities that would keep them away from their families. For instance, Flora Crawford, who lived in a newly developed working-class section of suburban Harvey, gave up all of her outside-the-home activities due to the guilt she felt after her daughter got sick after waiting outside for her mother to get home from a meeting. She "had gone to a club meeting and did not reach home in time to let the child in after school so the child played outdoors, and caught a cold which resulted in strep throat. Consequently, she is staying at home more than she did before."[54] Likewise, Nathaniel Parker, a trucker, did "not attend union meetings nor does he belong to any lodges in which he actively participates." He explained that he worked "six days a week, hard and long hours, so he is very glad to stay home and as he says 'sleep and eat.'" The Parkers spent quality time gardening, reading, and visiting friends in their somewhat rundown neighborhood in suburban Hillside instead of participating in organized groups.[55] Just as many working-class men passed up higher-paying jobs in exchange for more time at home, these couples also prioritized spending time with their families over civic participation.

Working-class applicants also expressed the belief that most community groups were more social than civic in nature—going so far as to question their utility for community improvement. Rebecca Compton, who lived in South Chicago, told her social worker that she "did not belong to any women's clubs or organizations, as she feels that many of these are rather useless because they simply furnished a means for a group of women to get together and gossip."[56] Earnest and Lucille Henry, who lived in Portage Park, avoided church activities and did not become involved with the church's board of directors "since they feel that there is a great deal of 'politicking' and that only the old-timers, those who have been in the community for a long time seem to be able to hold executive positions." They instead spent time with their children, friends, and relatives.[57] Similarly, Alton Paxton, a factory foreman who lived in a solidly white section of Englewood, said "he had never been particularly interested in belonging to a men's club . . . because of the drinking which goes on in so many of them." He also "enjoys his home and likes to spend as much of his time there as possible, so that he cannot see the point of belonging to a club where he would have to be away from home night after night and possibly not even have his wife along with him."[58] These applicants described organized clubs as primarily a social outlet, which could be a distraction from more meaningful time spent with family. Perhaps these couples were trying to convince their social workers of their family mindedness by suggesting that they always put family relationships over social and civic activities. But many middle-class white and African Americans applicants instead chose to link these activities to their families, which suggests that working-class applicants actually thought about this relationship differently—even if they were simply hoping to make a good impression.

These couples' focus on their families, friends, and neighbors instead of more formal civic participation does not, however, necessarily imply a rejection of community responsibility. Sociologists Pamela Herd and Madonna Harrington Meyer argue that unpaid care work, such as that provided for family members or an elderly neighbor, should also be considered part of civic activity rather than a separate, personal endeavor unrelated to public life. Bringing a feminist analysis to recent scholarship bemoaning the decline of American civic life in the last decades of the twentieth century, they contend that much of the literature has overlooked the ways in which providing care to others such as a family member or friend, work which is often done by women, builds the same kinds of "social capital"—the "social networks and norms of reciprocity and trustworthiness"—as does more formalized civic participation.[59] Their critique suggests that the working-class emphasis on relationships with family members and friends was a different strategy for contributing to one's community rather than a rejection of community obligation.

Working-class couples' skeptical attitudes about the role of civic activity for improving their communities and their own lives likely emerged out of the working class's very different relationship to civic activity in the first half of the twentieth century. The most prominent civic activities throughout much of the first half of the century often involved middle-class attempts to control working-class culture, values, and behavior. From the prohibition movement's attempts to regulate working-class male sociability to women reformers' campaigns to fight prostitution and contain working-class women's sexual and social lives, community engagement was frequently a veiled form of class conflict. Consequently, it is not surprising that working-class men and women placed a lower priority on civic work than they did on time spent with their families.[60] Further, their emphasis on the interpersonal and social rather than civic aspects of group activities reflects a different civic tradition among the working class. Just as middle-class civic activity often sought to control working-class culture, the working class in the early decades of the twentieth century had its own rich network of mutual aid societies and ethnic institutions. These associations served to mediate some of the perils of immigration and industrial capitalism. They further provided a sense of ethnic unity and group stability for working-class families. Although the crisis of the Depression depleted the resources of many ethnic institutions and aid groups, the appeal of social groups and fraternal organizations among some members of the postwar working class, with the organizations' focus on ritual, mutual aid, and close personal ties between members, reflects earlier twentieth-century working-class cultural patterns.[61]

Working-class men's and women's descriptions of their good citizenship reflected the city's long tradition of close-knit working-class neighborhoods by focusing on personal relationships within the family and between friends and neighbors. Rather than embracing organized civic activity as a way to provide a better life for their families, as did their middle-class and African American counterparts, white working-class men and women instead devoted their time and energy to their families and friends directly. They suggested to social workers that their goodwill, generosity, and neighborly trust were evidence enough of their citizenship and character. They presented themselves as good people and good potential parents by boasting about their ability to form solid interpersonal relationships and to prioritize their families within a wider network of social obligations and interests.

⌒

Domesticity shaped not only diverse families' lives within their households, but also their activities outside of their households. During the postwar years, community participation was often linked with family needs and desires. On the one hand, applicants to ICH&A invoked their engagement with their communities as evidence of their worthiness for a child. Applicants and workers alike equated examples of community and political participation with applicants' promise as good parents. On the other hand, applicants suggested that they got involved in civic and political affairs in order to create neighborhoods and networks that would best serve their family interests. A commitment to the family motivated a commitment to the community, for the well-being of one was served by the well-being of the other.

Yet even as domestic concerns tied people into the fabric of their communities and motivated civic and political activity, domesticity also reified social divides and differences along lines of race and class as men and women assessed the greatest hardships and dangers facing their children and thereby decided how to expend their civic energy. Among African Americans and working-class whites, the detrimental impact of inequality on their family lives was never far from their minds, and they sought to ameliorate its negative effects through their involvement with their communities. Working-class whites devoted their energies to building social networks that would assist in times of need, while African Americans sought redress for the ongoing racism they faced at all stages of life. Even white middle-class applicants saw room for improvement in their neighborhoods, and, as in the case of the residents of Hyde Park and Kenwood, often sought to stave off the potential disorder and family danger they saw in other areas of the city by becoming involved in local activities that would promote community standards. Diverse communities bred diverse domesticities and diverse assessments of how one's family life could best be served and improved through public participation.

The Postwar Family and American Politics

Emmett Till was lynched in Money, Mississippi, in 1955. He was accused of whistling at (or perhaps just speaking to) Carolyn Bryant, a white married woman, while shopping at a local convenience store. Only fourteen years old, he was taken from the home of relatives in the middle of the night and killed. His body was later discovered in the Tallahatchie River, weighed down with a cotton gin fan tied around his neck with barbed wire. Emmett Till, or Bo, as his mother called him, was from Chicago. Visiting family in the South for a few weeks over the summer, he had been unaccustomed to Mississippi's racial mores. His murder became, as historian Adam Green puts it, "for blacks, the first modern instance of simultaneity: an occasion in which northern city and southern delta seemed the same place, and the need for collective response among African Americans across the nation seemed urgent as never before."[1]

The murder was so galvanizing in part because Till's mother, Mamie Till Bradley Mobley, chose to make his funeral a public affair. She brought her son's body back to Chicago for burial, leaving the casket open and allowing thousands of mourners to view the gruesomely disfigured body. She explained later, "I wanted the whole world to see what they had done to my boy."[2] Local and national media, both black and white, covered the lynching and those on trial for Till's murder extensively that summer. Throughout, Mobley drew on her status as a mother as she fought for redress. As historian Ruth Feldstein explains, Mobley "explicitly politicized motherhood on a number of levels—challenging black women's exclusion from the racially specific discourse of white motherhood and challenging women's exclusion from the gendered discourse of politics."[3] Although Mobley's status as a mother did not protect her from ridicule and insult in the press, it did provide a vehicle through which she was able to make claims for justice—even as she also challenged the assumption that black women were supposed to know their place. In the process, she managed to make her son's murder a turning point in the postwar black freedom struggle.

When Mobley invoked her motherhood, and the harm done to her and her family, her claims resonated with Chicagoans in part because they were already accustomed to thinking about inequalities and privileges in relation to their family lives. During the postwar years, family played a central role in how diverse men and women understood and interacted with the world around them. Although scholars have generally associated the ideal postwar family with white, middle-class suburbanites, the case records from adoptive and foster care applicants at the time demonstrate that when we look at everybody else, we see that a much wider array of individuals ascribed intense personal and social significance to nuclear family membership—and they did so in ways that heightened their sense of social and racial inequality.

The nuclear family was central to diverse men's and women's sense of personal meaning and mission. This is particularly clear when one looks at the experiences of adoptive and foster care applicants at the time. Regardless of their race or class status, applicants drew upon their personal resources to demand from social workers and the state full inclusion in the benefits of postwar pronatalism. Their efforts reveal the importance of family membership to both their sense of personal well-being and their access to social citizenship, as well as the many ways the supposedly public sphere of politics, society, and the economy and the supposedly private sphere of family and household were intimately connected in the postwar years.

The significance of the family and its connection to the world outside the household during the postwar period were rooted in the upheavals and hardships that had come before: the Great Depression, migration, and the war itself. Family members had made sacrifices to help their loved ones through the Depression, husbands and wives had worked together to create better lives for themselves and their children outside of the Jim Crow South, and couples had looked to each other when facing the uncertainties of World War II. In the process, they had come to see the family as a central emotional and practical resource for managing adversity, suffering, and struggle—a belief that influenced the importance of the family in later decades. Emotionally, the family offered happiness, companionship, and security. Socially, it offered a sense of belonging and fitting in with one's peers and relatives, and a platform from which to participate in community affairs. While the family has always been a central institution in American life, during the baby boom it took on greater emotional and social meaning as diverse individuals embraced the family as a primary source of pleasure and purpose.

But the baby boom was a unique moment in American family history, and the nuclear family ideal of the postwar period was more of an anomaly than the epitome of long-standing American family traditions.[4] The changed political and economic environment of the 1960s and 1970s ruptured the immediate postwar consensus around the nuclear family. In the 1960s, the civil rights and Black Power movements, youth activism, growing skepticism about the war in

Vietnam, the sexual revolution, and the birth of second-wave feminism caused many Americans to question ideals and values they had once taken for granted. Moreover, as the economy began to falter in the 1970s, some of the very uncertainties that had long plagued working-class families and families of color penetrated the white middle class, creating less family stability throughout American society. Divorce rates began to climb, mothers and married women took paid jobs outside the home in ever-increasing numbers, and there was a rapid rise in female-headed households. These changes in the family gained widespread attention as feminists, alongside the emerging New Right, organized around the American family as an institution in need of repair.[5]

Yet the postwar nuclear family itself was riddled with significant political and social fractures even during the very decades it was most entrenched. Scholars have long suggested that much dissatisfaction lurked beneath its shiny surface: housewives faced boredom, husbands struggled to keep up with the Joneses, and teenagers felt trapped in a suburban dystopia.[6] But the tensions around the postwar family went beyond simply the discontent of family members who felt personally frustrated by the era's gender conservatism, focus on consumption, and restrictive sexual and behavioral norms. The postwar family consensus also inspired critiques of larger social inequalities.

Men and women from different racial and class backgrounds described a shared commitment to family membership in the postwar years, but the very democratization of family ideals made family a site where inequality was often painfully experienced. As diverse men labored to provide for their families and to stay involved in their children's lives, and their wives juggled the demands of housework, caregiving, and, increasingly, paid work, racial and structural inequalities permeated everyday family living. Although the privileged few found a sense of empowerment when providing and caring for their families, many others found their efforts to support and nurture their loved ones thwarted by inequality due to gender, race, and class. Mamie Till Bradley Mobley was not the only one who made the connection between her personal family tragedy and larger inequities. Everybody else did so as well.

Rather than turning people's attentions inward, away from social problems and politics, the family instead focused their attentions outward as people inscribed family meaning onto the world around them. As men and women worked on their homes and became involved in their communities, their families' needs were never far from their minds. In terms of housing, applicants used their domestic and residential spaces in a variety of ways to advance their families' interests, seeking out the best options they could, given their unequal circumstances. Some shared two-flats with relatives, others took in roomers and friends just to get by, and those who could purchased single-family homes with yards where they grew gardens and held barbecues. Imbuing their houses and neighborhoods with strong family significance, they evaluated their communities—and their neighbors—through the lens of the family's personal and financial stability.

Similarly, as they sought to improve the lives of their own and the community's children, diverse applicants embraced a variety of political and civic strategies. From running block groups, participating in the League of Women Voters, and running for office to simply being good friends and neighbors, applicants took a range of paths to make their communities and local authorities more responsive to their families' needs. Yet they defined their priorities—a more wholesome environment for their children, an end to racial discrimination, or a network of close friends and relatives to turn to in hard times—in relation to their circumstances. Applicants' experiences in their houses, neighborhoods, and larger communities served to reify social differences and inequalities even as they also reinforced the importance of the family itself.

The practice of adoption also changed in later decades in ways that reflected immediate postwar tensions. During the 1940s and 1950s, social workers built their professional authority on their attempts to hide the role of public authorities and state mandates in creating private adoptive and foster families. But as the pronatalist 1950s morphed into the rebellious 1960s, the practice of adoption fundamentally changed. It became more acceptable for white single mothers to raise their children themselves. Interracial and international adoptions also became more common, the practice of "matching" became passé, and the interpenetration of public and private spheres in adoptive family making became impossible to hide. By the late twentieth century, the difference of adoption was readily visible, creating both celebration and anxiety. But even during the 1940s and 1950s, social workers' efforts to cover up the difference of adoption were never entirely successful, for adoptive families were always reckoning with the particular joys and difficulties of forming kinship bonds through law rather than through birth. The pressures of matching, and of selecting deserving parents when the demand for children was so high but the supply was so low, put a strain on parents and social workers alike. Attempts to deny the difference of adoption ultimately reinvigorated the difference. In later decades, denial changed to acceptance, and difference was embraced as one of the many joys and difficulties of adoption as a means of family formation.

Politically, postwar family ideals shored up white middle-class privilege while also providing an inclusive platform from which diverse groups assessed and critiqued inequality. Understanding this paradox particularly clarifies the racial politics of the postwar family. Scholars have tended to focus on efforts to evaluate and regulate the black family in the postwar years by interrogating the Moynihan Report, the origins of the "underclass," and efforts to reform welfare.[7] But the family was not only a site where African Americans were judged by white (and sometimes black) authorities; it was also a site where African Americans themselves gave meaning to and critiqued racial inequality in the urban North.

Historians of emancipation have argued for the significance of, as historian Julie Saville puts it, the "protopolitical implications of slaves' kinship."[8] They have shown that the reconstitution of households was integral to freed slaves' conception of freedom: one's ability to have authority over and to support one's dependents was a key aspect of African Americans' personal and cultural autonomy, while household economies proved crucial to black economic independence. In the period after World War II, family self-determination continued to be an essential aspect of everyday racial politics among the black community. Financial self-sufficiency proved a particularly important goal for black families, but it was difficult to attain. For black men who encountered discrimination as they worked to support their families, and black women who wrestled with demands to both earn income and defer to male breadwinners, the family was a key site where the emotional impact of discrimination was acutely felt.

The family also served as a vehicle for racial uplift, and it was a crucial location where men and women sought autonomy from the political and social forces that otherwise limited their options. Black parents hoped to give their children the resources they would need to do better than themselves, but they also taught their children—and worked themselves—to help improve conditions for the race along the way. As African American parents labored to provide for their children in the face of racial discrimination, took needy friends and relatives into their homes, and participated in the political life of the black community, they were simultaneously crafting an oppositional definition of family ideals in the era of "domesticity." African Americans posited that the black family played a crucial social and political role alongside its personal pleasures: it was essential to both coping with and challenging racism.

For members of the white working class, meanwhile, family was a site where men and women worked out the meaning of class identity and inequality at a moment when these concepts were up for grabs. The case records reveal a persistent sense of anxiety about working-class people's inclusion in American prosperity. Doubts about one's ability to make life substantially better for oneself and one's children pervade these couples' records, even as they outlined the many choices they made on behalf of their families' welfare. Working-class men looked to their families for a sense of fulfillment and accomplishment they found lacking at work. Their wives, similarly, expressed a sense of disenchantment with their labors both inside and outside the household, but also valued their role as family caregivers. Lacking faith in promises of upward mobility, these couples prioritized time spent with each other and their children over higher incomes. Likewise, rather than pursuing civic improvement, they often looked instead to neighborhoods with relatives and friends to ensure their families' stability and security. For the white working class, family proved an essential lens for gauging their inclusion in national prosperity, while also serving as a source of meaning and purpose despite persistent inequalities.

For middle-class whites, however, family membership shored up racial and class privilege. The family offered warmth and succor while also boosting one's sense of confidence to pursue personal and family goals. While certainly some middle-class men and women felt trapped in unfulfilling family lives, the case records suggest that for many the family served as a springboard to other activities. It granted women a sense of purpose that ultimately inspired many to pursue happiness both inside and outside the household, and it gave men a retreat from the demands of the office while also providing a rationale for pursuing career success. Middle-class whites benefited from their social and moral authority as parents and spouses as they purchased homes, participated in their communities, and worked to build the best life possible for themselves and their children.

During the early postwar years, shared family ideals created multiple and competing worldviews in the everyday lives of ordinary men and women. These ideals foregrounded the importance of family membership to social belonging while also reinforcing profound social cleavages and political tensions that would come to the forefront of American life in later decades. During the 1960s and beyond, the personal became explicitly political, the family became laden with "family values," and the family became central to articulating political priorities and critiques for both left and right. But the stage for the growing importance of the family in American politics had already been set in previous decades. Men and women from different backgrounds expressed widespread agreement about the purpose and meaning of the family during the 1940s and 1950s, but they also encountered many privileges and inequalities while advancing the needs and interests of their families. The family was by then already an important site in which they thought about their rights and privileges, assessed economic, gendered, and racial disparities, and engaged in civic, social, and political affairs.

APPENDIX A
Note on Sources and Methodology

This book uses confidential case records from the Illinois Children's Home and Aid Society. I refer to this organization in the text as ICH&A, as it would have been called at the time, but it is now known as Children's Home + Aid (CH+A). (For more information about the organization today, see http://www.childrenshomeandaid.org/.) These case records form an unusual archive, and my research strategy and theoretical orientation deserve greater explication than I could provide in the text.

I analyzed 257 records from black and white couples that applied to ICH&A to adopt or provide foster care in Chicago and its suburbs in the 1940s and 1950s. These files were selected randomly from the over six thousand adoption and pre-adoptive foster care records that were closed by the agency across Illinois between 1940 and 1969. The agency filed adoption and foster care records from this period together and organized them alphabetically in seventy-three boxes. To select my sample, I pulled every fifth box (for a total of fifteen) so that I would have a spectrum of last names from across the alphabet, thereby increasing the odds of encountering diverse ethnicities within the records.

I then set up criteria by which to select particular records from these fifteen boxes. I only looked at families living in Cook County, which encompassed Chicago and, at the time, most of its new and existing suburbs.[1] In terms of dates, adoption and foster care records do not allow for precise sampling across time because records lasted anywhere from one year to several decades. Consequently, I selected records that closed during or after 1945 (which meant that I would have a number of records that opened well before 1945) and opened before or during 1959 (so that my sampling dates would extend into the early 1960s). This selection of dates allowed for the highest density of data during late 1940s and throughout the 1950s while still allowing me insight into the early 1940s (and even the 1930s) and the early 1960s. See appendix B, tables 1–4 for information on the kinds of records, racial breakdown, and years represented in my sample.

Because the majority of records produced during this period were those of white couples providing temporary foster care, I had different sampling rules for black and white families and for each kind of record. I used every black record, adoptive or foster care, which fit the above criteria as to date and location. I used every fifth white adoptive record fitting the sample criteria, and every seventh white foster care record. This selection process ensured that I would not simply select records that seemed especially rich or that either fit or challenged my preexisting ideas about the postwar family, but would instead encounter a variety of situations, dates, and kinds of families. It also ensured that I would have a large enough sample to see meaningful patterns in both social work practice and applicants' ideas and expectations.

These case records are anywhere from roughly ten single-spaced, typed pages to over fifty pages. The records recounting an adoption or foster home study usually follow a set pattern. Much of each file consists of narrative descriptions of every encounter between the agency and the applicants. Each case file begins with a contact sheet that was made after the couple's first encounter with the agency, which was usually a phone call. This sheet has identifying information about the family (name, address, phone number, religion, race, kind of application) on the front and the intake worker's description of their initial contact on the back. This description outlines who referred the couple to ICH&A or how they became interested in adoption or foster care, provides a bit of information about each spouse's job, and recounts the worker's first impressions. If the intake worker felt that this couple might be suitable for further study, she would arrange a formal interview at the agency's office with herself or another intake worker.

The criteria for accepting applicants were never hard-and-fast rules, and couples could be turned away at any time during the home study. As I have described in more detail throughout the text, workers saw it as their duty to evaluate each home in terms of the kind of security and warmth it could offer a child, and they made their decisions accordingly. Workers would deny applications of families that they believed could not offer a child stability because of intermittent unemployment or inadequate housing. They also turned away applicants whom they felt were not well suited for parenthood because they were too old (the agency preferred adoptive mothers to be under forty but had no age restrictions for foster parents), were unrealistic about the needs of a child, or desired a child simply for help around the house or for some other kind of work.[2]

For applicants who were invited to meet in-person with an intake worker, this first interview was a chance for the worker to better assess the family's prospects and for the family to learn about the foster care and adoption programs. Both members of a couple were expected to come to this initial meeting, and a description of this meeting is usually the first full entry in the case narrative. This first entry includes a description of the physical appearance of the couple—their complexions, eye color, height, age, et cetera. It continues with an account of the couple's attempts to have children (if they were infertile) and their desire for an adoptive or foster child—why they wanted children, what kind of child they imagined having (age, gender, coloring), and their experience with their own children or those of relatives and friends. The record then recounts the family background of each member of the couple, including how many siblings he or she had and their birth order, where he or she grew up, what the siblings did as adults and where they lived, how close each spouse was to his or her parents and in-laws, and each spouse's work history and education. This entry usually takes up roughly two to four single-spaced pages of the record. If the couple seemed like suitable applicants to the intake worker, she gave them an application and medical form at the end of this meeting to fill out and mail in if they desired to proceed with an adoptive or foster home study.

This entry and all others that recount a meeting between applicant and social worker begin with the date on which the interaction occurred and the name of the worker who met with the couple and wrote up the record. The typed record is usually based on dictation the worker recorded soon after the interview. The worker described the interview as she remembered it happening, including snippets of quotes from the conversation. She frequently recounted the questions she had asked and the applicants' replies, and she also noted the applicants' questions about the process and their concerns. Further, this entry, like most others, closes with a paragraph labeled "Worker's Impressions," where the worker recorded her reactions to the couple and recounted in more detail some of the specific topics of conversation during the first meeting that the worker deemed significant. As part of their effort to maintain accuracy and objectivity, workers always sought to separate their evaluations, proposals for areas needing further inquiry, and recommendations from their reconstructions of the interviews. Although the historian must always remain vigilant to the subtle judgments that seep into the texts of these records (for any historian who has worked with this kind of source knows that some social workers were particularly apt to forget this rule), workers generally did their best to recount their interviews completely and to then provide analysis and commentary.[3]

If, after the initial meeting with the agency, the couple decided to proceed with the home study and mailed in a completed application form, they were assigned to a placement social worker. This initial application form is included in every case file, and if a family applied to adopt or provide foster care for more than one child there is a form for each application. The form changed over time, but it generally includes information on the applicants' education (and their children's, if they had any), jobs and income, place of birth, religion, and marriage date. Couples were also asked to fill out a form with up to six references—a physician, a minister (if they had one, which many did not), a financial reference or the husband's employer, two personal references who were not relatives, and two personal references who were relatives. The intake social worker reviewed the couple's forms and sought out social agency and court records relating to the family's past, which could be anything from confirming a past divorce or checking test results for TB to a family's relief record during the Depression. The results of these inquiries were listed in the record after the forms were received.

Meanwhile, the placement worker usually made an appointment for the woman in the couple to come into the office for an interview without her husband. In her entry about this interview, which usually is around four or five pages in length, the social worker recounted in more detail the woman's desire for a child, her ideas about and experiences with childrearing and child care, her own childhood, her relationships with her siblings and parents, her schooling, and her career history or a description of jobs she had held. This entry also recounts the woman's description of her relationship with her husband, including how they met, her opinions of his family, her most and least favorite qualities about him, and any struggles or difficulties they had encountered in their marriage. In records that opened in the 1940s there is also usually some discussion of the woman's experiences during the war and the Depression. This entry also usually describes the wife's account of the couple's home—where they had lived together in the past and their current accommodations, as well as their plans for moving, purchasing, remodeling, or otherwise changing their housing situation. As always, this entry concludes with a paragraph labeled "Worker's Impressions," where the social worker provided her evaluation of the applicant and recorded any questions and concerns she wanted to explore more deeply at their next interview.

Following this first interview with the wife alone, there was an interview with the husband alone. The entry in the case record is usually parallel to that of the wife's solo interview, with the same topics discussed and recorded in the file. If, after meeting both spouses separately, the worker had uncertainties or felt she did not know a couple well enough, she would arrange for further interviews. She often conducted an additional in-office interview with the couple together, and in many cases met with each spouse individually again as well. When the worker and the couple were convinced that the application was worth pursuing further, the worker then usually visited the couple's home—most often when both spouses were present (though sometimes husbands could not get away from work). The couple showed the worker around the home, and the worker recounted the physical conditions of the house or apartment, as well as the furniture and general cleanliness of the domestic space, in the record. The worker also described her trip to and from the home, and her general impressions of the neighborhood. Further, while in the home, the worker conducted another interview with both spouses together. This interview usually explored in more detail topics that had come up in the earlier interviews. In her "impressions" section, the worker also used this interview to evaluate the give-and-take between the couple and to assess their relationship in the comfort of their own home.

If the worker felt very confident that this family should be approved, it was usually after visiting a couple's home that she began writing down her thoughts as to what kind of child to place in the home as far as age, gender, and coloring. In addition, she also usually gave the couple more detailed medical forms to be filled out by a doctor, and alerted them that she would begin contacting their references. If the worker was less certain about a couple's readiness for a child or felt that she needed more information about them, she conducted more interviews with the couple or would put the application on hold for a while, telling the applicants to contact the agency again when whatever problems they were having had been resolved (such as a husband's temporary unemployment or if the apartment was too small for a child but they planned to move soon). In many cases an application would be resumed at a later date with more interviews, and a child would eventually be placed.

Once an application was nearly approved, the worker interviewed the references the couple had listed on their initial application form. Workers usually talked with three to five references. Some references came into the office for an interview, the social worker visited others in their homes or workplaces, and a few were simply asked to write letters giving their impressions of the couple. In her entries describing these interviews, the worker recounted the references' evaluations of and insights into the applicants and the kind of life they would offer a child. These entries also often contain stories about the applicants—descriptions of family vacations taken with adult siblings, a coworker's account of the husband's kindness as a supervisor, or a father's description of his daughter's wedding and his hopes for grandchildren. For references who would likely be involved in a child's life in the home—such as relatives and close friends—the worker also asked direct questions about their feelings about adopted or foster children and sought to assess how welcoming and warm they would be to a child. In addition, employers were usually contacted by letter and wrote letters back confirming a husband's salary and giving a general impression of his performance and reliability in the workplace.

If the consultation with the references went well, the worker usually discussed the case with her supervisors and other social workers in a meeting where final approval was given. In the 1940s, the agency had some workers who were assigned to prospective adoptive and foster parents and others who were assigned to children in the agency's care who needed foster or adoptive care. While workers working with prospective parents were charged with inspecting homes and then helping families where children were placed adapt to one another, workers assigned to children were charged with getting to know each child and protecting his or her interests. These workers also worked with young mothers who wanted to place their children in adoption, as well as parents seeking foster care for their children during periods of family distress. It was during this final approval meeting that both sets of workers met, along with their supervisors, to decide on which, if any, child currently under agency care would fit with the newly approved family. In the 1950s this process was streamlined and adoption social workers handled both prospective parents and children available for adoption, and group meetings of all workers were held regularly to decide which child to place with which parents. If no child was deemed suitable under the dictates of the "matching" policy, the couple was told that they had been approved but would have to wait for the right child to come along.[4]

For adoption placements, once a child was selected, the couple was notified and came in to hear the child's history, which was essentially a brief sketch of the child's birth parents (their age, appearance, education, and perhaps something about their personalities) and a description of the child's experiences in foster care waiting for adoption. Parents were also told about any major illnesses or other problems a child might have had, as well as possible medical issues from the birth parents that might be significant in the child's life. If the prospective parents thought the child sounded like a good fit for their family, they made arrangements to meet the child. During this initial "showing," as it was called, the child's foster mother was usually there to help the child feel comfortable. Depending on a child's age and disposition, there might be anywhere from two to five showings for the child and adoptive parents to adjust to one another. Usually one or more of the showings took place at the foster home, and if the child was more than a year old, several showings involved taking the child to his or her new home for the afternoon or even a day before the final transition.

For pre-adoptive foster placements, a social worker instead usually came to the foster family's home to talk about the child the agency wanted to place. For infants, who represented most children placed in foster care in my sample, foster parents were not given much information about the child's birth parents, but they were given details about any previous foster homes and any problems the child might have had—such as slow speech development due to lack of interaction in the previous foster home. In rare instances in my sample, where birth parents were uncertain about whether to relinquish custody, which was often the case when older children were placed into pre-adoptive care, foster families were given much more thorough information about the child's family of origin and his or her birth parents. Further, in these cases, birth parents were expected and encouraged to visit with their children in foster homes while making up their minds, so foster families were told what to expect from them. Pre-adoptive infants were usually placed without much period of adjustment, although older children were introduced to a new foster home gradually.[5]

After a child was placed in an adoptive home, the worker supervised the home for six months to a year before the adoption could be legally consummated. The worker occasionally visited the home during this period, describing in the record the child's activities during her visit and interviewing the couple about their new lives as parents. The final placement report, which describes this probationary period, is always included in the record, as is a copy of the adoption decree. In foster homes, the social worker visited approximately once a month to check on how the placement was going, to witness the child's activities and development, and to see how the foster parents were adjusting. Each foster child also had his or her own social worker who also visited regularly, although I am not using those case records in this study. When it came time for a foster child to be removed—for adoption, to a different foster home, or (rarely) to return to his or her own parents—the placement social worker often recounted in the record the foster mother's distress about saying good-bye to the child. Some families quit providing foster care after the first child was removed because the experience was so traumatic. Many foster families of pre-adoptive infants begged to be allowed to keep a child who had been in the home since birth, but the agency rarely approved such an adoption. Foster families were only allowed to adopt their charges in the rare cases where the parents of older children relinquished them for adoption after the child had been in the foster home for some time, or in the case of special-needs and hard-to-place children.

The records also include any other items or documents relating to the family. Sometimes a distraught foster mother would write anguished letters to social workers begging to see a child who had been in her care. Or, if a foster child was having trouble at school or acting out in some way, a report from the child's teachers or school psychologist (or both) might have made its way into the file. In addition, adoptive parents often wrote letters accompanying donations to thank the agency for making them parents. These letters—often in the form of Christmas cards—usually describe the child's development and any new accomplishments or exciting events such as new teeth, new words, learning to ride a bike, or a family vacation. These letters often also include photographs of the child and of the family together. These letters usually trailed off by the time the child was four or five years old, but some families sent the agency yearly updates and donations until their children had graduated high school.

Finally, in the 1950s, the agency began including what it referred to as "yellow sheets" in the files. These pages are on yellow carbon paper and are included in the file but are separate from the case narrative. They recount the worker's interview with each spouse in even more detail than in the case record itself, and are organized by topic, including Family Relationships, Social Relationships, Marital Relationship, Housing, Vocational Adjustment, Attitude toward Adoptive Parenthood and Agency Service, and Finances. For instance, a page labeled "Family Relationships" would list the date of an interview, who was being interviewed (husband, wife, or both) and what the applicant said about his or her family of origin during that interview. These pages tend to have a number of direct quotes from the applicants. When yellow sheets were part of workers' standard practice, they tended to reserve their evaluations and impressions for the case record itself, using the yellow sheets to focus on recounting and sorting the information given in the interviews.

While conducting my research, Children's Home + Aid allowed me to take digital photographs of the case records as long as I blocked out any identifying information such as names and birthdates. In a painstaking process involving tiny slips of paper that I placed carefully over every name or birthdate for thousands of pages, I spent several weeks photographing records in the agency's main office in Chicago. I assigned each record a case number, which I also placed in every picture so that I would ensure that all of the pages from each record would be identifiable later on. This process was time consuming, but it has proved invaluable because I have been able to refer to the original case records throughout my research process. I have double-checked every quotation and situation I describe in the text, and I still have the records under lock and key in my home.

In order to make sense of so much information in so many records, I relied on qualitative research software called Nvivo to assist in my analysis. After converting my thousands of photographs into Microsoft Word documents, I used Nvivo to code each file for a number of traits, including information on family relationships, work, housing, leisure activities, community participation, comments about childrearing and the kind of child desired, and descriptions of applicants' own childhoods. The software allowed me to work with this data in a number of ways. I could obtain counts for the number of times certain words or phrases were used in the records, I could bring up every mention of a coded topic so that I could compare a variety of records and find patterns, and I could view each record individually with all of my coded headings highlighted. Further, because I had copies of the original case files, I was able to refer back to the originals if any questions arose about the coded text. For more information on Nvivo, which is a truly incredible resource for scholars, please refer to the website: http://www.qsrinternational .com/products_nvivo.aspx.

Children's Home + Aid was exceedingly generous to let me use their records in my research. As per my agreement with them, I have done all I can to protect the privacy of the families who used their services. I have no original names or identifying case numbers in my notes or in any written work about the records. In the text itself, all names and initials of adoptive or foster care applicants are pseudonyms. In addition, throughout this book I have omitted information that could identify or be easily linked to a particular individual. Although I mapped out these families using their real addresses to aid my analysis, I have given only neighborhoods or suburbs rather than more precise locations when describing people's housing. I have also only provided broad descriptions of people's jobs, and I have purposely left out company names and detailed job titles. I have omitted exact dates for births, marriages, deaths, or other public incidents that might compromise an individual's privacy. In all instances, I have done my best to retain the meaningful and telling aspects of people's daily lives as recounted in these records—including their family relationships, friendships, childhoods, ideas and ideals, homes, hobbies, and civic and political activities—without providing so much detail as to make it possible to connect these experiences back with particular individuals.

Because I have no original names or case numbers in my notes and research materials, I have assigned case numbers to these families for my personal use. These are the numbers cited in my footnotes along with any other information about where a quote or incident appears in that record and in what year it occurred. CH+A holds a key linking my numbers back to the original case files I used and will provide it to any qualified researcher who wishes to follow up on my work. Interested scholars should contact:

Hilary Freeman
Vice President of Quality and Planning
Children's Home + Aid
125 South Wacker Drive, 14th Floor
Chicago, IL 60606
312-424-0200

In order to contextualize the material I found in the case records, I also used a number of other published and archival sources. First, to better understand the history of ICH&A and the ideas of its social workers, I consulted the agency's papers at the Richard J. Daley Library Special Collections and Archives at the University of Illinois at Chicago. In addition, while I was initially reviewing the case files, staff members at CH+A recalled that there was a box of conference papers and articles written by agency social workers. After locating the box in a closet in their Evanston, Illinois, office, they allowed me to photocopy its contents, and I have cited material from these "Staff Papers" frequently in the text. I also reviewed social work textbooks and publications at the time, and particularly the *Social Service Review* and the *Child Welfare League of America Bulletin*.

Further, I learned that one of the agency's social workers and supervisors, Miriam Elson, who frequently appeared in the case records I used and in published and unpublished materials from the 1950s, was still alive and living in Hyde Park, Chicago, while I was researching this book. Elson had a distinguished career teaching at the University of Chicago's Social Service Administration and working in local social work agencies, and she published two books on integrating psychotherapy into clinical social work practice. I was fortunate enough to interview Elson, with the aid of her daughter, Karen Elson O'Niel, in July 2008. Although she was quite feeble at the time, the interview provided me a lens into the real dedication and professionalism of ICH&A workers in the postwar decades. Her description of working at ICH&A while raising young children also added nuance and depth to my understanding of social workers' ideas about the relationship between work and motherhood. I am so grateful that I had the opportunity to speak with her before she passed away at the age of ninety-nine in 2009.

To better understand community activism in black and white communities at the time, I consulted the Chicago Urban League Records at the Richard J. Daley Library Special Collections and Archives and the Hyde Park–Kenwood Community Conference Papers at the Special Collections Research Center in the Joseph Regenstein Library at the University of Chicago. I also searched the *Chicago Defender* and the *Chicago Tribune* for articles about family life and community activity at the time, and I read a number of sermons about the family that these papers published during the postwar years. In order to get a richer sense of the texture of black life in Chicago at the time, I also consulted sociologist Horace Cayton's papers and the Illinois Writers' Project/"Negro in Illinois" Papers in the Vivian G. Harsh Research Collection at the Woodson Regional Library of the Chicago Public Library.

Likewise, to get a better sense of how other people at the time experienced family and marriage—not just foster care and adoptive applicants, I particularly relied on published works of sociology, which I cite throughout the text. I also reviewed material in the Ernest Watson Burgess Papers and Addenda, as well as the Allison Davis Papers, at the Special Collections Research Center in the Regenstein Library at the University of Chicago. Burgess, Davis, and their students documented a wide variety of aspects of life in Chicago in the middle of the twentieth century, including extensive interviews with families and couples. Although only a few examples from this research appear in the text, it certainly shaped my larger understanding of the time period.

Theoretically, this project draws on the insights of Thomas Holt. In his analysis of the persistence of racism in America, Holt suggests that historians can best address the meaning and production of race, racism, and ideas about racial difference through the "study of everyday life and 'everydayness.'" It is in the everyday, Holt argues, that "the levels problem" is solved—"that is, the problem of establishing the continuity between behavioral explanations sited at the individual level of human experience and those at the level of society and social forces." It is in the everyday "that race is reproduced via the marking of the racial Other and that racist ideas and practices are naturalized, made self-evident, and thus seemingly beyond audible challenge. It is at that level that race is reproduced long after its original historical stimulus—the slave trade and slavery—have faded."[6]

Holt goes on to suggest that unraveling the levels problem to understand "how the large and 'important' are articulated with and expressed through the small and 'unimportant,' and vice versa . . . requires that we explicate more precisely the relation between individual agency and structural frameworks, on the one hand, and that we conceptualize more clearly just how one's consciousness of self and other are formed, on the other."[7] I seek to fulfill Holt's prescription by exploring how everyday ideas about the family and experiences of the family intersected with structural inequality and people's understanding of the social differences of gender, race, and class. The resulting book is a social history, but my analysis is discursive. The case records let us see how family was described and given meaning in a certain context, not how it was actually lived. Yet this was a discourse produced in the everyday, not at the level of popular culture, policy, or formal politics. By providing a discursive analysis of the everyday ideas of ordinary people, I demonstrate that what seems excessively small, intimate, and "unimportant"— the day-to-day family relationships of ordinary men and women—actually served to inform people's expectations for their communities, organize their lives, and mediate their assessment of their place within the larger social world.

APPENDIX B

Tables

TABLE 1   Type of Record, White, ICH&A Sample

Kind of Record	Number
Adoptive	79
Foster Care	85
Both	13
Total	177

TABLE 2   Type of Record, African American, ICH&A Sample

Kind of Record	Number
Adoptive	28
Foster Care	44
Both	5
Total	77

TABLE 3   Years Records Opened and Closed, White, ICH&A Sample

Year Opened or Closed	Number
Opened in 1920s or 1930s	23
Opened in 1940s	116
Closed in 1940s	96
Opened in 1950s	37
Closed in 1950s	59
Closed in 1960s	22

Note: This table includes data on when records both opened and closed because records could last anywhere from one year to two decades or more. This means that a record that opened in 1945 and closed in 1955 has information about the 1940s and the 1950s, and listing it by just its opening or closing date would misrepresent its data. Consequently, in order for the reader to have a sense of how many records I have that pertain to any single moment in time, I have listed records by opening and closing dates.

TABLE 4   Years Records Opened and Closed, African American, ICH&A Sample

Year Opened or Closed	Number
Opened in 1920s or 1930s	18
Opened in 1940s	32
Closed in 1940s	24
Opened in 1950s	27
Closed in 1950s	43
Closed in 1960s	10

Note: This table includes data on when records both opened and closed because records could last anywhere from one year to two decades or more. This means that a record that opened in 1945 and closed in 1955 has information about the 1940s and the 1950s, and listing it by just its opening or closing date would misrepresent its data. Consequently, in order for the reader to have a sense of how many records I have that pertain to any single moment in time, I have listed records by opening and closing dates.

TABLE 5 Religion Given on Intake Form, White, ICH&A Sample

	Number (total)	Number in City	Number in Suburbs
Protestant (both members of couple)	144	84	60
Catholic (both members of couple)	11	6	5
Jewish (both members of couple)	1	1	0
Catholic/Protestant Marriage	11	5	6
Jewish/Protestant Marriage	2	2	0
Jewish/Catholic Marriage	1	1	0
Greek Orthodox (both members of couple)	2	1	1
Christian Scientist (both members of couple)	2	1	1
Freethinker/No Religion Stated Marriage	1	0	1
No religion stated (both members of couple)	2	1	1

TABLE 6 Religion Given on Intake Form, African American, ICH&A Sample

	Number (total)	Number in City	Number in Suburbs
Protestant (both members of couple)	73	67	6
Catholic (both members of couple)	1	1	0
Catholic/Protestant Marriage	3	3	0

TABLE 7 Income by Race, ICH&A Sample, as Reported on Application

	1940–1945	1946–1950	1951–1955	1956–1960
White Men (177 white families in sample)*				
Median	$2,884	$3,890	$6,250	$13,750
Lowest	$1,560	$1,976	$2,000	$5,700
Highest	$6,500	$20,000	$9,000	$28,000
Black Men (77 black families in sample)				
Median	$1,800	$3,208	$4,030	$5,055
Lowest	$1,000	$2,080	$2,173	$4,410
Highest	$2,600	$5,200	$9,100	$7,500

* As this table shows, white men's incomes in particular went up dramatically in the late 1950s. This change represents not only shifts in the economy, but also a change within the practice of adoption in the later 1950s, when adoption received much more press coverage, the demand for white adoptive infants far outpaced the supply, and foster care was less common. Consequently, the applicant pool self-selected toward more affluent couples more frequently than it had before. However, because many of my records span a number of years (from either long-term foster care placements or the adoption of several children over a decade), I have information into the late 1950s from white families with lower incomes who applied in earlier years.

TABLE 8   Median Income in Chicago by Race: Selected Census Data

	1939	1949	1959
White Men (1939 and 1949; all men in 1959)	*Median yearly income for white men, experienced workers age 14 and over*: between $1,000–1,199	*Median yearly income for white men with income, age 14 and over*: $3,247	*Median yearly income for ALL males (white and nonwhite) in the experienced civilian labor force, age 14 and over*: $5,615
Nonwhite Men	*Median yearly income for nonwhite males, experienced workers age 14 and over*: between $600–799	*Median yearly income for "negro" males with income, age 14 and over*: $2,340	*Median yearly income for nonwhite males in the experienced civilian labor force, age 14 and over*: $4,104

Sources: Data from Wirth, Sheldon, and Chicago Community Inventory, *Local Community Fact Book of Chicago*, "Table C: Wages and Salaries of Experienced Workers, Age 14 Years and Over by Race and Sex, 1939, City of Chicago"; Bureau of the Census, *U.S. Census of the Population: 1950* (Washington, D.C.: Government Printing Office, 1953), vol. 2, pt. 13, table 87; Bureau of the Census, *U.S. Census of the Population: 1960* (Washington, D.C., Government Printing Office, 1963), vol. 1, pt. 15, table 124.

TABLE 9   Housing Locations by Race, ICH&A Sample

	City	Suburb
African American (percentage of all black families)	71 (92.2%)	6 (7.8%)
White (percentage of all white families)	102 (57.6%)	75 (42.4%)

TABLE 10   Tenancy Status by Race, ICH&A Sample

	Own	Rent	Share Home with Others*
White	131 (74.0%)	79 (44.6%)†	79 (44.6%)
Black	54 (70.1%)	40 (51.9%)	55 (71.4%)

* These families shared their living quarters with roomers or relatives, or rented a separate apartment in their home to others (duplex, three-flat, basement apartment, et cetera). When looking at these numbers, keep in mind that black families were much more likely to be sharing their actual living quarters with relatives, friends, and strangers than their white counterparts. In addition, among whites, the practice of sharing homes with anyone other than relatives declined sharply in my records as the housing shortage eased in the later 1940s, while for African Americans the practice continued unabated.

† These figures add up to over 100 percent because some families both rented and owned during the course of their adoption or foster care record. Many began their records renting, but as their financial stability increased, they purchased a home. In addition, several families, due to preference or circumstance, sold their homes and began renting during their contact with ICH&A.

TABLE 11   Tenancy Status in Chicago by Race, Selected Census Data

	1940		1950		1960	
	Own	Tenant	Own	Tenant	Own	Tenant
White	25.8%	74.2%*	32.9%	67.1%†	39.0%	61.0%‡
Nonwhite	7.5%	92.5%§	12.1%	87.9%‖	15.7%	84.3%#

Sources: Data from Bureau of the Census, *Sixteenth Census of the United States: 1940: Housing* (Washington, D.C.: Government Printing Office, 1943), vol. 2, pt. 2, table 1; Bureau of the Census, *Seventeenth Decennial Census of the United States: Census of Housing: 1950* (Washington, D.C.: Government Printing Office, 1953), vol. 1, pt. 3, table 17; Bureau of the Census, *Eighteenth Decennial Census of the United States: Census of Housing: 1960* (Washington, D.C.: Government Printing Office, 1963), vol. 1, pt. 3, table 12; Bureau of the Census, *Sixteenth Census of the United States: 1940: Housing* (Washington, D.C.: Government Printing Office, 1943), vol. 2, pt. 2, table 1.

* These figures represent the percentage of white owner-occupied and tenant-occupied dwelling units for all dwelling units occupied by whites in the city of Chicago.

† These figures represent the percentage of white owner-occupied and tenant-occupied dwelling units for all dwelling units occupied by whites in the city of Chicago.

‡ These figures represent the percentage of white owner-occupied and tenant-occupied dwelling units for all dwelling units occupied by whites in the city of Chicago.

§ These figures represent the percentage of nonwhite owner-occupied and tenant-occupied dwelling units for all dwelling units occupied by nonwhites in the city of Chicago.

‖ These figures represent the percentage of "Negro" owner-occupied and tenant-occupied dwelling units for all dwelling units occupied by "Negroes" in the city of Chicago.

These figures represent the percentage of nonwhite owner-occupied and tenant-occupied dwelling units for all dwelling units occupied by nonwhites in the city of Chicago.

NOTES

Introduction

1. "The Adoption," *The Honeymooners*, on *The Jackie Gleason Show*, season 3, episode 19, March 26, 1955.

2. "Beaver Gets Adopted," *Leave it to Beaver*, season 2, episode 61, February 26, 1959; "Adopted Daughter," *Father Knows Best*, season 2, episode 36, May 23, 1956.

3. For statistical information on marriage, divorce, and fertility rates at this time, see May, *Homeward Bound*, xiii–xvi, tables 1–6; Mintz and Kellogg, *Domestic Revolutions*, 180; Chafe, *The American Woman*, 217; and Coontz, *The Way We Never Were*, 24.

4. See, for instance, Berebitsky, *Like Our Very Own*; Carp, *Family Matters*; Fessler, *The Girls Who Went Away*; Herman, The Adoption History Project; Herman, "Families Made by Science"; Herman, "The Paradoxical Rationalization of Modern Adoption"; Herman, "Child Adoption in a Therapeutic Culture"; Herman, "Supervising Spoiled Selfhood"; Herman, *Kinship by Design*; Kunzel, *Fallen Women, Problem Girls*; May, *Barren in the Promised Land*, chaps. 4–5; Melosh, *Strangers and Kin*; Solinger, *Wake Up Little Susie*.

5. The figure for those making below a middle-class income in 1950 reflects the percentage of the population making less than $2,000, and it is therefore a conservative figure. Bureau of the Census, *U.S. Census of the Population: 1950* (Washington, D.C.: Government Printing Office, 1953), vol. 2, pt. 1, "Table 57: Income in 1949 of Families and Unrelated Individuals, for the United States, Urban and Rural: 1950," 1–104. Figure on African American population from Campbell Gibson and Kay Jung, Population Division, U.S. Census Bureau, "Historical Census Statistics on Population Totals by Race, 1790 to 1990, and by Origin, 1970 to 1990, for the United States, Regions, Divisions, and States," Working Paper Series No. 56, September 2002, Table 1: United States—Race and Hispanic Origin: 1790–1990.

6. May, *Homeward Bound*. See also Friedan, *The Feminine Mystique*; Chafe, *The American Woman*; Hartmann, "Prescriptions for Penelope"; Hartmann, *The Home Front and Beyond*; Campbell, *Women at War with America*; Honey, *Creating Rosie the Riveter*; Coontz, *The Way We Never Were*; Lewis, *Prescription for Heterosexuality*.

7. Scholars generally know very little about the experiences of postwar families of color and working-class families, nor has there been much consideration of these families' relationship with middle-class family ideals. There are a number of useful studies that show how mainstream domestic ideals were used to evaluate, control, and discipline families of color, but they pay little attention to how those families responded to domestic norms. See, for instance, Feldstein, *Motherhood in Black and White*; Shah, *Contagious*

Divides. Likewise, some works consider domestic and gender diversity at the time, but they focus more exclusively on women or on popular culture than on the social world and ideas of diverse families. See Meyerowitz, ed., *Not June Cleaver*; Smith, *Visions of Belonging*; Nelson, *Gender and Culture in the 1950s*. One notable exception to this trend is Lisa Levenstein's *A Movement without Marches*.

8. Weiss, *To Have and to Hold.*

9. Plant, *Mom.*

10. See, for instance, Murray, *The Progressive Housewife*; Reumann, *American Sexual Character*; Meyerowitz, ed., *Not June Cleaver*; Nelson, *Gender and Culture in the 1950s*; Levenstein, *A Movement without Marches.*

11. Arnold R. Hirsch, *Making the Second Ghetto*; Sugrue, *The Origins of the Urban Crisis*; Nicolaides, *My Blue Heaven.*

12. See, for instance, Sugrue, *Sweet Land of Liberty*, Bates, *Pullman Porters and the Rise of Protest Politics in Black America*; Biondi, *To Stand and Fight*; Phillips, *AlabamaNorth.*

13. Petigny, *The Permissive Society*. See also Breines, *Young, White, and Miserable.*

14. Lizabeth Cohen, *A Consumer's Republic.*

15. Reagan, "Republican National Convention Acceptance Speech," July 17, 1980, in *The Great Communicator*, 5, 6. Cited in Zaretsky, *No Direction Home*, 227–40.

16. Zaretsky, *No Direction Home*, 227–40.

17. Zaretsky, *No Direction Home*, 240. See also Self, *All in the Family*; Schulman, *The Seventies*, 159–89; Bailey, "She 'Can Bring Home the Bacon,'" 107–28; Lassiter, "Inventing Family Values," 13–28; and Spruill, "Gender and America's Right Turn," 71–89.

18. Pacyga, *Chicago*, chaps. 8–10; Ehrenhalt, *The Lost City*; Spinney, *City of Big Shoulders*, chaps. 10 and 11.

19. For instance, Drake, Cayton, and Wright, *Black Metropolis*; Grossman, *Land of Hope*; Green, *Selling the Race*. The Mapping the Stacks project at the University of Chicago (http://mts.lib.uchicago.edu) and Black Metropolis Research Consortium have also done a wonderful job making material on African American life and politics in Chicago more accessible to scholars.

20. See also Cohen and Taylor, *American Pharaoh*; Biles, *Richard J. Daley*. Housing conflicts in particular will be discussed at some length in chapter 6.

Chapter 1. The Difference of Adoption

1. U.S. Senate Committee on the Judiciary, Subcommittee to Investigate Juvenile Delinquency, *Juvenile Delinquency (Interstate Adoption Practices—Miami, Florida): Hearings Before the Subcommittee to Investigate Juvenile Delinquency of the Committee on the Judiciary United States Senate*, 84th Congress, 1st sess., November 14 and 15, 1955, 4.

2. Bizantz, *The Baby Thief*; Austin, *Babies for Sale* and "Babies for Sale"; Herman, *Kinship by Design*, 142–43.

3. For more on the ways that the difference of adoption can illuminate family norms, see Melosh, *Strangers and Kin*, 5; and all of Herman, *Kinship by Design*. Likewise, some of the anxiety around the black market in babies also stemmed from the perceived physical and emotional vulnerability of children during this time period. See, for instance, Tuttle, *"Daddy's Gone to War"*; Mintz, *Huck's Raft*, 302–308.

4. Briggs, *Somebody's Children*, 24. See also Balcom, *The Traffic in Babies*, 11.

5. Berebitsky, *Like Our Very Own*, 19–20; Carp, *Family Matters*, 5–7.

6. Berebitsky, *Like Our Very Own*, 20–23; Carp, *Family Matters*, 7.

7. Berebitsky, *Like Our Very Own*, 20–23; Carp, *Family Matters*, 7.

8. Carp, *Family Matters*, 8.

9. This shift away from institutional care is best exemplified by Charles Loring Brace's orphan trains, which sent institutionalized children from New York City to the supposedly more wholesome environs of Christian families in the rural Midwest and West. See Carp, *Family Matters*, 9–11; Gordon, *The Great Arizona Orphan Abduction*. See also Cmiel, *A Home of Another Kind*; Herman, The Adoption History Project; Herman, "The Paradoxical Rationalization of Modern Adoption."

10. Carp, *Family Matters*, 11, 14.

11. Herman, "The Paradoxical Rationalization of Modern Adoption," 354.

12. Field, "The Impact of Psychodynamic Theory on Social Casework, 1917–1949," 121–25. ICH&A continued to care for and place boarding and adoptive children across the state of Illinois throughout the century, and it still operates today as the oldest child-placing agency outside the Northeast. For more on the history and practice of adoption in Chicago, see Pfeffer, "A Historical Comparison of Catholic and Jewish Adoption Practices in Chicago"; and Cmiel, *A Home of Another Kind*.

13. Social work schools had been professionalizing and standardizing social work practice throughout the early twentieth century, but there was still a great deal of variability in foster care and adoption protocols. In fact, private, nonagency adoptions were the most common form of adoption throughout the century. Melosh, *Strangers and Kin*, 36–37; Herman, "The Paradoxical Rationalization of Modern Adoption"; Herman, *Kinship by Design*, 55–81. See also Gill, "The Jurisprudence of Good Parenting." For a case study of the formalization of the relationship between the care of orphaned children and the state in the first decades of twentieth century, see Cmiel, *A Home of Another Kind*, 75–85.

14. Berebitsky, *Like Our Very Own*, 129; Herman, "The Paradoxical Rationalization of Modern Adoption," 341.

15. See Melosh, *Strangers and Kin*, 5. For other histories of adoption in the postwar United States, see Carp, *Family Matters*, chap. 4; Kunzel, *Fallen Women, Problem Girls*, chap. 6, and "White Neurosis, Black Pathology", 304–33; May, *Barren in the Promised Land*, chap. 4, and "Nonmothers as Bad Mothers", 198–219; Solinger, "Race and 'Value,'" 343–63, and *Wake up Little Susie*, chap. 5; Berebitsky, *Like Our Very Own*, chap. 5.

16. Herman, *Kinship by Design*; Herman, "Families Made by Science;" Herman, "The Paradoxical Rationalization of Modern Adoption;" Herman, "Child Adoption in a Therapeutic Culture;" Herman, "Supervising Spoiled Selfhood." On social workers' professionalization in other contexts, see Kunzel, *Fallen Women, Problem Girls*; Abrams and Curran, "Between Women"; and Tice, *Tales of Wayward Girls and Immoral Women*.

17. "The Gray Market in Child Adoption," *The University of Chicago Round Table*, pamphlet no. 879, February 13, 1955, 1, 11. See also "Adoption . . . through a Licensed Social Agency" (Washington, D.C.: Children's Protective Association, 1950). These papers are located at the Metropolitan Regional Office of Children's Home and Aid, located in Evanston, Illinois. They are the staff papers remaining from ICH&A's staff library. They will be cited hereafter as ICH&A Staff Papers, Evanston, Ill.

18. ICH&A director Lois Wildy made a concerted effort in the 1950s to increase the professionalism of her social work staff by requiring graduate coursework for new hires and by forcing the resignations of many workers who were not familiar with the latest trends in social work theory. Adoption social workers at ICH&A also had occasional special training sessions with psychologists and psychiatrists about aspects of their work.

Further, the city of Chicago offered considerable resources for social work and psychological training, including the University of Chicago's School of Social Service Administration and the Chicago Institute for Psychoanalysis, and ICH&A social workers and their supervisors were linked to these institutions as well as the area's variety of child welfare organizations, such as the Institute for Juvenile Research, the Chicago Orphan Asylum, and a child guidance clinic affiliated with the University of Chicago's medical complex. Field, "The Impact of Psychodynamic Theory on Social Casework," 121–25, 198–99. "Semi Annual Report, Adoption Division of the Illinois Children's Home and Aid Society," June 30, 1947; "Illinois Children's Home and Aid Society, Adoption Division Service Report, 1958," folder 1, box 73, Children's Home and Aid Society of Illinois Papers, Richard J. Daley Library Special Collections and Archives (RJDL), University of Illinois at Chicago (UIC).

19. Field, "Social Casework Practice during the 'Psychiatric Deluge,'" 497. See also paper prepared by Marjorie Ferguson and Draza Kline (director, Foster Care Division, ICH&A) for Child Welfare League Midwest Regional Conference, Chicago, 1954; Irene Josselyn, MD (staff member of the Institute for Psychoanalysis, Chicago), "The Dynamic Process of the Foster Home Study," paper presented at the First Annual Homefinding Institute, sponsored by Committee on Foster Homes for Children of the Welfare Council of Metropolitan Chicago, Chicago, October 1951; Irene Josselyn, MD, "Evaluating Motives of Foster Parents," with "Discussion," by Charlotte Towle (professor, School of Social Service Administration, University of Chicago), ICH&A Staff Papers, Evanston, Ill.

20. Illinois Children's Home and Aid Society Adoption Division Service Report for 1958, p. 3; Adoption Division Service Report, 1961, p. 6; Adoption Services Service Report draft, 1963, p. 4; Adoption Services Service Report, 1963, p. 7, folder 1, box 73, Children's Home and Aid Society of Illinois Papers, RJDL, UIC. See also the following case records, which describe fee structures in some detail: files 50260, 56262, 58822, 60071, 60105, 60349, 61088, 61196, 61197, 61322, 62034, 63219, ICH&A Adoption Program Applications (Children's Home + Aid, Chicago).

21. Melosh, *Strangers and Kin*, chap. 2; Herman, *Kinship by Design*, 121–91; Berebitsky, *Like Our Very Own*, 137–42.

22. Richard B. Gehman, "Preparing Parents for Adoption," *Tomorrow*, June 1949, 40, ICH&A Staff Papers, Evanston, Ill. See also Herman, *Kinship by Design*, chap. 4; Melosh, *Strangers and Kin*, chap. 2.

23. File 56262, p. 5, 1954, ICH&A Adoption Program Applications (Children's Home + Aid, Chicago). Throughout this book, I use pseudonyms to identify couples. These names have no relationship to the original applicants' names, although I do try to reflect their ethnicity in their last names. I used the Social Security Administration's registry of popular names in the first decades of the century to choose first names. Further, I often identify couples by race or by the husband's job or both. I do not wish to essentialize racial differences or suggest that women's identities were necessarily subsumed by their husbands. My intention is instead to suggest the class, social, and racial diversity of men and women who shared the same views and ideas about adoption, as well as the pleasures, rewards, and social benefits of family membership. I also use these identifiers to highlight these same social differences when couples espoused differing ideals and expectations. I will mention it when a wife works outside the home, but I frequently use the husband's job when referring to these couples because, as chapter 4 will elaborate, it was his income and kind of work that had the greatest impact on the couple's class status and their modes for family living. I will also explore women's ideas about their

gender, race, and class status and their sense of resistance to, or acceptance of, gender roles within marriage in chapter 5.

24. File 56131, "Attitude toward Adoptive Parenthood and Agency Service" yellow sheet, 1954, ICH&A Adoption Program Applications (Children's Home + Aid, Chicago).

25. On the expectations of social workers and foster mothers regarding foster care arrangements, see Curran, "Feminine Women, Hard Workers." For more on the foster program at ICH&A and the persistence of late adoptive placements throughout the 1940s, see Field, "The Impact of Psychodynamic Theory on Social Casework." For more on the policies governing state-mandated foster care systems, see Rymph, "From 'Economic Want' to 'Family Pathology,'" 7–25.

26. At the society's annual meeting for 1922, the director of the program spoke about the role of the agency in helping the city's growing number of African American children. "Speech for Annual Meeting," February 14, 1922, folder 15, box 68, Children's Home and Aid Society of Illinois Papers, RJDL, UIC. There is extensive documentation of the agency's efforts to attract more African American foster and adoptive parents in the agency's records, which was an unusual stance for an adoption agency during this period. See folders 4 and 7, box 30, Children's Home and Aid Society of Illinois Papers, RJDL, UIC. These efforts included hiring a more diverse staff. The director of the adoption program, beginning in 1942, recounted the hiring and activities of African American caseworkers as part of the society's attempts to place more children in the African American community. Although the agency always had a handful of black social workers who dealt primarily with black applicants, the majority of the agency's social workers during the middle decades of the century were unmarried, white, Protestant women. There were also a few male social workers on staff during the 1940s and 1950s, and a growing number of Catholics. After World War II, several Jewish and Japanese American social workers joined the staff. In 1955, the agency had five white workers and three African American workers, while in 1951 it had eight white workers and five African American workers. "Service Report—Adoption Division," December 1, 1955, and "Semi-Annual Report—Adoption Department," December 4, 1951, folder 1, box 73, Children's Home and Aid Society of Illinois Papers, RJDL, UIC. On the Negro Adoption Project, see Dukette and Thompson, *Adoptive Resources for Negro Children*. For more on the changes in ICH&A's staff, see Field, "The Impact of Psychodynamic Theory on Social Casework," chaps. 3 and 6. On the relative scarcity of interest in African American children in the professional adoption community and among many in the black community prior to the 1960s, see Briggs, *Somebody's Children*, 27–58; Solinger, "Race and 'Value'"; and Solinger, *Wake up Little Susie*, chap. 5.

27. Herman, *Kinship by Design*, 122.

28. Carp, *Family Matters*, 102–37.

29. Strong-Boag, *Finding Families, Finding Ourselves*, viii–x.

30. Much has been written about these changes in adoption practice. From a professional historical perspective, see the following for information on how adoption changed in the later postwar decades, and particularly the growth of interracial and international adoption: Herman, *Kinship by Design*, chaps. 6–7; Melosh, *Strangers and Kin*, chap. 4; Carp, *Family Matters*, chaps. 5–7; Balcom, *The Traffic in Babies*; Briggs, *Somebody's Children*; Oh, "From War Waif to Ideal Immigrant," 34–55; Dubinsky, *Babies without Borders*.

31. For another description of the home study, see Melosh, *Strangers and Kin*, 46–49. For descriptions of the practice at ICH&A, see pamphlet by Rita Dukette (director, Adoptive Division, ICH&A), "Some Casework Implications in Adoptive Home Intake Proce-

dures," reprinted from article of same title in *Child Welfare* (January 1954), ICH&A Staff Papers, Evanston, Ill.; Marjorie Ferguson and Draza Kline (director, Foster Care Division, ICH&A), "The Dynamic Process of the Foster Home Study," paper presented at the Child Welfare League Midwest Regional Conference, Chicago, 1954, ICH&A Staff Papers, Evanston, Ill. For the small changes in the Adoption Divisions practices and procedures during this period, see also the Narrative Reports of the Adoption Division, 1943–1963, and in particular "Supplement to Semi-Annual Report, August 1953" and "Narrative Report 1951, Adoption Division," box 73, folder 1, Children's Home and Aid Society of Illinois Papers, RJDL, UIC. I also describe the process in much greater detail in appendix A.

32. Tice, *Tales of Wayward Girls and Immoral Women*, 190.

33. These meetings and the high degree of staff supervision were discussed throughout the Adoption Division's "Narrative Reports" during these years. Folder 1, box 73, Children's Home and Aid Society of Illinois Papers, RJDL, UIC. See also Tice, *Tales of Wayward Girls and Immoral Women*; Herman, "The Paradoxical Rationalization of Modern Adoption"; Herman, *Kinship by Design*, 62–64.

34. A psychodynamic orientation also encouraged workers to examine their own behaviors and motivation, and to be on the lookout for transference and identification that might cloud their attempts to provide objective and nonjudgmental evaluations. In practice, ICH&A workers displayed an array of attitudes toward applicants during this period. Some were quite critical of applicants, expressing very little empathy with their clients and pointing out every flaw in their personalities and living situations, while others instead were quite positive and praised applicants for their appealing family lives. No generalizations can be made, and instead each record must be read carefully to assess the particularities of each social worker and each family. For more on the evaluations of foster and adoptive parents at this time, see Ruth F. Brenner, *A Follow-up Study of Adoptive Families* (New York: Child Adoption Research Committee, 1951), 98–101; Donald Brieland, *An Experimental Study of the Selection of Adoptive Parents at Intake* (New York: Child Welfare League of America, 1959), 24; and pamphlet by Rita Dukette (director, Adoptive Division, ICH&A), "Some Casework Implications in Adoptive Home Intake Procedures," reprinted from article of same title in *Child Welfare* (January 1954), ICH&A Staff Papers, Evanston, Ill.

35. During this period many agencies encouraged telling adopted children of their status when they were still very young, so they would grow up with the knowledge rather than being surprised by it later in life or hearing it from someone other than their parents. Workers repeatedly recounted in the records their efforts to convince parents to tell, but they were often unsuccessful. For more on the process, see Ellen Herman's Adoption History Project entry on "Telling." Workers often suggested that parents use the children's storybook "The Chosen Baby" with their young children to explain the process. Wasson, *The Chosen Baby*.

36. See also Herman, "The Paradoxical Rationalization of Modern Adoption." For examples of lack of compliance and anger at social workers' practices in the records, see, for instance, files 46035, 46285, 47025, 47139, 48238, 49228, 50031, 50198, 50230, 52101, 53089, 54310, ICH&A Adoption Program Applications (Children's Home + Aid, Chicago).

37. Gordon, *Heroes of Their Own Lives*, 291.

38. Ibid., 295. For more on Gordon's ideas about social control and case records, see Gordon, "Response to Scott."

39. Ferguson and Kline, "The Dynamic Process of the Foster Home Study," p. 1, ICH&A Staff Papers, Evanston, Ill.

40. Ibid., p. 2, ICH&A Staff Papers, Evanston, Ill. See also Irene Josselyn, MD, "Evaluating Motives of Foster Parents," with "Discussion" by Charlotte Towle; and Norman Herstein, "The Child Placement Process: An Overview," presented at the Minnesota Welfare Conference, St. Paul, Minn., 1961 ICH&A Staff Papers, Evanston, Ill. For a similar analysis of this problem at another agency, see Melosh, *Strangers and Kin*, 207–13.

Chapter 2. Embracing Domesticity

1. File 51122, p. 4, 1949, ICH&A Adoption Program Applications (Children's Home + Aid, Chicago).

2. May, *Homeward Bound*, xiii.

3. Lizabeth Cohen, *Making a New Deal*, 217.

4. Pacyga, *Chicago*, 253.

5. Ibid., 251–52; Lizabeth Cohen, *Making a New Deal*, 218–30.

6. Pacyga, *Chicago*, 268–73; Cohen and Taylor, *American Pharaoh*, 68.

7. Cavan and Ranck, *The Family and the Depression*, 86–90. See also Lizabeth Cohen, *Making a New Deal*, 214–18, 246–49; and Ware, *Holding Their Own*.

8. Elder, *Children of the Great Depression*, 197, 226, 282.

9. File 47207, ICH&A Adoption Program Applications (Children's Home + Aid, Chicago).

10. For instance, files 50312, 56103, and 62113, ICH&A Adoption Program Applications (Children's Home + Aid, Chicago).

11. File 47239, p. 4–5, 1941, ICH&A Adoption Program Applications (Children's Home + Aid, Chicago).

12. Ibid., p. 6.

13. File 49343, p. 7, 1949, ICH&A Adoption Program Applications (Children's Home + Aid, Chicago).

14. File 54349, "family relationships," 1952, ICH&A Adoption Program Applications (Children's Home + Aid, Chicago).

15. File 48041, p. 8, 1946; 53302, pp. 11, 12, 1948, ICH&A Adoption Program Applications (Children's Home + Aid, Chicago).

16. Arnold R. Hirsch, *Making the Second Ghetto*, 16–17. See also Grossman, *Land of Hope*; Lemann, *The Promised Land*; and Gregory, *The Southern Diaspora*.

17. Graham, "The Negro Family in a Northern City," 49, 51.

18. Frazier, *The Negro Family the United States*; Drake and Cayton, *Black Metropolis*, especially 526–715. See also Frazier, *Black Bourgeoisie*.

19. Grossman, *Land of Hope*. See also Phillips, *AlabamaNorth*; Wilkerson, *The Warmth of Other Suns*.

20. There are too many instances of these kinds of relationships and living arrangements in the records to list here, but for a few examples, see files 50198, 51164, 52336, 54349, 56050, 56262, 60071, 68298, ICH&A Adoption Program Applications (Children's Home + Aid, Chicago). Housing will be discussed in more detail in chapter 6.

21. File 61279, 1959, ICH&A Adoption Program Applications (Children's Home + Aid, Chicago).

22. File 50312, p. 12, 1948; see also files 51267, 52316, ICH&A Adoption Program Applications (Children's Home + Aid, Chicago). See also Jones, *Labor of Love, Labor of Sorrow*.

23. File 53320, p. 5, 1951, ICH&A Adoption Program Applications (Children's Home + Aid, Chicago).

24. File 58062, "adoption application" yellow sheet, 1956, ICH&A Adoption Program Applications (Children's Home + Aid, Chicago).

25. For more on the black community's relationship with the Chicago Democratic machine during these years, see Biles, *Richard J. Daley*, chaps. 1–4; Cohen and Taylor, *American Pharaoh*, chaps. 1–8.

26. For Davis's published work on this family, see Allison Davis, *Father of the Man*.

27. Washington Family, December 1, 1943, Allison Davis Papers, box 38, folder 12, Special Collections Research Center, University of Chicago Library; Claudette and Ruth-Topeka, Allison Davis Papers, box 38, folder 17, Special Collections Research Center, University of Chicago Library; T. S. Downs, notes, March 3, 1943, Allison Davis Papers, box 38, folder 19, Special Collections Research Center, University of Chicago Library; J. L. Neely, notes, July 26, 1943, Allison Davis Papers, box 38, folder 20, Special Collections Research Center, University of Chicago Library.

28. Claudette and Ruth-Topeka, Allison Davis Papers, box 38, folder 17, Special Collections Research Center, University of Chicago Library; T. S. Downs, notes, March 29, 1943, Allison Davis Papers, box 39, folder 2, Special Collections Research Center, University of Chicago Library.

29. T. S. Downs, notes, March 3, 1943, Allison Davis Papers, box 38, folder 19, Special Collections Research Center, University of Chicago Library.

30. J. L. Neely, notes, July 26, 1943, Allison Davis Papers, box 38, folder 20, Special Collections Research Center, University of Chicago Library.

31. On the American home front during World War II, see Blum, *V Was for Victory*; Erenberg and Hirsch, *The War in American Culture*; Lingeman, *Don't You Know There's a War On*. On women and family during the war, see Campbell, *Women at War with America*; Chafe, *The American Woman*; Hartmann, "Prescriptions for Penelope;" Hartmann, *The Home Front and Beyond*; Honey, *Creating Rosie the Riveter*; May, *Homeward Bound*; Westbrook, "I Want a Girl, Just Like the Girl That Married Harry James."

32. Kozol, *Life's America*, 58, 69.

33. Honey, *Creating Rosie the Riveter*. See also Westbrook, "I Want a Girl, Just Like the Girl That Married Harry James."

34. J. Edgar Hoover, "Mothers . . . Our Only Hope," *Women's Home Companion*, January 1944, 20, printed in Walker, ed., *Women's Magazines 1940–1960*, 44–47.

35. "When Your Soldier Comes Home," *Ladies Home Journal*, October 1945, 183, printed in Walker, *Women's Magazines 1940–1960*, 56–62.

36. Burgess, "The Effect of War on the American Family," 343–52.

37. Burgess, "Postwar Problems of the Family," 47–50. See also Celello, *Making Marriage Work*, chap. 2; Rebecca Davis, *More Perfect Unions*, chap. 2.

38. Spinney, *City of Big Shoulders*, 200.

39. For more on Chicago during the war, see Pacyga, *Chicago*, 273–85; Spinney, *City of Big Shoulders*, 198–203; and Duis and LaFrance, *We've Got a Job to Do*.

40. File 50308, p. 14, 1949, ICH&A Adoption Program Applications (Children's Home + Aid, Chicago).

41. For more on the marriage boom during the early years of the war, see, for example, Campbell, *Women at War with America*, 63–100, 163–86; Cott, *Public Vows*, 180–190; Hartmann, *The Home Front and Beyond*, 163–86; May, *Homeward Bound*, 49–79.

42. File 58222, p. 4, 1954, ICH&A Adoption Program Applications (Children's Home + Aid, Chicago).

43. File 57039, "family relationships" yellow sheet, 1953, ICH&A Adoption Program

Applications (Children's Home + Aid, Chicago). See also Hartmann, "Prescriptions for Penelope;" Westbrook, "I Want a Girl, Just Like the Girl That Married Harry James"; LaRossa, *Of War and Men*, 81–97.

44. File 56350, "first interview in office," 1949, ICH&A Adoption Program Applications (Children's Home + Aid, Chicago).

45. File 53351, 1948, ICH&A Adoption Program Applications (Children's Home + Aid, Chicago).

Chapter 3. Defining Domesticity

1. File 49146, p. 16, 1948, ICH&A Adoption Program Applications (Children's Home + Aid, Chicago).

2. See, for instance, Meyerowitz, "Beyond the Feminine Mystique"; Ehrenreich, *The Hearts of Men*; Feldstein, *Motherhood in Black and White*; May, *Homeward Bound*; Smith, *Visions of Belonging*; Weiss, *To Have and to Hold*; Kline, *Building a Better Race*, chap. 5.

3. The companionate family had begun to dominate upper-middle-class and elite families in the 1920s but became much more widespread by the postwar years. See Mintz and Kellogg, *Domestic Revolutions*, 107–31, 186.

4. Irene Josselyn, MD, "Evaluating Motives of Foster Parents," with "Discussion," by Charlotte Towle (professor, School of Social Service Administration, University of Chicago), ICH&A Staff Papers, Evanston, Ill.; Rita Dukette, "Panel on Reduction in Adoptive Applications—Implications for Practice," National Conference of Social Work, Cleveland, May 23, 1963; "Adoption . . . through a Licensed Social Agency," Children's Protective Association, 1950; Richard B. Gehman, "Preparing Parents for Adoption," reprinted from *Tomorrow Magazine* (June 1949), ICH&A Staff Papers, Evanston, Ill. For discussions of criteria for adoptive and foster parents at other agencies, see, for instance, Rathbun, "The Adoptive Foster Parent"; Brenner, "The Selection of Adoptive Parents."

5. Marjorie Ferguson and Draza Kline (director, Foster Care Division, ICH&A), "The Dynamic Process of the Foster Home Study," paper presented at the Child Welfare League Midwest Regional Conference, Chicago, 1954, ICH&A Staff Papers, Evanston, Ill.

6. File 49146, p. 16, 1948, ICH&A Adoption Program Applications (Children's Home + Aid, Chicago).

7. File 53305, page 1 of Formulation, 1952, ICH&A Adoption Program Applications (Children's Home + Aid, Chicago).

8. File 55202, pp. 3, 6, 1947, ICH&A Adoption Program Applications (Children's Home + Aid, Chicago). On the origins of companionate marriage across race, see Simmons, *Making Marriage Modern*. Simmons points out that companionate marriage during the interwar period was understood as a marriage without children, or a stage of marriage prior to having children (122–23). I suggest that applicants in the postwar period instead saw children as an extension of the companionate marriage, rather than a new stage of marriage. Children heightened intimacy and gave both partners a greater stake in the joys of marriage.

9. File 59225, p. 12, 1957, ICH&A Adoption Program Applications (Children's Home + Aid, Chicago).

10. File 51122, p. 7, 1949, ICH&A Adoption Program Applications (Children's Home + Aid, Chicago).

11. File 59287, p. 3, 1959, ICH&A Adoption Program Applications (Children's Home + Aid, Chicago).

12. Ibid.

13. File 60142, "adoption application," 1954, ICH&A Adoption Program Applications (Children's Home + Aid, Chicago).

14. File 46271, p. 4, 1943, ICH&A Adoption Program Applications (Children's Home + Aid, Chicago).

15. File 52288, p. 1, 1950, ICH&A Adoption Program Applications (Children's Home + Aid, Chicago).

16. File 52288, p. 22, 1951, ICH&A Adoption Program Applications (Children's Home + Aid, Chicago).

17. File 53110, "family relationships," 1952, ICH&A Adoption Program Applications (Children's Home + Aid, Chicago).

18. File 56131, "experiences w/ son" yellow sheet, 1954, ICH&A Adoption Program Applications (Children's Home + Aid, Chicago).

19. File 56050, p. 11–12, 1951; also 53342, ICH&A Adoption Program Applications (Children's Home + Aid, Chicago).

20. File 53342, "adoption application" and "children" yellow sheet, 1952, ICH&A Adoption Program Applications (Children's Home + Aid, Chicago).

21. File 52167, p. 24, 1951, ICH&A Adoption Program Applications (Children's Home + Aid, Chicago).

22. File 53320, p. 2, 1951; 61296, p. 13, 1950, ICH&A Adoption Program Applications (Children's Home + Aid, Chicago).

23. File 49107, p. 7, 1947, ICH&A Adoption Program Applications (Children's Home + Aid, Chicago).

24. File 49146, p. 25, 1951, ICH&A Adoption Program Applications (Children's Home + Aid, Chicago).

25. File 61088, p. 2, 1959, ICH&A Adoption Program Applications (Children's Home + Aid, Chicago).

26. File 50081, p. 21, 1948, ICH&A Adoption Program Applications (Children's Home + Aid, Chicago).

27. File 51314, p. 6, 1948, ICH&A Adoption Program Applications (Children's Home + Aid, Chicago).

28. File 60142, p. 8, 1956, ICH&A Adoption Program Applications (Children's Home + Aid, Chicago).

29. File 53110, "attitudes towards children," 1952, ICH&A Adoption Program Applications (Children's Home + Aid, Chicago).

30. File 60338, p. 10, 1955, ICH&A Adoption Program Applications (Children's Home + Aid, Chicago).

31. File 51164, p. 4, 1949, ICH&A Adoption Program Applications (Children's Home + Aid, Chicago).

32. For a thorough analysis of gender preferences in adoption at this time, see Melosh, *Strangers and Kin*, 55–69.

33. File 57121, "adoption application" yellow sheets, ICH&A Adoption Program Applications (Children's Home + Aid, Chicago).

34. File 62034, pp. 1, 14, 1951, ICH&A Adoption Program Applications (Children's Home + Aid, Chicago).

35. File 50355, p. 1, "discharge summary," 1948, ICH&A Adoption Program Applications (Children's Home + Aid, Chicago).

36. File 49090, pp. 3–4, 1942, ICH&A Adoption Program Applications (Children's Home + Aid, Chicago). The dangers of "momism" were proposed in Philip Wylie's 1942

Generation of Vipers, and the concept had some traction in my records although the word "momism" was never used explicitly. But several parents, including this woman and a black father who feared his wife was turning their son in a "Little Lord Fauntleroy," brought up the perceived dangers of overmothering their children. See also Feldstein, *Motherhood in Black and White*; Ladd-Taylor and Umansky, *"Bad" Mothers*; Plant, *Mom*; Wylie, *Generation of Vipers*.

37. See also Zelizer, *Pricing the Priceless Child*.

38. File 50230, p. 20, 1952, ICH&A Adoption Program Applications (Children's Home + Aid, Chicago).

39. File 51324, p. 15, 1948, ICH&A Adoption Program Applications (Children's Home + Aid, Chicago).

40. File 58222, "family relationships," 1954, ICH&A Adoption Program Applications (Children's Home + Aid, Chicago).

41. File 58326, p. 14, 1952, ICH&A Adoption Program Applications (Children's Home + Aid, Chicago).

42. File 51324, p. 1, 1947, ICH&A Adoption Program Applications (Children's Home + Aid, Chicago).

43. File 49328, p. 9, 1946, ICH&A Adoption Program Applications (Children's Home + Aid, Chicago).

44. These values fit in with the trends in parenting advice at the time. See, for instance, Hulbert, *Raising America*; Spock, *The Common Sense Book of Baby and Child Care*; Stearns, *Anxious Parents*; Weiss, *To Have and to Hold*, chap. 4.

45. Weiss, *To Have and to Hold*, 17. Likewise, scholars have shown that young people across race really did accomplish the key transitions to adulthood at younger ages and in quicker succession during the postwar years. Stranger-Ross, Collins, and Stern, "Falling Far from the Tree," 625–48.

46. File 60349, pp. 5, 8, 1959, ICH&A Adoption Program Applications (Children's Home + Aid, Chicago).

47. File 61088, p. 18, 1960, married in 1947, ICH&A Adoption Program Applications (Children's Home + Aid, Chicago).

48. May, *Homeward Bound*, xi, 163–85; Weiss, *To Have and to Hold*, 177–201.

49. For example, files 45065, 46012, and 53245 ICH&A Adoption Program Applications (Children's Home + Aid, Chicago).

50. File 52319, p. 21, 1951; see also 51267, 55171, ICH&A Adoption Program Applications (Children's Home + Aid, Chicago).

51. May, *Barren in the Promised Land*, 127.

52. Ibid., 129.

53. Ibid., 153.

54. File 57121, "adoption application," 1955, ICH&A Adoption Program Applications (Children's Home + Aid, Chicago).

55. File 49124, p. 7, 1947, ICH&A Adoption Program Applications (Children's Home + Aid, Chicago).

56. File 53187, "adoptive study summary," 1952, ICH&A Adoption Program Applications (Children's Home + Aid, Chicago).

57. File 53302, p. 13, 1948, ICH&A Adoption Program Applications (Children's Home + Aid, Chicago).

58. File 58059, "adoption application" yellow sheet, 1953, ICH&A Adoption Program Applications (Children's Home + Aid, Chicago).

59. File 56262, p. 12, 1955, ICH&A Adoption Program Applications (Children's Home + Aid, Chicago). See also May, *Barren in the Promised Land*, 127–79; May, "Nonmothers as Bad Mothers"; Ehrenreich, *The Hearts of Men*.

60. File 50109, p. 2, 1948, ICH&A Adoption Program Applications (Children's Home + Aid, Chicago).

61. File 62143, ICH&A Adoption Program Applications (Children's Home + Aid, Chicago).

62. File 50081, p. 20, 1948, ICH&A Adoption Program Applications (Children's Home + Aid, Chicago). For a similar story, see Marsh and Ronner, *The Empty Cradle*, 206.

63. File 50081, p. 20, 1948, ICH&A Adoption Program Applications (Children's Home + Aid, Chicago).

64. File 59287, "intake interview," 1957, ICH&A Adoption Program Applications (Children's Home + Aid, Chicago).

65. File 45158, p. 2, 1944, ICH&A Adoption Program Applications (Children's Home + Aid, Chicago).

66. File 58094, p. 9, 1957, ICH&A Adoption Program Applications (Children's Home + Aid, Chicago).

67. File 51314, p. 4, 1948, ICH&A Adoption Program Applications (Children's Home + Aid, Chicago).

68. File 50109, ICH&A Adoption Program Applications (Children's Home + Aid, Chicago).

69. Komarovsky, *Blue-Collar Marriage*, 237, 208.

70. File 47025, ICH&A Adoption Program Applications (Children's Home + Aid, Chicago).

71. File 51122, ICH&A Adoption Program Applications (Children's Home + Aid, Chicago).

72. File 54166, "family relationships," 1952; see also 60157, p. 17, 1958, ICH&A Adoption Program Applications (Children's Home + Aid, Chicago).

73. File 56131, ICH&A Adoption Program Applications (Children's Home + Aid, Chicago).

74. File 49146, p. 11, 1948, ICH&A Adoption Program Applications (Children's Home + Aid, Chicago).

75. For instance, files 53089, 58062, 58093, ICH&A Adoption Program Applications (Children's Home + Aid, Chicago).

76. File 49146, p. 16, 1948, ICH&A Adoption Program Applications (Children's Home + Aid, Chicago).

77. File 47045, p. 18, 1946; 45261; 56262, "social relationships," 1955, ICH&A Adoption Program Applications (Children's Home + Aid, Chicago).

78. On the glorification of family in popular culture and Cold War politics during the 1950s, see Coontz, *The Way We Never Were*, May, *Homeward Bound*; Weiss, *To Have and to Hold*.

Chapter 4. Providing Anxiety and Optimism

1. Berger, *Working-Class Suburb*, v. See also Halle, *America's Working Man*.

2. Berger, *Working-Class Suburb*, 24. Emphasis in original.

3. Ibid., 25.

4. There is a wealth of literature on the changes described in this paragraph and the one above. For sociological studies, see, for instance, Drake and Cayton, *Black Me-*

tropolis; Mills, *White Collar*; Whyte, *The Organization Man*; Rainwater, Coleman, and Handel, *Workingman's Wife*; Shostak and Gomberg, *Blue-Collar World*; Frazier, *Black Bourgeoisie*; Gans, *The Levittowners*; Komarovsky, *Blue-Collar Marriage*; Riesman, *The Lonely Crowd*; Berger, *Working-Class Suburb*; Halle, *America's Working Man*. Historical studies are too numerous to list here, but see, for instance, Lizabeth Cohen, *A Consumer's Republic*; Fones-Wolf, *Selling Free Enterprise*; Lassiter, *The Silent Majority*; Lipsitz, *Rainbow at Midnight*; Sugrue, *The Origins of the Urban Crisis*; McGirr, *Suburban Warriors*; Mettler, *Soldiers to Citizens*; Gregory, *The Southern Diaspora*; Nicolaides, *My Blue Heaven*; Green, *Selling the Race*; Wiese, *Places of Their Own*. On workers' depictions in *Life*, see Quirke, *Eyes on Labor*, 51–107.

5. Weiss, *To Have and to Hold*, chaps. 1, 2, and 3; May, *Homeward Bound*. For more on the increasing involvement of fathers within the family, see also Griswold, *Fatherhood in America*, 161–218.

6. Melosh and Herman also offer extensive discussions of the selection criteria for prospective applicants. Melosh, *Strangers and Kin*, 112–13; Herman, *Kinship by Design*, 150–53.

7. File 60157, p. 9, 1958, ICH&A Adoption Program Applications (Children's Home + Aid, Chicago).

8. File 61197, p. 21, 1959, ICH&A Adoption Program Applications (Children's Home + Aid, Chicago).

9. File 57039, "evaluation of first child's adjustment," p. 5, 1955, ICH&A Adoption Program Applications (Children's Home + Aid, Chicago).

10. Melosh describes a similar practice at the Children's Bureau of Delaware in the 1950s. Melosh, *Strangers and Kin*, 113–14.

11. File 46079, p. 12, 1943; p. 14, 1944, ICH&A Adoption Program Applications (Children's Home + Aid, Chicago).

12. Griswold, *Fatherhood in America*, 4. Sociologist Ralph LaRossa also argues that there was a great variety among men's (and women's) ideas about fatherhood in the postwar years. LaRossa, *Of War and Men*, particularly 101–31. Likewise, historian James Gilbert suggests that, even among the white middle class, masculinity was varied and diverse, rarely fitting into stereotypes we might have about men at the time. Gilbert, *Men in the Middle*.

13. In the mid-1950s, ICH&A started a "Negro Adoption Project" to recruit more black adoptive families. The project made a point of reaching out to the black community and particularly emphasized that large incomes and spacious apartments were not necessary for approval. Workers involved in the project, as will be discussed in the next chapter, were much more accommodating of working wives and mothers than were social workers dealing with white applicants. The project emerged from the agency's recognition that Chicago's black community approached adoption differently than did white couples. Workers believed that African American couples would be less likely to apply for fear of rejection, given how much hardship and rejection these couples faced on a regular basis already due to racism. They also noted that informal adoption by friends and relatives was fairly common in black communities, and therefore childless couples were somewhat suspicious of children available for adoption by strangers. They wondered who these children were who had no one available to care for them already, and they assumed that there must be something wrong with them. Workers also recognized that due to migration, poverty, and discrimination, many black applicants had enjoyed less stable family lives as children and so might have different parenting attitudes than white

applicants. Despite these many differences noted by the project, workers held black applicants to similar standards as white applicants when it came to character and emotional attitudes toward the family. They still believed that the best interests of the child would be served by fulfilling workers' expectations as to proper family attitudes. They would accommodate different work patterns among black parents, but they sought the same gender characteristics in black men and women and the same degree of commitment to family engagement. It was not until the mid-1960s that workers at ICH&A began to consider more deeply the important linkages between class, race, and applicants' values and patterns of family living. During the 1960s the agency began to be more flexible in their evaluations of applicants' motives for taking in a child and the probable care they would provide to that child. Rather than holding diverse applicants to similar standards, they began to accommodate differences. On the Negro Adoption Project, see Dukette and Thompson, *Adoptive Resources for Negro Children*. The numbers of African American applicants and strategies to recruit more African Americans to the adoption and foster care programs were also recurring themes in nearly every yearly report from the Adoption and Home Finding departments at ICH&A during these years. See Narrative Yearly Reports—Adoption Division, box 73, folder 1; and Narrative Yearly Reports—Home Finding Division, box 74, folder 1, Children's Home and Aid Society of Illinois Papers, Richard J. Daley Library Special Collections and Archives (RJDL), University of Illinois at Chicago (UIC). For agency files outlining ICH&A's various efforts to recruit more black applicants, see also box 38, folders 4 and 7, Children's Home and Aid Society of Illinois Papers, RJDL, UIC. On changing standards at the agency in the 1960s, see Rita Dukette, "Drift or Design," paper presented at the TIP Session of the Midwest Regional Conference of the Child Welfare League of America, March 24, 1965, particularly pages 18–19, ICH&A Staff Papers, Evanston, Ill.

14. Categorizing white families by class is particularly difficult during this period because blue-collar incomes were rising, sometimes matching or even surpassing those of white-collar workers who would have before made up the bulk of the middle class. Also, the expansion of mass consumption made more goods available to families across class. In my analysis, I use income as one aspect of class status, but I also rely heavily on factors other than income in order to categorize these men and women. Middle-class men and women, in my classification, had white- or pink-collar jobs and had finished high school if not one to four years of college. Some came from families where their parents had a similar background, but many came from working-class backgrounds as well (although many of these tended to be from more stable and financially secure working-class backgrounds). See tables 7–11 in appendix B for more on these families' incomes, tenancy status, and suburban/urban location.

15. Just as it is difficult to precisely categorize who was middle-class at this time, it is also difficult to categorize who was working-class. The embourgeoisement of the white working class during this period caused many sociologists to wonder at the time (and ever since) how to best understand what it meant (and currently means) to be working class in the United States. For my purposes, I largely relied on the type of work people did (blue collar), their educational background (nothing beyond high school, and many of these men and women did not finish high school), union membership, and indications within the records that they believed themselves to be working class or, as one husband put it, "for the working man." File 48120, ICH&A Adoption Program Applications (Children's Home + Aid, Chicago).

16. File 61197, p. 8, 1956, ICH&A Adoption Program Applications (Children's Home + Aid, Chicago).

17. File 52232, p. 45, 1950, ICH&A Adoption Program Applications (Children's Home + Aid, Chicago).

18. File 60067, p. 7, 1958, ICH&A Adoption Program Applications (Children's Home + Aid, Chicago).

19. File 58066, p. 3, 1948, ICH&A Adoption Program Applications (Children's Home + Aid, Chicago).

20. For instance, see file 48046; file 47096, adoption discharge summary, 1947, ICH&A Adoption Program Applications (Children's Home + Aid, Chicago). On the growing importance of fathers' positive and playful interactions with their children during this period, see also Weiss, *To Have and to Hold*, 83–101; Hulbert, *Raising America*, 249, 253; Stearns, *Anxious Parents*, 57–58.

21. File 50308, p. 27, 1950, ICH&A Adoption Program Applications (Children's Home + Aid, Chicago).

22. File 45065, p. 21, 1953, ICH&A Adoption Program Applications (Children's Home + Aid, Chicago).

23. Susan E. Hirsch, "Economic Geography," 72–75.

24. File 43084, ICH&A Adoption Program Applications (Children's Home + Aid, Chicago).

25. Files 45030, 49077, 50042, ICH&A Adoption Program Applications (Children's Home + Aid, Chicago).

26. File 47239, ICH&A Adoption Program Applications (Children's Home + Aid, Chicago).

27. File 63251, ICH&A Adoption Program Applications (Children's Home + Aid, Chicago).

28. File 58326, p. 6, 1952, ICH&A Adoption Program Applications (Children's Home + Aid, Chicago).

29. Chinoy, *Automobile Workers and the American Dream*, 67, 70.

30. Ibid., 111.

31. Ibid., 110–21.

32. File 45159, p. 17, 1945, ICH&A Adoption Program Applications (Children's Home + Aid, Chicago).

33. File 51083, p. 3, 1949, ICH&A Adoption Program Applications (Children's Home + Aid, Chicago).

34. File 50115, ICH&A Adoption Program Applications (Children's Home + Aid, Chicago).

35. File 51314, p. 12, 1948, ICH&A Adoption Program Applications (Children's Home + Aid, Chicago).

36. Chinoy, *Automobile Workers and the American Dream*, 43–61; Lichtenstein, *State of the Union*, 118–20.

37. Chinoy, *Automobile Workers and the American Dream*, 43–61; Mills, *White Collar*, 89.

38. Berger, *Working-Class Suburb*, 80–90; Chinoy, *Automobile Workers and the American Dream*, 125. See also Quirke, *Eyes on Labor*, 186–224.

39. On involved middle-class fathers, see Griswold, *Fatherhood in America*, 185–218; Weiss, *To Have and to Hold*, 83–113.

40. File 49077, p. 6, 1946, ICH&A Adoption Program Applications (Children's Home + Aid, Chicago).

41. File 46005, ICH&A Adoption Program Applications (Children's Home + Aid, Chicago).

42. File 60142, pp. 13, 20, 1958, ICH&A Adoption Program Applications (Children's Home + Aid, Chicago).

43. Files 47118, 48049, ICH&A Adoption Program Applications (Children's Home + Aid, Chicago).

44. File 53342, 1952, "adoptive father" yellow sheets, ICH&A Adoption Program Applications (Children's Home + Aid, Chicago). See also Rubin, *Worlds of Pain*, 155–66.

45. Bodnar, "Immigration, Kinship, and the Rise of Working-Class Realism in Industrial America," 56. There is a rich literature on the meaning of social mobility for American workers. Inspired by the early work of Stephan Thernstrom, much of this literature focuses on an earlier time period and on immigrants and their children. This scholarship emphasizes a similar point to the one I'm making here: workers sought advancement for themselves and their offspring, but security was an equally if not more important goal. For an overview, see Chudacoff, "Success and Security," 101–12.

46. File 49077, p. 17, 1949, ICH&A Adoption Program Applications (Children's Home + Aid, Chicago).

47. File 55064, pp. 9–10, 1953, ICH&A Adoption Program Applications (Children's Home + Aid, Chicago).

48. File 53291, p. 2, 1951, ICH&A Adoption Program Applications (Children's Home + Aid, Chicago).

49. File 60323, p. 8, 1958, ICH&A Adoption Program Applications (Children's Home + Aid, Chicago).

50. File 62321, p. 17, 1953, ICH&A Adoption Program Applications (Children's Home + Aid, Chicago).

51. File 50260, page 8, 1948, ICH&A Adoption Program Applications (Children's Home + Aid, Chicago).

52. File 50081, p. 7, 1948, ICH&A Adoption Program Applications (Children's Home + Aid, Chicago).

53. See Hulbert, *Raising America*, 225–55.

54. File 48268, p. 11, 1947, ICH&A Adoption Program Applications (Children's Home + Aid, Chicago).

55. File 49107, p. 6, 1947, ICH&A Adoption Program Applications (Children's Home + Aid, Chicago).

56. File 49001, p. 7, 1948, ICH&A Adoption Program Applications (Children's Home + Aid, Chicago).

57. File 48041, p. 4, 1946, ICH&A Adoption Program Applications (Children's Home + Aid, Chicago).

58. Sociological studies from the time also make this argument. See Berger, *Working-Class Suburb*, 20–21; Chinoy, *Automobile Workers and the American Dream*, 126–28; Komarovsky, *Blue-Collar Marriage*, 287–88.

59. While the median yearly income for white men in 1950 was $2,709, growing to $4,296 in 1960, black men's median yearly income was $1,471 and $2,260 in those years. Bureau of the Census, *Historical Income Tables: People* (Washington, D.C.: Government Printing Office, 2011), table P-2: Race and Hispanic Origin of People by Medial In-

come and Sex: 1947 to 2011, http://www.census.gov/hhes/www/income/data/historical/people/2011/P02_2011.xls (accessed January 6, 2013). For more on discrimination in job markets during this period in the urban North, see Sugrue, *The Origins of the Urban Crisis*; Drake and Cayton, *Black Metropolis*, chaps. 9, 11, 12.

60. For more on these families' incomes and comparative data on Chicago, see appendix B, tables 7 and 8.

61. File 53320, ICH&A Adoption Program Applications (Children's Home + Aid, Chicago).

62. File 63219, ICH&A Adoption Program Applications (Children's Home + Aid, Chicago).

63. File 58062, pp. 6–7, "adoption application" yellow sheets, 1956, ICH&A Adoption Program Applications (Children's Home + Aid, Chicago).

64. File 58062, p. 3, "vocational adjustment" yellow sheets, 1956, ICH&A Adoption Program Applications (Children's Home + Aid, Chicago).

65. File 55125, p. 3, "vocational adjustment" yellow sheet, 1953, ICH&A Adoption Program Applications (Children's Home + Aid, Chicago).

66. On earlier race consciousness and black workers' attitudes toward work in Chicago, see Street, "The 'Best Union Members,'" 18–49.

67. File 53110, p. 5, "attitude towards children" yellow sheet, 1952, ICH&A Adoption Program Applications (Children's Home + Aid, Chicago).

68. File 60157, p. 2, 1958, ICH&A Adoption Program Applications (Children's Home + Aid, Chicago).

69. 50312, p. 13, 1948, ICH&A Adoption Program Applications (Children's Home + Aid, Chicago).

70. File 56262, p. 3, "family relationships" yellow sheet, 1955, ICH&A Adoption Program Applications (Children's Home + Aid, Chicago).

71. Ibid., p. 2.

72. File 49328, p. 9, ICH&A Adoption Program Applications (Children's Home + Aid, Chicago).

73. File 61091, p. 2, 1955; p. 5, 1956, ICH&A Adoption Program Applications (Children's Home + Aid, Chicago).

74. File 52316, p. 24, 1952, ICH&A Adoption Program Applications (Children's Home + Aid, Chicago).

75. File 46285, p. 19, 1946, ICH&A Adoption Program Applications (Children's Home + Aid, Chicago).

76. File 55202, p. 21, ICH&A Adoption Program Applications (Children's Home + Aid, Chicago).

77. File 54162, p. 18, 1950, ICH&A Adoption Program Applications (Children's Home + Aid, Chicago).

78. File 52140, p. 4, 1949, ICH&A Adoption Program Applications (Children's Home + Aid, Chicago).

79. File 51164, p. 2, 1949, ICH&A Adoption Program Applications (Children's Home + Aid, Chicago). See also Drake and Cayton, *Black Metropolis*, 664–67.

80. File 54166, "reasons for boarding application," 1952, ICH&A Adoption Program Applications (Children's Home + Aid, Chicago).

81. Ritterhouse, *Growing up Jim Crow*, 82–107.

82. LaRossa, *Of War and Men*, 170–86. See also Payne, *I've Got the Light of Freedom*, 207–35.

83. File 51344, pp. 6–7, 1949, ICH&A Adoption Program Applications (Children's Home + Aid, Chicago).

84. See also Gregory, *The Southern Diaspora*.

85. File 56050, p. 15, 1951, ICH&A Adoption Program Applications (Children's Home + Aid, Chicago). For a contemporary account of the multiple meanings of, and strategies for, uplifting or otherwise "advancing" the race, see Drake and Cayton, *Black Metropolis*, chap. 23.

Chapter 5. Nurturing Frustration and Entitlement

1. Friedan, *The Feminine Mystique*, 18.

2. In her study of the impact of Friedan's text on women's lives at the time, Stephanie Coontz suggests that even though the book restated much that had been said before and Friedan herself overstated her case in both the book and her later writings and interviews about it, it still resonated with a number of women and provided a meaningful exposition of a situation in which they felt trapped. Coontz, *A Strange Stirring*, xxi–xxii. Elaine Tyler May's *Homeward Bound* also supports Friedan's analysis. May documents the unhappiness of many white middle-class housewives but suggests that most felt they had no other options. These women remained committed to making their marriages last even when doing so left them sad, lonely, and frustrated. May, *Homeward Bound*, 163–85.

3. Weiss, *To Have and to Hold*, chaps. 1, 2, and 3. See also Griswold, *Fatherhood in America*, 161–218.

4. Goldin, *Understanding the Gender Gap*, 17. See also Weiss, *To Have and to Hold*, chap. 2.

5. Meyerowitz, "Beyond the Feminine Mystique."

6. Moskowitz, "It's Good to Blow Your Top," 88.

7. Meyerowitz, "Beyond the Feminine Mystique," 252.

8. For other iterations of this claim, see Horowitz, *Betty Friedan and the Making of "The Feminine Mystique"*; Plant, *Mom*, particularly chap. 5.

9. Social workers' views of femininity mirrored those of marriage counselors and other family "experts" at the time, though social workers tended to be considerably more sympathetic to working women than their counterparts. Rebecca Davis, *More Perfect Unions*, chap. 4.

10. File 49273, p. 4, 1945, ICH&A Adoption Program Applications (Children's Home + Aid, Chicago).

11. This line of questions also reflects social workers' ongoing suspicions about applicants' possible psychological sterility, in which a woman's infertility was attributed to psychological causes such as frigidity, anxiety, or a deep ambivalence about motherhood. Workers at ICH&A occasionally mentioned this problem in their writings and in the records when there was no obvious physical cause for a couple's infertility. They generally believed, however, that the process of the home study could uncover these problems if they were there. Similarly, when applicants became pregnant during a home study, workers suggested that this was the happy result of working through in the study whatever worries or fears had prevented them from becoming pregnant before. Herman, *Kinship by Design*, 113–17; Marsh and Ronner, *The Empty Cradle*, 196–97, 205. For attitudes toward infertility at another agency, see Melosh, *Strangers and Kin*, 111–12, 210–12.

12. File 61322, p. 10, 1960, ICH&A Adoption Program Applications (Children's Home + Aid, Chicago).

13. File 58222, Formulation, p. 6, 1955, ICH&A Adoption Program Applications (Children's Home + Aid, Chicago).

14. File 58059, p. 15, 1956, ICH&A Adoption Program Applications (Children's Home + Aid, Chicago).

15. As the secondary literature has demonstrated, social workers prized their professional competence and enjoyed their work. But they were also subject to some of the same social pressures they imposed on applicants: many were expected to prioritize the needs of their husbands and children over their own commitment to their profession. Though the ICH&A case records and agency archives lack detailed information on the personal lives of staff social workers, the Adoption Division's yearly reports described the reasons for all staff departures during the year, which often included pregnancy or moving when a worker's husband got a job elsewhere. See, for instance, "Adoption Division Service Report 1957," p. 1, and "Service Report—Adoption Division—12-1-55," p. 1, folder 1, box 73, Children's Home and Aid Society of Illinois Papers, Richard J. Daley, Library Special Collections and Archives (RJDL), University of Illinois at Chicago (UIC). Further, at least one social worker at ICH&A from this time, Miriam Elson, had a very successful career as a social worker and lecturer at the University of Chicago's School of Social Service Administration beside being a mother, though agency archives suggest that she took summers off from her work at ICH&A during the years she was caring for school-aged children. Miriam Elson, interview by author, digital recording, Chicago, July 1, 2008; "Semi-Annual Report to the General Director, Illinois Children's Home and Aid Society, first draft, September 3, 1946," p. 3, folder 1, box 73, Children's Home and Aid Society of Illinois Papers, RJDL, UIC. On professional competence, see, for instance, Kunzel, *Fallen Women, Problem Girls*, chap. 5; Herman, *Kinship by Design*, chap. 1.

16. Melosh, *Strangers and Kin*, 116.

17. For more on my categorization of families by class, see chap. 4, notes 14 and 15. See also appendix B, tables 7–11, for more on these families' incomes, tenancy status, and suburban or urban location.

18. File 60067, p. 4, 1958, ICH&A Adoption Program Applications (Children's Home + Aid, Chicago).

19. Hartmann, "Women's Employment and the Domestic Ideal in the Early Cold War Years," 86.

20. Weiss, *To Have and to Hold*, chap. 2.

21. File 49146, p. 2, 1948, ICH&A Adoption Program Applications (Children's Home + Aid, Chicago).

22. Ibid., p. 5.

23. Friedan, *The Feminine Mystique*, 22–26.

24. File 53302, p. 6, 1948, ICH&A Adoption Program Applications (Children's Home + Aid, Chicago).

25. File 49228, pp. 26–27, 1944, ICH&A Adoption Program Applications (Children's Home + Aid, Chicago).

26. This woman's situation and my underlying argument in this chapter about the centrality of white middle-class women's personal happiness to their postwar family ideals resonate with Elaine Tyler May's analysis of the "childfree" movement of the 1970s. May notes that although those who were childfree by choice in the 1970s seemed on the surface to be rebelling against postwar pronatalism, there was in fact an important continuity between these two ideologies: "the preoccupation with private life fueled both the nuclear family ideal and the reaction against it." May, *Barren in the Promised Land*, 185.

27. Komarovsky, *Blue-Collar Marriage*, 49.

28. Rainwater, Coleman, and Handel, *Workingman's Wife*, 86.

29. File 55064, p. 6, 1953, ICH&A Adoption Program Applications (Children's Home + Aid, Chicago).

30. File 55257, p. 5, 1954, ICH&A Adoption Program Applications (Children's Home + Aid, Chicago).

31. Komarovsky, *Blue-Collar Marriage*, 60, 112–77. See also Rainwater, Coleman, and Handel, *Workingman's Wife*, 67–87; Rubin, *Worlds of Pain*, 93–133.

32. File 48120, p. 11, 1939, ICH&A Adoption Program Applications (Children's Home + Aid, Chicago).

33. Benson, "Living on the Margin," 220–24. Benson expanded on "good managers," as well as the other important networks on which working-class families relied in the interwar years, in a book published posthumously: Benson, *Household Accounts*.

34. File 48049, ICH&A Adoption Program Applications (Children's Home + Aid, Chicago). Bureau of the Census, *U.S. Census of the Population: 1950* (Washington, D.C.: Government Printing Office, 1953), vol. 2, pt. 13, table 87.

35. File 48049, pp. 14–15, 1948, ICH&A Adoption Program Applications (Children's Home + Aid, Chicago).

36. File 46189, p. 2, 1945, ICH&A Adoption Program Applications (Children's Home + Aid, Chicago).

37. Ibid. See also file 53342, "adoptive mother" yellow sheet, 1952, ICH&A Adoption Program Applications (Children's Home + Aid, Chicago).

38. File 60338, p. 7, 1955, ICH&A Adoption Program Applications (Children's Home + Aid, Chicago).

39. Weiss, *To Have and to Hold*, 51–81. See also May, *Homeward Bound*, 49–79. Dorothy Sue Cobble elaborates on the political implications of working-class women's experiences as wives, mothers, and workers. Cobble, *The Other Women's Movement*, 121–44.

40. Komarovsky, *Blue-Collar Marriage*, 68–69. See also Damaske, *For the Family*.

41. File 61196, pp. 3, 5, 1956, ICH&A Adoption Program Applications (Children's Home + Aid, Chicago).

42. File 50260, p. 7, 1948, ICH&A Adoption Program Applications (Children's Home + Aid, Chicago).

43. File 50081, p. 20, 1948, ICH&A Adoption Program Applications (Children's Home + Aid, Chicago).

44. File 46134, p. 14, 1945, ICH&A Adoption Program Applications (Children's Home + Aid, Chicago).

45. File 50115, p. 3, 1946, ICH&A Adoption Program Applications (Children's Home + Aid, Chicago).

46. Jones, *Labor of Love, Labor of Sorrow*, 264, 269.

47. Landry, *Black Working Wives*. See also Simmons, *Making Marriage Modern*, 150–64.

48. Collins, *Black Feminist Thought*, 75.

49. "Goodbye Mammy, Hello Mom," *Ebony*, March 1947, 36–37.

50. Ibid. See also Feldstein, *Motherhood in Black and White, 1930–1965*.

51. File 53320, p. 12, 1951, ICH&A Adoption Program Applications (Children's Home + Aid, Chicago).

52. File 45152, p. 5, 1944, ICH&A Adoption Program Applications (Children's Home + Aid, Chicago).

53. Ibid.

54. File 57168, p. 7, 1952, ICH&A Adoption Program Applications (Children's Home + Aid, Chicago).

55. File 48238, 46237, ICH&A Adoption Program Applications (Children's Home + Aid, Chicago).

56. File 46319, ICH&A Adoption Program Applications (Children's Home + Aid, Chicago).

57. File 50198, ICH&A Adoption Program Applications (Children's Home + Aid, Chicago). Although creative ways of making ends meet were common among African American women in the case records, Lisa Levenstein suggests the limitations of this strategy for very poor women, pointing out that they rarely led to significant financial stability, much less class mobility. She suggests that a number of women also looked to the state to provide kinds of assistance they could not achieve through odd jobs and networks of family and friends. Levenstein, *A Movement without Marches*, 20–23.

58. Tera Hunter's *To 'Joy My Freedom* provides an excellent example of the ways in which black families organized their labor so as to gain greater autonomy from employers. By working in their own homes rather than in the homes of white employers, Atlanta washerwomen in particular gained racial and familial autonomy and created better working and family conditions for themselves.

59. File 60157, p. 22, 1958, ICH&A Adoption Program Applications (Children's Home + Aid, Chicago).

60. File 61088, p. 21, 1960, ICH&A Adoption Program Applications (Children's Home + Aid, Chicago).

61. File 51306, "Joint Service Bureau, Sheet: 9," 1936, ICH&A Adoption Program Applications (Children's Home + Aid, Chicago). See also Anderson, "Last Hired, First Fired." For more on the professional options available to black women, see Drake and Cayton, *Black Metropolis*, 214–62.

62. File 59356, p. 21, 1957, ICH&A Adoption Program Applications (Children's Home + Aid, Chicago).

63. File 52127, p. 12, 1950, ICH&A Adoption Program Applications (Children's Home + Aid, Chicago).

64. Harley, "For the Good of Family and Race," 337.

Chapter 6. Constructing Domesticity

1. Hansberry, *A Raisin in the Sun*.

2. Green, *Selling the Race*, 183.

3. On the centrality of suburban single-family homes to "domesticity," see, for instance, May, *Homeward Bound*; Weiss, *To Have and to Hold*. On the policies and politics of race and housing, see, for instance, Arnold R. Hirsch, "Massive Resistance in the Urban North;" Jackson, *Crabgrass Frontier*; Arnold R. Hirsch, *Making the Second Ghetto*; Kruse, *White Flight*; Lassiter, *The Silent Majority*; Nicolaides, *My Blue Heaven*; Sugrue, *The Origins of the Urban Crisis*.

4. Kenneth T. Jackson, "America's Rush to Suburbia," *New York Times*, June 9, 1996.

5. Jackson, *Crabgrass Frontier*; Lizabeth Cohen, *A Consumer's Republic*, chap. 5; Baxandall and Ewen, *Picture Windows*.

6. Pacyga, *Chicago*, 308–21.

7. Drake and Cayton, *Black Metropolis*; Green, *Selling the Race*.

8. For a more detailed account, see Arnold R. Hirsch, *Making the Second Ghetto*, 17–39. See also McEnaney, "Nightmares on Elm Street."

9. Arnold R. Hirsch, *Making the Second Ghetto*, 24.

10. Chicago Community Inventory, Chicago Plan Commission, *Census Statistics on Housing for Chicago: 1950, 1940*, ii.

11. Arnold R. Hirsch, *Making the Second Ghetto*, 29.

12. The Chicago metropolitan area added 688,222 new homes in the first fifteen years after World War II. Of these new units, over 77 percent were located in the suburbs, and 76 percent of them were single-family dwellings. The rest of the new building was within the city, but mostly along its undeveloped edges, in areas more suburban than urban in feel. Almost all new building in the city center was related to "government programs, public housing, or private institutional redevelopment plans." This rush of new suburban building had a profound effect on the city's population. Although the population of the metropolitan area grew by over 1.5 million people between 1940 and 1960, the city's share went from 74 percent to 57 percent, and the city itself began losing population by 1950. Further, new suburban building was primarily restricted to white residents, which dramatically shifted the city's racial demographics. In 1940, blacks were 6.6 percent of the metropolitan area's residents and 2.1 percent of the suburban population. In 1960, blacks were 14.3 percent of the overall metropolitan population but still only 2.9 percent of the suburban population. Arnold R. Hirsch, *Making the Second Ghetto*, 27–28.

13. Arnold R. Hirsch, *Making the Second Ghetto*, 29–32. On blockbusting in Chicago during the first half of the century, see Garb, "Drawing The 'Color Line.'" For a nuanced analysis of postwar blockbusting and contract selling, see Satter, *Family Properties*.

14. Lizabeth Cohen, *A Consumer's Republic*, 212–27. For a spatial analysis of racism and urban change, see Sugrue, *The Origins of the Urban Crisis*. See also Seligman, *Block by Block*.

15. Cohen and Taylor, *American Pharaoh*, 10.

16. For a racial breakdown of the proportion of urban and suburban dwellers in my sample, as well as a racial breakdown of tenancy status in my sample and in Chicago during this period, see appendix B, tables 9–11.

17. File 50230, p. 4, 1948, ICH&A Adoption Program Applications (Children's Home + Aid, Chicago).

18. File 54310, p. 12, 1946, ICH&A Adoption Program Applications (Children's Home + Aid, Chicago).

19. File 50355, p. 5, 1948, ICH&A Adoption Program Applications (Children's Home + Aid, Chicago).

20. File 48234, p. 9, ICH&A Adoption Program Applications (Children's Home + Aid, Chicago). See file 43084, ICH&A Adoption Program Applications (Children's Home + Aid, Chicago).

21. File 53089, p. 13, 1950, ICH&A Adoption Program Applications (Children's Home + Aid, Chicago).

22. File 52140, p. 3, 1949, also 51344, p. 4, 1949, ICH&A Adoption Program Applications (Children's Home + Aid, Chicago).

23. Files 46102, 47239, 47334, 49001, 49218, 49273, 51003, 51209, 62113, 62321, 65174, ICH&A Adoption Program Applications (Children's Home + Aid, Chicago). For more on self-built housing in Chicago, see Harris, "Chicago's Other Suburbs."

24. Lizabeth Cohen, *A Consumer's Republic*, 202.

25. Files 48309, 49335, 50190, 62034, ICH&A Adoption Program Applications (Children's Home + Aid, Chicago).

26. File 49146, ICH&A Adoption Program Applications (Children's Home + Aid, Chicago). See also file 50308, ICH&A Adoption Program Applications (Children's Home + Aid, Chicago).

27. File 51119, p. 15, 1949, ICH&A Adoption Program Applications (Children's Home + Aid, Chicago). See also files 49146, 50308, 51003, 53187, 59287, ICH&A Adoption Program Applications (Children's Home + Aid, Chicago).

28. File 50260, p. 3, 1948, ICH&A Adoption Program Applications (Children's Home + Aid, Chicago).

29. File 50230, p. 4, 1948, ICH&A Adoption Program Applications (Children's Home + Aid, Chicago). See also file 59087, p. 15, ICH&A Adoption Program Applications (Children's Home + Aid, Chicago).

30. See also Kelly, *Expanding the American Dream*; and Baxandall and Ewen, *Picture Windows*, 164–65.

31. File 51119, p. 15, ICH&A Adoption Program Applications (Children's Home + Aid, Chicago).

32. File 51209, pp. 2, 4, ICH&A Adoption Program Applications (Children's Home + Aid, Chicago).

33. For more on the ideology of "togetherness," see Weiss, *To Have and to Hold*, 115–39.

34. Files 52127, 54162, 56213, ICH&A Adoption Program Applications (Children's Home + Aid, Chicago). Wiese also discusses urban black families' interest in farms in relation to the advertising of suburban homes in black newspapers, which often employed farm imagery. Wiese, *Places of Their Own*, 145–54.

35. See also Gelber, "Do-It-Yourself," 66–112.

36. File 51122, p. 7, 1949, ICH&A Adoption Program Applications (Children's Home + Aid, Chicago).

37. Ibid., p. 11.

38. Although there is not space to develop the claim here, I have explored elsewhere the nuances of social workers' and applicants' assessments of residential space. I argue that ordinary Chicagoans thought about their family's housing in relation to particular neighborhoods and their amenities, rather than in terms of broad categories of suburban and urban space, which scholars typically use to discuss the relationship between family ideals and housing during the postwar years. See Sarah Potter, "Family Ideals."

39. File 49343, pp. 4–5, 15, 1949, ICH&A Adoption Program Applications (Children's Home + Aid, Chicago).

40. Spinney, *City of Big Shoulders*, 210.

41. File 61150, p. 1, 1959, ICH&A Adoption Program Applications (Children's Home + Aid, Chicago).

42. File 53302, p. 10, 1948. See also file 47249, p. 6, 1946; 62321, p. 4, 1948, and 62143, p. 3, 1957, ICH&A Adoption Program Applications (Children's Home + Aid, Chicago).

43. File 62034, p. 4, 1951, ICH&A Adoption Program Applications (Children's Home + Aid, Chicago . See also files 43084 and 51083, ICH&A Adoption Program Applications (Children's Home + Aid, Chicago); Perry, "Portage Park," 642. These couples were certainly not the norm in Chicago at the time. Chicago's suburbs expanded rapidly during

the postwar years, with more than three-quarters of new homes built in the area between 1945 and 1959 constructed outside of the city limits. Further, unlike those most studied in the historical literature, these families were not Catholic or part of a tight-knit ethnic immigrant community. Instead, they described important family benefits to living in a city neighborhood. Biles, *Richard J. Daley*, 4. See also McGreevy, *Parish Boundaries*; Gamm, *Urban Exodus*; Pritchett, *Brownsville, Brooklyn*.

44. Ehrenhalt, *The Lost City*, 92–98. See also Harris, "Working-Class Home Ownership in the American Metropolis," 46–69.

45. Files 45185, 48041, 51242, 51255, 61196, ICH&A Adoption Program Applications (Children's Home + Aid, Chicago).

46. File 53291, p. 9, ICH&A Adoption Program Applications (Children's Home + Aid, Chicago). See also files 45013, 45185, 46015, 46172, 46189, 47008, 48041, 48120, 48241, 49090, 51255, 52232, 60338, 61196, 63251, ICH&A Adoption Program Applications (Children's Home + Aid, Chicago).

47. File 50198, pp. 5–6, 1947, ICH&A Adoption Program Applications (Children's Home + Aid, Chicago).

48. Ibid., p. 6.

49. File 58270, pp. 11–12, 1958, ICH&A Adoption Program Applications (Children's Home + Aid, Chicago); Wallace Best, "Chatham," in *The Encyclopedia of Chicago*, 128–29. See also 63164, pp. 12–13, 1961, ICH&A Adoption Program Applications (Children's Home + Aid, Chicago).

50. File 63154, pp. 12–13, 1961, ICH&A Adoption Program Applications (Children's Home + Aid, Chicago).

51. File 62321, ICH&A Adoption Program Applications (Children's Home + Aid, Chicago).

52. Files 50081, 53305, 58222, 60323, ICH&A Adoption Program Applications (Children's Home + Aid, Chicago).

53. File 51242, ICH&A Adoption Program Applications (Children's Home + Aid, Chicago).

54. File 61196, ICH&A Adoption Program Applications (Children's Home + Aid, Chicago).

55. Sociologist Mirra Komarovsky found a similar pattern in her 1967 study of blue-collar marriages. Komarovsky, *Blue-Collar Marriage*, 208, 237.

56. File 47193, p. 6, 1945, ICH&A Adoption Program Applications (Children's Home + Aid, Chicago).

57. Kitagawa and Taeuber, *Local Community Fact Book*, 150–51. For more on racial violence in Englewood, see Pacyga, *Chicago*, 293–95; Spinney, *City of Big Shoulders*, 205.

58. File 60142, p. 12, ICH&A Adoption Program Applications (Children's Home + Aid, Chicago).

59. Ibid., p. 13.

60. Stockwell, "Englewood," 269.

61. Capehart, "Douglas," 244.

62. File 60071, pp. 3, 11, 1959, ICH&A Adoption Program Applications (Children's Home + Aid, Chicago).

63. File 53282, ICH&A Adoption Program Applications (Children's Home + Aid, Chicago). For other accounts of the prevalence of taking in roomers in black communities, see Gregory, *The Southern Diaspora*, 105; Satter, *Family Properties*, 36–63; Weise, *Places of Their Own*, 146.

64. File 50348, p. 11, ICH&A Adoption Program Applications (Children's Home + Aid, Chicago).

65. File 53282, pp. 18–19, 1952, ICH&A Adoption Program Applications (Children's Home + Aid, Chicago).

66. Ibid.

67. File 51164, p. 5, 1949, ICH&A Adoption Program Applications (Children's Home + Aid, Chicago).

68. File 49328, ICH&A Adoption Program Applications (Children's Home + Aid, Chicago). See also Stack, *All Our Kin*.

69. Abrahamson, *A Neighborhood Finds Itself*, ix. I would like to thank former University of Chicago student Lisa Furchtgott, whose fantastic undergraduate essay "Talking in the City: Gender, Language, and the Work of Rumor in the Hyde Park-Kenwood Community Conference, 1949–1958" pointed me to the HPKCC as a potentially rich source for this analysis.

70. Hyde Park-Kenwood Community Conference, *Newsletter* (July 1956), 1. Available at the Joseph Regenstein Library, University of Chicago.

71. Hyde Park-Kenwood Community Conference, *Newsletter*, 1952–1964. For an in-depth analysis of the HPKCC and its role in urban renewal, see Arnold R. Hirsch, *Making the Second Ghetto*, 135–70.

72. Arnold R. Hirsch, *Making the Second Ghetto*, 136–39, 166.

73. Abrahamson, *A Neighborhood Finds Itself*, 292–93.

74. "Organization of Block Groups for Neighborhood Improvement: The Hyde Park-Kenwood Community Conference," undated but most likely from the mid-1950s, published by ACTION, American Council To Improve Our Neighborhoods, Inc., New York, box 96, folder 4, Hyde Park Kenwood Community Conference, Special Collections Research Center, Joseph Regenstein Library, University of Chicago. Hereafter cited as HPKCC, SCRC, Regenstein Library, University of Chicago.

75. Abrahamson, *A Neighborhood Finds Itself*, 24.

76. "It Can Happen Right Here," slide show script, box 64, folder 5, HPKCC, SCRC, Regenstein Library, University of Chicago.

77. Abrahamson, *A Neighborhood Finds Itself*, 34.

78. Ibid., 36.

79. "Are You Getting Good Neighbors?" pamphlet, undated (likely from the mid-1950s), published by Community Relations Service, New York, N.Y., box 153, folder 6, HPKCC, SCRC, Regenstein Library, University of Chicago.

80. Mr. Lewis James, 6356 S. Ingleside, October 20, 1952, report, p. 3, box 92, folder 6, HPKCC, SCRC, Regenstein Library, University of Chicago.

81. Hyde Park-Kenwood Community Conference, *Newsletter* no. 8 (April 16, 1953), 2.

82. Hyde Park-Kenwood Community Conference, *Newsletter* 10, no. 8 (December 1958), 1.

83. "Hyde Park Youth Project Progress Report," June 1956–December 1956, p. 1, box 236, folder 4 or 5, HPKCC, SCRC, Regenstein Library, University of Chicago. The HPKCC took over the youth project in 1958. See Hyde Park-Kenwood Community Conference, *Newsletter* 10, no. 8 (December 1958); and "Hyde Park-Kenwood Community Conference Summary of Annual Report for Year Ending November, 1958," box 95, folder 14, HPKCC, SCRC, Regenstein Library, University of Chicago.

84. See, for instance, Hyde Park-Kenwood Community Conference, *Newsletter*, July 1956, 1; Hyde Park-Kenwood Community Conference, *Newsletter* 10, no. 2 (February

1958), pp. 1–2; Hyde Park-Kenwood Community Conference, *Newsletter* 11, no. 1 (February 1959), 2.

85. Abrahamson, *A Neighborhood Finds Itself*, 282.

Chapter 7. To Take Some Responsibility for Community Problems

1. File 56050, pp. 8, 15, 1951, ICH&A Adoption Program Applications (Children's Home + Aid, Chicago). This is very similar to analyses of uplift and respectability among African Americans in the earlier decades of the century, and particularly during the early years of migration. See, for instance, Carby, "Policing the Black Woman's Body in an Urban Context"; and Higginbotham, *Righteous Discontent*. For more on the relationship between Chicago city politics, the deterioration of West Side neighborhoods, and neighborhood racial change, see Seligman, *Block by Block*.

2. File 46339, p. 6, 1945, ICH&A Adoption Program Applications (Children's Home + Aid, Chicago).

3. File 50198, p. 11, 1947, ICH&A Adoption Program Applications (Children's Home + Aid, Chicago).

4. File 56050, p. 17, 1951, ICH&A Adoption Program Applications (Children's Home + Aid, Chicago).

5. Ibid., p. 15.

6. Berebitsky, *Like Our Very Own*, 51–74; Hart, "A Nation's Need for Adoption and Competing Realities," 151.

7. Berebitsky, *Like Our Very Own*, 81–83.

8. Ibid., 88–101.

9. See, for instance, Hawes, *Children between the Wars*; Lindenmeyer, *The Greatest Generation Grows Up*; Mintz, *Huck's Raft*; Zelizer, *Pricing the Priceless Child*.

10. Stearns, *Anxious Parents*. For another account of changing trends in childrearing literature, see Hulbert, *Raising America*.

11. Mintz, *Huck's Raft*, 297–302.

12. Tuttle, *"Daddy's Gone to War."*

13. Mintz, *Huck's Raft*, 302–8.

14. Richard B. Gehman, "Preparing Parents for Adoption," reprinted from *Tomorrow* magazine (June 1949), ICH&A Staff Papers, Evanston, Ill.

15. File 46079, adoption decree, 1946; p. 15, 1944, ICH&A Adoption Program Applications (Children's Home + Aid, Chicago).

16. File 50312, p. 13, 1948, ICH&A Adoption Program Applications (Children's Home + Aid, Chicago).

17. Whyte, *The Organization Man*, 280.

18. Ibid., 287.

19. Riesman, *The Lonely Crowd*; Sloan Wilson, *The Man in the Gray Flannel Suit*; Murray, *The Progressive Housewife*, 2–3.

20. File 61197, "social relationships" yellow sheet, 1956, ICH&A Adoption Program Applications (Children's Home + Aid, Chicago). See also Charles, *Service Clubs in American Society*. For recent interpretations of the impact of civic engagement on democracy and community vitality in the postwar period, see Putnam, *Bowling Alone*; Skocpol, *Diminished Democracy*.

21. File 48268, p. 12, 1947, ICH&A Adoption Program Applications (Children's Home + Aid, Chicago).

22. File 58169, p. 5, 1957, ICH&A Adoption Program Applications (Children's Home + Aid, Chicago).

23. File 58059, p. 6, 1953, ICH&A Adoption Program Applications (Children's Home + Aid, Chicago).

24. File 50308, p. 30, 1950, ICH&A Adoption Program Applications (Children's Home + Aid, Chicago).

25. File 51324, ICH&A Adoption Program Applications (Children's Home + Aid, Chicago).

26. File 61150, p. 7, 1960, ICH&A Adoption Program Applications (Children's Home + Aid, Chicago).

27. File 56131, "vocational adjustment" yellow sheets, 1954, ICH&A Adoption Program Applications (Children's Home + Aid, Chicago).

28. File 50230, p. 5, 1948; p. 10, 1949, ICH&A Adoption Program Applications (Children's Home + Aid, Chicago). This woman was certainly not alone in creating her own club. To help women manage their club memberships and to create new clubs, some authors wrote handbooks with tips and advice. See, for instance, McElroy and Houghton, *The Compete Book for Clubwomen*.

29. There is a wealth of scholarship on maternalism in women's history from the eighteenth through the twentieth centuries—far more than I can cite here. For a few selected works, see Kerber, *Women of the Republic*; Ginzberg, *Women and the Work of Benevolence*; Ryan, *Cradle of the Middle Class*; Kunzel, *Fallen Women, Problem Girls*; Storrs, *Civilizing Capitalism*.

30. Their activity was also likely to have far-reaching effects. As historian Susan Ware has demonstrated, participation in the League of Women Voters during the 1950s led many women to become involved in electoral and activist politics in later decades. See Ware, "American Women in the 1950s," 281–99; Lynn, "Gender and Post World War II Progressive Politics," 215–39. For other examples of women's political activity at the time, see Swerdlow, *Women Strike for Peace*, and Murray, *The Progressive Housewife*.

31. Cohen and Taylor, *American Pharaoh*, chaps. 1–4; Pacyga, *Chicago*, chaps. 9–10; Biles, *Richard J. Daley*, chaps. 1–4.

32. Cohen and Taylor, *American Pharaoh*, 81, 92–104, 126, 134, 171–74, 183–215, 303–8, 312–15; Pacyga, *Chicago*, chaps. 9–10; Biles, *Richard J. Daley*, chaps. 1–4.

33. Drake and Cayton, *Black Metropolis*, 390.

34. Knupfer, *The Chicago Black Renaissance and Women's Activism*; and Green, *Selling the Race*.

35. File 52101, p. 4, 1942, ICH&A Adoption Program Applications (Children's Home + Aid, Chicago).

36. File 55148, p. 8, 1955, ICH&A Adoption Program Applications (Children's Home + Aid, Chicago).

37. File 54322, p. 2, 1952, ICH&A Adoption Program Applications (Children's Home + Aid, Chicago).

38. On the activities of the block clubs organized by the Chicago Urban League during this period, see their reports in Chicago Urban League Records, series II, subseries 4.I, boxes II-234, II-235, II-236, Richard J. Daley Library Special Collections and Archives, University of Illinois at Chicago.

39. Skocpol, *Diminished Democracy*, 130.

40. Danns, *Something Better for Our Children*; Homel, *Down from Equality*; Seligman, *Block by Block*, chap. 5; Cohen and Taylor, *American Pharaoh*, 303–8, 312–15; Biles,

Richard J. Daley, 97–101. Chicago was not the only northern city where African Americans demanded better service from their public schools. See also Levenstein, *A Movement without Marches*, chap. 4.

41. Skocpol, Liazos, and Ganz, *What a Mighty Power We Can Be*, 209. See also Mettler, *Soldiers to Citizens*, chaps. 7 and 8.

42. Cohen and Taylor, *American Pharaoh*, 57–61, 92–98, 204–7.

43. File 63219, p. 11, 1959, ICH&A Adoption Program Applications (Children's Home + Aid, Chicago). The age of Du Bois here appears to be a typo in the adoption record, as Du Bois would have been ninety-one in 1959 when this statement was made. Du Bois gave fairly regular speeches in Chicago during the 1950s and this family would have had ample opportunity to see him. Though I found no evidence of his having spoken in the city in 1959, he gave lectures in Chicago at least twice in 1958, one of which was a widely publicized tribute to him in honor of his ninetieth birthday. The *Chicago Defender* covered the activities of Du Bois regularly and announced these events. See, for instance, "African Students Meeting Here to Weigh Unification," *Chicago Defender*, June 16, 1958, A6; "DuBois Tribute Lauded by Daley," *Chicago Defender*, May 19, 1958, A4.

44. Gillon, *Politics and Vision*.

45. File 53110, "social relationships" yellow sheet, 1952, ICH&A Adoption Program Applications (Children's Home + Aid, Chicago).

46. File 52336, p. 7, 1946, ICH&A Adoption Program Applications (Children's Home + Aid, Chicago). For more on the family's relationship with civil rights activism, see LaRossa, *Of War and Men*, 170–86; Payne, *I've Got the Light of Freedom*, 207–35.

47. Berger, *Working-Class Suburb*, 59.

48. Ibid., 59–64. See also Shostak and Gomberg, *Blue-Collar World*, especially pp. 193–306 ("The Community") and 406–57 ("Leisure").

49. Rainwater, Coleman, and Handel, *Workingman's Wife*, 114. In her recent analysis of large membership organizations in the twentieth-century United States, Theda Skocpol suggests that most of the largest groups in the 1950s recruited across class and occupational lines for their membership. Veterans groups (and their female auxiliaries), churches, fraternal organizations, and national service groups enlisted people from a range of locales, diverse educational experiences, and social backgrounds. Although many were segregated by sex or race or both, they did frequently bring people of different backgrounds together to participate in rituals, provide mutual aid, and otherwise serve their membership and the community around them. Skocpol's conclusions suggest that perhaps Rainwater, et al, were correct in their analysis that generally Americans across class engaged in similar activities, but not always to the same degree. Skocpol, *Diminished Democracy*, 129–33.

50. Ibid., 115.

51. Ibid., 119.

52. File 50031, pp. 11, 16, 1947, ICH&A Adoption Program Applications (Children's Home + Aid, Chicago).

53. While Chicago's many working-class white Catholics might have espoused a wholehearted commitment to community participation through being involved in the church, participating in the life and well-being of the parish, and practicing the social gospel, the many Protestant or more secular Catholic working-class families in my sample instead envisioned their communities as primarily consisting of their friends and neighbors. For more on the importance of church and parish in Catholics' attachments

to and involvement in their neighborhoods during this period, see Gamm, *Urban Exodus*; McGreevy, *Parish Boundaries*.

54. File 46230, p. 3, 1941, ICH&A Adoption Program Applications (Children's Home + Aid, Chicago).

55. File 53086, p. 5, 1940, ICH&A Adoption Program Applications (Children's Home + Aid, Chicago).

56. File 51255, p. 12, 1949, ICH&A Adoption Program Applications (Children's Home + Aid, Chicago).

57. File 62034, p. 36, 1961, ICH&A Adoption Program Applications (Children's Home + Aid, Chicago).

58. File 54307, p. 10, 1950, ICH&A Adoption Program Applications (Children's Home + Aid, Chicago).

59. Quote from Putnam, cited in Herd and Meyer. Putnam, *Bowling Alone*, 19; Herd and Meyer, "Care Work," 667.

60. See, for instance, Alexander, *The Girl Problem*; Gamm and Putnam, "The Growth of Voluntary Associations in America, 1840–1940"; Rosenzweig, *Eight Hours for What We Will*.

61. Lizabeth Cohen, *Making a New Deal*, chap. 2. Similarly, historian Susan Porter Benson has demonstrated the centrality of relationships of reciprocity among community and kin networks for working-class family survival during the interwar period. Benson, *Household Accounts*.

Conclusion

1. Green, *Selling the Race*, 182. See also Feldstein, "I Wanted the Whole World to See," 263–303.

2. Feldstein, "I Wanted the Whole World to See," 271.

3. Ibid., 266. Emmett Till's mother also positioned herself as a grieving and deserving mother in the memoir she wrote with Christopher Benson. See Till-Mobley and Benson, *Death of Innocence*, especially 128–37.

4. May, *Homeward Bound*; Coontz, *The Way We Never Were*; Weiss, *To Have and to Hold*; Breines, *Young, White, and Miserable*.

5. On disputes over the family in the 1960s and 1970s, see especially Self, *All in the Family*; Zaretsky, *No Direction Home*; Critchlow, *Phyllis Schlafly and Grassroots Conservatism*; Rebecca Davis, *More Perfect Unions*, chaps. 6–7; Lassiter, "Inventing Family Values"; and Bailey, "She 'Can Bring Home the Bacon.'"

6. May, *Homeward Bound*; Coontz, *The Way We Never Were*; Weiss, *To Have and to Hold*; Breines, *Young, White, and Miserable*; Douglas, *Where the Girls Are*.

7. The Moynihan Report, which is officially entitled "The Negro Family: The Case for National Action," was produced in 1965 by Daniel Patrick Moynihan for the Department of Labor. Building on the work of scholars such as E. Franklin Frazier and others, the Report made provocative claims about the interconnections between poverty, the history of slavery and racism, and black family structures that have incited debate and discussion ever since. The Report and analyses of it are part of a much larger and diverse literature on the relationship between the underclass, welfare, poverty, and the black family. For historians, the most influential texts on this topic include Katz, ed., *The "Underclass" Debate*; Sugrue, *Origins of the Urban Crisis*; and William Julius Wilson, *The Truly Dis-*

advantaged. For recent interpretations, see Levenstein, *A Movement without Marches*; Patterson, *Freedom Is Not Enough.*

8. Saville, *The Work of Reconstruction*, 110.

Appendix A. Note on Sources and Methodology

1. I relied on the Chicago *Community Fact Book* editions from 1940, 1950, and 1960 to make this decision. The fact books provide census data for Chicago and its suburbs, including housing and population densities. See Wirth, Sheldon, and Chicago Community Inventory, *Local Community Fact Book of Chicago*; Hauser, Kitagawa, Wirth, and Chicago Community Inventory, *Local Community Fact Book for Chicago, 1950*; Kitagawa and Taeuber, *Local Community Fact Book: Chicago Metropolitan Area, 1960*.

2. For more on criteria used to judge applicants, see, in addition to the adoption and foster care records themselves, "Service Report, Adoption Division—1951," "Semi-Annual Report, Adoption Division of the Illinois Children's Home and Aid Society," December 31, 1948, and June 30, 1947, box 73, folder 1; and Annual and Semi-Annual Reports of the Home Finding Division, box 74, folder 1, Children's Home and Aid Society of Illinois Papers, Richard J. Daley Library Special Collections and Archives (RJDL), University of Illinois at Chicago (UIC).

3. For a discussion of how workers understood their role in the creation of case records at a time when records were becoming increasingly elaborate, see Barbara Harrison, Helen Lampe, and Myra Thomas, *Recording III* (New York: Family Welfare Association of America, 1939), located in ICH&A Staff Papers, Evanston, Ill. For more on the origins of adoption records, see Carp, *Family Matters*, chap. 2.

4. For these procedures, and particularly the merger of the Infant Division and Adoption Division in 1950, see "Semi-Annual Report," January 1951, and "Semi-Annual Report," August 1951, Children's Home and Aid Society of Illinois Papers, box 73, folder 1, RJDL, UIC.

5. For policies on placement, see "Supplement to Semi-Annual Report," August 1953, Children's Home and Aid Society of Illinois Papers, box 73, folder 1, RJDL, UIC.

6. Holt, "Marking," 7.

7. Ibid., 8.

BIBLIOGRAPHY

Manuscript Collections Consulted

Children's Home and Aid Society of Illinois
  Records of adoptive and foster care applicants filed before 1970, Chicago
  Staff papers from staff library, Evanston
Richard J. Daley Library Special Collections and University Archives, University of
  Illinois at Chicago
  Papers of Children's Home and Aid Society of Illinois
  Chicago Urban League Records
Special Collections Research Center, University of Chicago Library
  Allison Davis Papers
  Earnest Watson Burgess Papers
  Earnest Watson Burgess Papers, Addenda
  Hyde Park–Kenwood Community Conference
Vivian G. Harsh Research Collection of Afro-American History & Literature,
  Woodson Regional Library, Chicago Public Library
  Horace Cayton Papers
  Illinois Writers Project / "Negro in Illinois" Papers

Works Cited

Abrahamson, Julia. *A Neighborhood Finds Itself.* New York: Harper & Brothers, 1959.
Abrams, Laura S., and Laura Curran. "Between Women: Gender and Social Work in
  Historical Perspective." *Social Service Review* 78, no. 3 (2004): 429–46.
Alexander, Ruth M. *The Girl Problem: Female Sexual Delinquency in New York,
  1900–1930.* Ithaca, N.Y.: Cornell University Press, 1995.
Anderson, Karen Tucker. "Last Hired, First Fired: Black Women Workers during
  World War II." *Journal of American History* 69, no. 1 (1982): 82–97.
Austin, Linda T. "Babies for Sale: The Tennessee Children's Home Adoption Scandal."
  PhD diss., Memphis State University, 1992.
———. *Babies for Sale: The Tennessee Children's Home Adoption Scandal.* Westport,
  Conn.: Praeger Publishers, 1993.
Bailey, Beth. "She 'Can Bring Home the Bacon': Negotiating Gender in the 1970s." In
  America in the Seventies, edited by Beth Bailey and David Farber, 107–28. Lawrence:
  University Press of Kansas, 2004.
Balcom, Karen A. *The Traffic in Babies: Cross-Border Adoption and Baby-Selling*

between the United States and Canada, 1930–1972. Toronto: University of Toronto Press, 2011.

Bates, Beth Tompkins. *Pullman Porters and the Rise of Protest Politics in Black America, 1925–1945*. Chapel Hill: University of North Carolina Press, 2001.

Baxandall, Rosalyn Fraad, and Elizabeth Ewen. *Picture Windows: How the Suburbs Happened*. New York: Basic Books, 2000.

Benson, Susan Porter. *Household Accounts: Working-Class Family Economics in the Interwar United States*. Ithaca, N.Y.: Cornell University Press, 2007.

———. "Living on the Margin: Working-Class Marriages and Family Survival Strategies in the United States, 1919–1941." In *The Sex of Things: Gender and Consumption in Historical Perspective*, edited by Victoria De Grazia and Ellen Furlough, 212–43. Berkeley: University of California Press, 1996.

Berebitsky, Julie. *Like Our Very Own: Adoption and the Changing Culture of Motherhood, 1851–1950*. Lawrence: University Press of Kansas, 2000.

Berger, Bennett M. *Working-Class Suburb: A Study of Auto Workers in Suburbia*. 1960. Reprint, Berkeley: University of California Press, 1971.

Best, Wallace. "Chatham." In *The Encyclopedia of Chicago*, edited by James R. Grossman, Ann Durkin Keating, and Janice L. Reiff, 128–29. Chicago: University of Chicago Press, 2004.

Biles, Roger. *Richard J. Daley: Politics, Race, and the Governing of Chicago*. DeKalb: Northern Illinois University Press, 1995.

Biondi, Martha. *To Stand and Fight: The Struggle for Civil Rights in Postwar New York City*. Cambridge, Mass.: Harvard University Press, 2003.

Bisantz, Barbara. *The Baby Thief: The Untold Story of Georgia Tann, the Baby Seller Who Corrupted Adoption*. New York: Union Square Press, 2007.

Blum, John Morton. *V Was for Victory: Politics and American Culture during World War II*. New York: Harcourt Brace Jovanovich, 1976.

Bodnar, John. "Immigration, Kinship, and the Rise of Working-Class Realism in Industrial America." *Journal of Social History* 14, no. 1 (1980): 45–65.

Breines, Wini. *Young, White, and Miserable: Growing up Female in the 1950s*. Chicago: University of Chicago Press, 1992.

Brenner, Ruth F. "The Selection of Adoptive Parents: A Casework Responsibility." *Child Welfare League of America Bulletin* 25 (December 1946): 1–6.

Briggs, Laura. *Somebody's Children: The Politics of Transracial and Transnational Adoption*. Durham, N.C.: Duke University Press, 2012.

Burgess, Ernest. "The Effect of War on the American Family." *American Journal of Sociology* 48, no. 3 (November 1942): 343–52.

———. "Postwar Problems of the Family." *Marriage and Family Living* 6, no. 3 (August 1944): 47–50.

Campbell, D'Ann. *Women at War with America: Private Lives in a Patriotic Era*. Cambridge, Mass.: Harvard University Press, 1984.

Capehart, Adrian. "Douglas." In *The Encyclopedia of Chicago*, edited by James R. Grossman, Ann Durkin Keating, and Janice L. Reiff, 244. Chicago: University of Chicago Press, 2004.

Carby, Hazel. "Policing the Black Woman's Body in an Urban Context." *Critical Inquiry* 18, no. 4 (1992): 738–55.

Carp, E. Wayne. *Family Matters: Secrecy and Disclosure in the History of Adoption*. Cambridge, Mass.: Harvard University Press, 1998.

Cavan, Ruth Shonle, and Katherine Howland Ranck. *The Family and the Depression: A Study of One Hundred Chicago Families*. 1938. Reprint, Freeport, N.Y.: Books for Libraries Press, 1969.

Celello, Kristin. *Making Marriage Work: A History of Marriage and Divorce in the Twentieth-Century United States*. Chapel Hill: University of North Carolina Press, 2009.

Chafe, William Henry. *The American Woman: Her Changing Social, Economic, and Political Roles, 1920–1970*. New York: Oxford University Press, 1972.

Charles, Jeffrey A. *Service Clubs in American Society: Rotary, Kiwanis, and Lions*. Urbana: University of Illinois Press, 1993.

Chicago Community Inventory, Office of Housing and Redevelopment Coordinator, Chicago Plan Commission. *Census Statistics on Housing for Chicago, 1950, 1940: A Report to the Housing and Redevelopment Coordinator and the Chicago Plan Commission*. Chicago Plan Commission, 1954.

Chinoy, Ely. *Automobile Workers and the American Dream*. 1955. Reprint, Boston, Mass.: Beacon Press, 1965.

Chudacoff, Howard P. "Success and Security: The Meaning of Social Mobility in America." *Reviews in American History* 10, no. 4 (December 1982), 101–12.

Cmiel, Kenneth. *A Home of Another Kind: One Chicago Orphanage and the Tangle of Child Welfare*. Chicago: University of Chicago Press, 1995.

Cobble, Dorothy Sue. *The Other Women's Movement: Workplace Justice and Social Rights in Modern America*. Princeton, N.J.: Princeton University Press, 2004.

Cohen, Adam, and Elizabeth Taylor. *American Pharaoh: Mayor Richard J. Daley: His Battle for Chicago and the Nation*. Boston: Little, Brown, 2000.

Cohen, Lizabeth. *A Consumer's Republic: The Politics of Mass Consumption in Postwar America*. New York: Alfred A. Knopf, 2003.

———. *Making a New Deal: Industrial Workers in Chicago, 1919–1939*. New York: Cambridge University Press, 1990.

Collins, Patricia Hill. *Black Feminist Thought: Knowledge, Consciousness, and the Politics of Empowerment*. New York: HarperCollins, 1990.

Coontz, Stephanie. *A Strange Stirring: The Feminine Mystique and American Women at the Dawn of the 1960s*. New York: Basic Books, 2011.

———. *The Way We Never Were: American Families and the Nostalgia Trap*. New York: Basic Books, 1992.

Cott, Nancy F. *Public Vows: A History of Marriage and the Nation*. Cambridge, Mass.: Harvard University Press, 2000.

Critchlow, Donald T. *Phyllis Schlafly and Grassroots Conservatism: A Woman's Crusade*. Princeton, N.J.: Princeton University Press, 2005.

Curran, Laura. "Feminine Women, Hard Workers: Foster Motherhood in Midcentury America (1946–1963)." *Journal of Family History* 31, no. 4 (2006): 386–412.

Damaske, Sarah. *For the Family? How Class and Gender Shape Women's Work*. New York: Oxford University Press, 2011.

Danns, Dionne. *Something Better for Our Children: Black Organizing in Chicago Public Schools, 1963–1971*. New York: Routledge, 2003.

Davis, Allison. *Father of the Man: How Your Child Gets His Personality*. Boston: Houghton Mifflin, 1947.

Davis, Rebecca. *More Perfect Unions: The American Search for Marital Bliss*. Cambridge, Mass.: Harvard University Press, 2010.

Douglas, Susan. *Where the Girls Are: Growing up Female with the Mass Media.* New York: Three Rivers Press, 1995.

Drake, St. Clair, and Horace R. Cayton. *Black Metropolis: A Study of Negro Life in a Northern City.* 1945. Reprint. Chicago: University of Chicago Press, 1993.

Dubinsky, Karen. *Babies without Borders: Adoption and Migration across the Americas.* Toronto: University of Toronto Press, 2010.

Duis, Perry, and Scott LaFrance. *We've Got a Job to Do: Chicagoans and World War II.* Chicago: Chicago Historical Society, 1992.

Dukette, Rita, and Thelma G. Thompson. *Adoptive Resources for Negro Children.* New York: Child Welfare League of America, 1959.

Ehrenhalt, Alan. *The Lost City: Discovering the Forgotten Virtues of Community: The Chicago of the 1950s.* New York: Basic Books, 1995.

Ehrenreich, Barbara. *The Hearts of Men: American Dreams and the Flight from Commitment.* Garden City, N.Y.: Anchor Press/Doubleday, 1983.

Elder, Glen H. *Children of the Great Depression: Social Change in Life Experience.* Chicago: University of Chicago Press, 1974.

Erenberg, Lewis A., and Susan E. Hirsch. *The War in American Culture: Society and Consciousness during World War II.* Chicago: University of Chicago Press, 1996.

Feldstein, Ruth, "'I Wanted the Whole World to See': Race, Gender, and Constructions of Motherhood in the Death of Emmett Till." In *Not June Cleaver: Women and Gender in Postwar America, 1945–1960,* edited by Joanne J. Meyerowitz, 263–303. Philadelphia: Temple University Press, 1994.

———. *Motherhood in Black and White: Race and Sex in American Liberalism, 1930–1965.* Ithaca, N.Y.: Cornell University Press, 2000.

Fessler, Ann. *The Girls Who Went Away: The Hidden History of Women Who Surrendered Children for Adoption in the Decades before Roe v. Wade.* New York: Penguin, 2007.

Field, Martha Heineman. "The Impact of Psychodynamic Theory on Social Casework, 1917–1949." PhD diss., University of Chicago Social Service Administration, 1979.

———. "Social Casework Practice during the 'Psychodynamic Deluge.'" *Social Service Review* 54, no. 4 (1980): 482–507.

Fones-Wolf, Elizabeth A. *Selling Free Enterprise: The Business Assault on Labor and Liberalism, 1945–60.* Urbana: University of Illinois Press, 1994.

Frazier, Edward Franklin. *Black Bourgeoisie.* Glencoe, Ill.: Free Press, 1957.

———. *The Negro Family in the United States.* Revised and abridged edition, 1948. Reprint, Chicago: University of Chicago Press, 1966.

Friedan, Betty. *The Feminine Mystique.* New York: Norton, 1963.

Gamm, Gerald H. *Urban Exodus: Why the Jews Left Boston and the Catholics Stayed.* Cambridge, Mass.: Harvard University Press, 1999.

Gamm, Gerald, and Robert D. Putnam. "The Growth of Voluntary Associations in America, 1840–1940." *Journal of Interdisciplinary History* 29, no. 4 (1999): 511–57.

Gans, Herbert J. *The Levittowners: Ways of Life and Politics in a New Suburban Community.* New York: Pantheon Books, 1967.

Garb, Margaret. "Drawing The 'Color Line': Race and Real Estate in Early Twentieth-Century Chicago." *Journal of Urban History* 32, no. 5 (2006): 773–87.

Gelber, Steven M. "Do-It-Yourself: Constructing, Repairing and Maintaining Domestic Masculinity." *American Quarterly* 49, no. 1 (1997): 66–112.

Gilbert, James. *Men in the Middle: Searching for Masculinity in the 1950s*. Chicago: University of Chicago Press, 2005.

Gill, Brian Paul. "The Jurisprudence of Good Parenting: The Selection of Adoptive Parents, 1894–1964." PhD diss., University of California, Berkeley, 1997.

Gillon, Steven M. *Politics and Vision: The ADA and American Liberalism, 1947–1985*. New York: Oxford University Press, 1987.

Ginzberg, Lori D. *Women and the Work of Benevolence: Morality, Politics, and Class in the Nineteenth-Century United States*. New Haven, Conn.: Yale University Press, 1990.

Goldin, Claudia. *Understanding the Gender Gap: An Economic History of American Women*. New York: Oxford University Press, 1990.

Gordon, Linda. *The Great Arizona Orphan Abduction*. Cambridge, Mass.: Harvard University Press, 1999.

———. *Heroes of Their Own Lives: The Politics and History of Family Violence, Boston, 1880–1960*. Urbana: University of Illinois Press, 2002.

———. "Response to Scott." *Signs* 15, no. 4 (1990): 852–53.

Graham, Irene. "The Negro Family in a Northern City." *Opportunity* 8, no. 2 (February 1930): 48–51.

Green, Adam. *Selling the Race: Culture, Community, and Black Chicago, 1940–1955*. Chicago: University of Chicago Press, 2007.

Gregory, James N. *The Southern Diaspora: How the Great Migrations of Black and White Southerners Transformed America*. Chapel Hill: University of North Carolina Press, 2005.

Griswold, Robert L. *Fatherhood in America: A History*. New York: Basic Books, 1993.

Grossman, James R. *Land of Hope: Chicago, Black Southerners, and the Great Migration*. Chicago: University of Chicago Press, 1989.

Halle, David. *America's Working Man: Work, Home, and Politics among Blue-Collar Property Owners*. Chicago: University of Chicago Press, 1984.

Hansberry, Lorraine. *A Raisin in the Sun*. New York: New American Library, 1988.

Harley, Sharon. "For the Good of Family and Race: Gender, Work, and Domestic Roles in the Black Community, 1880–1930." *Signs* 15, no. 2 (1990): 336–49.

Harris, Richard. "Chicago's Other Suburbs." *Geographical Review* 84, no. 4 (1994): 394–410.

———. "Working-Class Home Ownership in the American Metropolis." *Journal of Urban History* 17, no. 1 (1990): 46–69.

Hart, Patricia S. "A Nation's Need for Adoption and Competing Realities: The Washington Children's Home Society, 1895–1915." In *Adoption in America: Historical Perspectives*, edited by E. Wayne Carp, 140–59. Ann Arbor: University of Michigan Press, 2002.

Hartmann, Susan M. *The Home Front and Beyond: American Women in the 1940s*. Boston: Twayne Publishers, 1982.

———. "Prescriptions for Penelope." *Women's Studies* 5, no. 3 (1978): 223–239.

———. "Women's Employment and the Domestic Ideal in the Early Cold War Years." In *Not June Cleaver: Women and Gender in Postwar America, 1945–1960*, edited by Joanne J. Meyerowitz, 84–100. Philadelphia: Temple University Press, 1994.

Hauser, Philip Morris, Evelyn Mae Kitagawa, Louis Wirth, and Chicago Community Inventory. *Local Community Fact Book for Chicago, 1950*. Chicago: Chicago Community Inventory, University of Chicago, 1953.

Hawes, Joseph M. *Children between the Wars: American Childhood, 1920–1940.* New York: Twayne; London, Prentice Hall International, 1997.

Herd, Pamela, and Madonna Harrington Meyer. "Care Work: Invisible Civic Engagement." *Gender and Society* 16, no. 5 (2002): 665–88.

Herman, Ellen. The Adoption History Project. Department of History, University of Oregon. http://www.uoregon.edu/~adoption/index.html.

———. "Child Adoption in a Therapeutic Culture." *Society* 39, no. 2 (2002): 11–18.

———. "Families Made by Science: Arnold Gesell and the Technologies of Modern Child Adoption." *Isis* 92, no. 4 (2001): 684–715.

———. *Kinship by Design: A History of Adoption in the Modern United States.* Chicago: University of Chicago Press, 2008.

———. "The Paradoxical Rationalization of Modern Adoption." *Journal of Social History* 36, no. 2 (2002): 339–85.

———. "Supervising Spoiled Selfhood: Inquiry and Interpretation in the History of Modern American Child Adoption." *Osiris* 22, no. 1 (2007): 158–79.

Higginbotham, Evelyn Brooks. *Righteous Discontent: The Women's Movement in the Black Baptist Church, 1880–1920.* Cambridge, Mass.: Harvard University Press, 1993.

Hirsch, Arnold R. *Making the Second Ghetto: Race and Housing in Chicago, 1940–1960.* Chicago: University of Chicago Press, 1998.

———. "Massive Resistance in the Urban North: Trumbull Park, Chicago, 1953–1966" *Journal of American History* 82, no. 2 (1995): 522–50.

Hirsch, Susan E. "Economic Geography." In *Chicago Neighborhoods and Suburbs: A Historical Guide,* edited by Ann Durkin Keating, 64–75. Chicago: University of Chicago Press, 2008.

Holt, Thomas C. "Marking: Race, Race-Making, and the Writing of History." *American Historical Review* 100, no. 1 (1995): 1–20.

Homel, Michael W. *Down from Equality: Black Chicagoans and the Public Schools, 1920–41.* Urbana: University of Illinois Press, 1984.

Honey, Maureen. *Creating Rosie the Riveter: Class, Gender, and Propaganda during World War II.* Amherst: University of Massachusetts Press, 1984.

Horowitz, Daniel. *Betty Friedan and the Making of "The Feminine Mystique": The American Left, The Cold War, and Modern Feminism.* Amherst: University of Massachusetts Press, 1998.

Hulbert, Ann. *Raising America: Experts, Parents, and a Century of Advice about Children.* New York: Alfred A. Knopf, 2003.

Hunter, Tera W. *To 'Joy My Freedom: Southern Black Women's Lives and Labors after the Civil War.* Cambridge, Mass.: Harvard University Press, 1997.

Hyde Park–Kenwood Community Conference. *Newsletter.* 1952–1964.

Jackson, Kenneth. *Crabgrass Frontier: The Suburbanization of the United States.* New York: Oxford University Press, 1985.

Jones, Jacqueline. *Labor of Love, Labor of Sorrow: Black Women, Work, and the Family from Slavery to the Present.* New York: Basic Books, 1985.

Katz, Michael B., ed. *The "Underclass" Debate: Views from History.* Princeton, N.J.: Princeton University Press, 1993.

Kelly, Barbara M. *Expanding the American Dream: Building and Rebuilding Levittown.* Albany: State University of New York Press, 1993.

Kerber, Linda K. *Women of the Republic: Intellect and Ideology in Revolutionary America*. New York: Norton, 1986.

Kitagawa, Evelyn Mae, and Karl E. Taeuber. *Local Community Fact Book: Chicago Metropolitan Area, 1960*. Chicago: Chicago Community Inventory, University of Chicago, 1963.

Kline, Wendy. *Building a Better Race: Gender, Sexuality, and Eugenics from the Turn of the Century to the Baby Boom*. Berkeley: University of California Press, 2001.

Knupfer, Anne Meis. *The Chicago Black Renaissance and Women's Activism*. Urbana: University of Illinois Press, 2006.

Komarovsky, Mirra. *Blue-Collar Marriage*. New York: Vintage Books, 1967.

Kozol, Wendy. *Life's America: Family and Nation in Postwar Photojournalism*. Philadelphia: Temple University Press, 1994.

Kruse, Kevin Michael. *White Flight: Atlanta and the Making of Modern Conservatism*. Princeton, N.J.: Princeton University Press, 2005.

Kunzel, Regina G. *Fallen Women, Problem Girls: Unmarried Mothers and the Professionalization of Social Work, 1890–1945*. New Haven, Conn.: Yale University Press, 1993.

———. "White Neurosis, Black Pathology: Constructing Out-of-Wedlock Pregnancy in the Wartime and Postwar United States." In *Not June Cleaver: Women and Gender in Postwar America, 1945–1960*, edited by Joanne J. Meyerowitz, 304–31. Philadelphia: Temple University Press, 1994.

Ladd-Taylor, Molly, and Lauri Umansky, eds. *"Bad" Mothers: The Politics of Blame in Twentieth-Century America*. New York: New York University Press, 1998.

Landry, Bart. *Black Working Wives: Pioneers of the American Family Revolution*. Berkeley: University of California Press, 2000.

LaRossa, Ralph. *Of War and Men: World War II in the Lives of Fathers and Their Families*. Chicago: University of Chicago Press, 2011.

Lassiter, Matthew D. "Inventing Family Values." In *Rightward Bound: Making America Conservative in the 1970s*, edited by Bruce Schulman and Julian Zelizer, 13–28. Cambridge, Mass.: Harvard University Press, 2008.

———. *The Silent Majority: Suburban Politics in the Sunbelt South*. Princeton, N.J.: Princeton University Press, 2006.

Lemann, Nicholas. *The Promised Land: The Great Black Migration and How It Changed America*. New York: Vintage Books, 1991.

Levenstein, Lisa. *A Movement without Marches: African American Women and the Politics of Poverty in Postwar Philadelphia*. Chapel Hill: University of North Carolina Press, 2009.

Lewis, Carolyn Herbst. *Prescription for Heterosexuality: Sexual Citizenship in the Cold War Era*. Chapel Hill: University of North Carolina Press, 2010.

Lichtenstein, Nelson. *State of the Union: A Century of American Labor*. Princeton, N.J.: Princeton University Press, 2002.

Lindenmeyer, Kriste. *The Greatest Generation Grows Up: American Childhood in the 1930s*. Chicago: Ivan R. Dee, 2005.

Lingeman, Richard R. *Don't You Know There's a War On? The American Home Front, 1941–1945*. 2nd ed. New York: Thunder's Mouth Press/Nation Books, 2003.

Lipsitz, George. *Rainbow at Midnight: Labor and Culture in the 1940s*. Urbana: University of Illinois Press, 1994.

Lynn, Susan. "Gender and Post World War II Progressive Politics: A Bridge to Social Activism in the 1960s USA." *Gender and History* 4, no. 2 (June 1992): 215–39.

Marsh, Margaret, and Wanda Ronner. *The Empty Cradle: Infertility in America from Colonial Times to the Present.* Baltimore, Md.: Johns Hopkins University Press, 1996.

May, Elaine Tyler. *Barren in the Promised Land: Childless Americans and the Pursuit of Happiness.* New York: Basic Books, 1995.

———. *Homeward Bound: American Families in the Cold War Era.* New York: Basic Books, 1988.

———. "Nonmothers as Bad Mothers: Infertility and the 'Maternal Instinct.'" In *"Bad" Mothers: The Politics of Blame in Twentieth-Century America*, edited by Molly Ladd-Taylor and Lauri Umansky, 198–219. New York: New York University Press, 1998.

McElroy, Edith Wasson, and Dorothy Deemer Houghton. *The Complete Book for Clubwomen.* New York: Ronald Press: 1957.

McEnaney, Laura. "Nightmares on Elm Street: Demobilizing in Chicago, 1945–1953." *Journal of American History* 92, no. 4 (2006): 1265–91.

McGirr, Lisa. *Suburban Warriors: The Origins of the New American Right.* Princeton, N.J.: Princeton University Press, 2001.

McGreevy, John T. *Parish Boundaries: The Catholic Encounter with Race in the Twentieth-Century Urban North.* Chicago: University of Chicago Press, 1996.

Melosh, Barbara. *Strangers and Kin: The American Way of Adoption.* Cambridge, Mass.: Harvard University Press, 2002.

Mettler, Suzanne. *Soldiers to Citizens: The G.I. Bill and the Making of the Greatest Generation.* New York: Oxford University Press, 2005.

Meyerowitz, Joanne J. "Beyond the Feminine Mystique: A Reassessment of Postwar Mass Culture, 1946–1958." In *Not June Cleaver: Women and Gender in Postwar America, 1945–1960*, edited by Joanne J. Meyerowitz, 229–62. Philadelphia: Temple University Press, 1994.

———, ed. *Not June Cleaver: Women and Gender in Postwar America, 1945–1960.* Philadelphia: Temple University Press, 1994.

Mills, C. Wright. *White Collar: The American Middle Classes.* New York: Oxford University Press, 1951.

Mintz, Steven. *Huck's Raft: A History of American Childhood.* Cambridge, Mass.: Belknap Press of Harvard University Press, 2004.

Mintz, Steven, and Susan Kellogg. *Domestic Revolutions: A Social History of American Family Life.* New York: Free Press, 1988.

Moskowitz, Eva. "'It's Good to Blow Your Top': Women's Magazines and a Discourse of Discontent, 1945–1965." *Journal of Women's History* 8, no. 3 (Fall 1996): 66–98.

Murray, Sylvie. *The Progressive Housewife: Community Activism in Suburban Queens, 1945–1965.* Philadelphia: University of Pennsylvania Press, 2003.

Nelson, Deborah L. *Gender and Culture in the 1950s.* New York: Feminist Press at the City University of New York, 2005.

Nicolaides, Becky M. *My Blue Heaven: Life and Politics in the Working-Class Suburbs of Los Angeles, 1920–1965.* Chicago: University of Chicago Press, 2002.

Oh, Arissa. "From War Waif to Ideal Immigrant: The Cold War Transformation of the Korean Orphan." *Journal of American Ethnic History* 31, no. 4 (Summer 2012): 34–55.

Pacyga, Dominic. *Chicago: A Biography.* Chicago: University of Chicago Press, 2009.

Patterson, James T. *Freedom Is Not Enough: The Moynihan Report and the Struggle over Black Family Life from LBJ to Obama.* New York: Basic Books, 2010.

Payne, Charles. *I've Got the Light of Freedom: The Organizing Tradition and the Mississippi Freedom Struggle*. Berkeley: University of California Press, 1995.

Perry, Marilyn Elizabeth. "Portage Park." In *The Encyclopedia of Chicago*, edited by James R. Grossman, Ann Durkin Keating, and Janice L. Reiff, 642. Chicago: University of Chicago Press, 2004.

Petigny, Alan. *The Permissive Society: America, 1941–1965*. New York: Cambridge University Press, 2009.

Pfeffer, Paula E. "A Historical Comparison of Catholic and Jewish Adoption Practices in Chicago, 1833–1933." In *Adoption in America: Historical Perspectives*, edited by E. Wayne Carp, 101–23. Ann Arbor: University of Michigan Press, 2002.

Phillips, Kimberley L. *AlabamaNorth: African-American Migrants, Community, and Working-Class Activism in Cleveland, 1915–45*. Urbana: University of Illinois Press, 1999.

Plant, Rebecca Jo. *Mom: The Transformation of Motherhood in Modern America*. Chicago: University of Chicago Press, 2010.

Potter, Sarah. "Family Ideals: The Diverse Meanings of Residential Space in Chicago during the Baby Boom." *Journal of Urban History* 39, no. 1 (Winter 2013): 59–78.

Pritchett, Wendell E. *Brownsville, Brooklyn: Blacks, Jews, and the Changing Face of the Ghetto*. Chicago: University of Chicago Press, 2002.

Putnam, Robert D. *Bowling Alone: The Collapse and Revival of American Community*. New York: Simon & Schuster, 2000.

Quirke, Carol. *Eyes on Labor: News Photography and America's Working Class*. New York: Oxford University Press, 2012.

Rainwater, Lee, Richard P. Coleman, and Gerald Handel. *Workingman's Wife: Her Personality, World and Life Style*. New York: Oceana Publications, 1959.

Rathbun, Constance. "The Adoptive Foster Parent: A Basis for Evaluation." *Child Welfare League of America Bulletin* 23 (November 1944): 5–7.

Reagan, Ronald. *The Great Communicator: Selected Speeches of President Ronald Reagan*. St. Petersburg, Fla.: Red and Black Publishers, 2010.

Reumann, Miriam G. *American Sexual Character: Sex, Gender, and National Identity in the Kinsey Reports*. Berkeley: University of California Press, 2005.

Riesman, David. *The Lonely Crowd: A Study of the Changing American Character*. Abridged ed. New Haven, Conn.: Yale University Press, 1969.

Ritterhouse, Jennifer. *Growing up Jim Crow: How Black and White Southern Children Learned Race*. Chapel Hill: University of North Carolina Press, 2006.

Rosenzweig, Roy. *Eight Hours for What We Will: Workers and Leisure in an Industrial City, 1870–1920*. New York: Cambridge University Press, 1983.

Rubin, Lillian Breslow. *Worlds of Pain: Life in the Working-Class Family*. New York: Basic Books, 1976.

Ryan, Mary P. *Cradle of the Middle Class: The Family in Oneida County, New York, 1790–1865*. New York: Cambridge University Press, 1981.

Rymph, Catherine E. "From 'Economic Want' to 'Family Pathology': Foster Family Care, the New Deal, and the Emergence of a Public Child Welfare System." *Journal of Policy History* 24, no. 1 (2012): 7–25.

Satter, Beryl. *Family Properties: How the Struggle over Race and Real Estate Transformed Chicago and Urban America*. New York: Metropolitan Books, 2009.

Saville, Julie. *The Work of Reconstruction: From Slave to Wage Laborer in South Carolina, 1860–1870*. New York: Cambridge University Press, 1996.

Schulman, Bruce. *The Seventies: The Great Shift in American Culture, Society, and Politics*. Cambridge, Mass.: Da Capo Press, 2001.

Self, Robert O. *All in the Family: The Realignment of American Democracy since the 1960s*. New York: Hill and Wang, 2012.

Seligman, Amanda I. *Block by Block: Neighborhoods and Public Policy on Chicago's West Side*. Chicago: University of Chicago Press, 2005.

Shah, Nayan. *Contagious Divides: Epidemics and Race in San Francisco's Chinatown*. Berkeley: University of California Press, 2001.

Shostak, Arthur B., and William Gomberg. *Blue-Collar World: Studies of the American Worker*. Englewood Cliffs, N.J.: Prentice-Hall, 1964.

Simmons, Christina. *Making Marriage Modern: Women's Sexuality from the Progressive Era to World War II*. New York: Oxford University Press, 2009.

Skocpol, Theda. *Diminished Democracy: From Membership to Management in American Civic Life*. Norman: University of Oklahoma Press, 2003.

Skocpol, Theda, Ariane Liazos, and Marshall Ganz. *What a Mighty Power We Can Be: African American Fraternal Groups and the Struggle for Racial Equality*. Princeton, N.J.: Princeton University Press, 2006.

Smith, Judith E. *Visions of Belonging: Family Stories, Popular Culture, and Postwar Democracy, 1940–1960*. New York: Columbia University Press, 2004.

Solinger, Rickie. "Race and 'Value': Black and White Illegitimate Babies, 1945–1965." In *Mothering: Ideology, Experience & Agency*, edited by Evelyn Nakano Glenn, Grace Chang, and Linda Rennie Forcey, 287–310. New York: Routledge, 1994.

———. *Wake up Little Susie: Single Pregnancy and Race before "Roe v. Wade."* 2nd ed. New York: Routledge, 2000.

Spinney, Robert G. *City of Big Shoulders: A History of Chicago*. DeKalb: Northern Illinois University Press, 2000.

Spock, Benjamin. *The Common Sense Book of Baby and Child Care*. New York: Duell, Sloan and Pearce, 1946.

Spruill, Marjorie J. "Gender and America's Right Turn." In *Rightward Bound: Making America Conservative in the 1970s*, edited by Bruce Schulman and Julian Zelizer, 71–89. Cambridge, Mass.: Harvard University Press, 2008.

Stack, Carol B. *All Our Kin*. New York: Basic Books, 1997.

Stearns, Peter N. *Anxious Parents: A History of Modern Childrearing in America*. New York: New York University Press, 2003.

Stockwell, Clinton E. "Englewood." In *The Encyclopedia of Chicago*, edited by James R. Grossman, Ann Durkin Keating, and Janice L. Reiff, 269. Chicago: University of Chicago Press, 2004.

Storrs, Landon R. Y. *Civilizing Capitalism: The National Consumers' League, Women's Activism, and Labor Standards in the New Deal Era*. Chapel Hill: University of North Carolina Press, 2000.

Stranger-Ross, Jordan, Christina Collins, and Mark Stern, "Falling Far from the Tree: Transitions to Adulthood and the Social History of Twentieth-Century America." *Social Science History* 29, no. 4 (Winter 2005): 625–48.

Street, Paul. "The 'Best Union Members': Class, Race, Culture, and Black Worker Militancy in Chicago Stockyards during the 1930s." *Journal of American Ethnic History* 20, no. 1 (2000): 18–49.

Strong-Boag, Veronica. *Finding Families, Finding Ourselves: English Canada Encounters*

Adoption from the Nineteenth Century to the 1990s. New York: Oxford University Press, 2006.

Sugrue, Thomas J. *The Origins of the Urban Crisis: Race and Inequality in Postwar Detroit.* Princeton, N.J.: Princeton University Press, 1996.

——. *Sweet Land of Liberty: The Forgotten Struggle for Civil Rights in the North.* New York: Random House, 2008.

Swerdlow, Amy. *Women Strike for Peace: Traditional Motherhood and Radical Politics in the 1960s.* Chicago: University of Chicago Press, 1993.

Tice, Karen Whitney. *Tales of Wayward Girls and Immoral Women: Case Records and the Professionalization of Social Work.* Urbana: University of Illinois Press, 1998.

Till-Mobley, Mamie, and Christopher Benson. *Death of Innocence: The Story of the Hate Crime that Changed America.* New York: Random House, 2003.

Tuttle, William M. *"Daddy's Gone to War": The Second World War in the Lives of America's Children.* New York: Oxford University Press, 1993.

U.S. Senate Committee on the Judiciary, Subcommittee to Investigate Juvenile Delinquency. *Juvenile Delinquency (Interstate Adoption Practices—Miami, Florida): Hearings before the Subcommittee to Investigate Juvenile Delinquency of the Committee on the Judiciary United States Senate,* 84th Congress, 1st sess., November 14 and 15, 1955.

Walker, Nancy, ed. *Women's Magazines, 1940–1960: Gender Roles and the Popular Press.* Boston: Bedford/St. Martin's Press, 1998.

Ware, Susan. "American Women in the 1950s: Nonpartisan Politics and Women's Politicization." In *Women, Politics, and Change,* edited by Louise A Tilly and Patricia Gurin, 281–99. New York: Russell Sage Foundation, 1990.

——. *Holding Their Own: American Women in the 1930s.* Boston: Twayne, 1982.

Wasson, Valentina Pavlovna. *The Chosen Baby.* New York: Carrick and Evans, 1939.

Weiss, Jessica. *To Have and to Hold: Marriage, the Baby Boom, and Social Change.* Chicago: University of Chicago Press, 2000.

Westbrook, Robert B. "'I Want a Girl, Just Like the Girl That Married Harry James': American Women and the Problem of Political Obligation in World War II." *American Quarterly* 42, no. 4 (1990): 587–614.

Whyte, William Hollingsworth. *The Organization Man.* New York: Simon and Schuster, 1956.

Wiese, Andrew. *Places of Their Own: African American Suburbanization in the Twentieth Century.* Chicago: University of Chicago Press, 2004.

Wilkerson, Isabel. *The Warmth of Other Suns: The Epic Story of America's Great Migration.* New York: Vintage Books, 2010.

Wilson, Sloan. *The Man in the Gray Flannel Suit.* New York: Simon and Schuster, 1955.

Wilson, William Julius. *The Truly Disadvantaged: The Inner City, the Underclass, and Public Policy.* Chicago: University of Chicago Press, 1990.

Wirth, Louis, Eleanor Harriet Sheldon, and Chicago Community Inventory. *Local Community Fact Book of Chicago.* Chicago: University of Chicago Press, 1949.

Wylie, Philip. *Generation of Vipers.* New York: Rinehart, 1955.

Zaretsky, Natasha. *No Direction Home: The American Family and the Fear of National Decline.* Chapel Hill: University of North Carolina Press, 2007.

Zelizer, Viviana A. *Pricing the Priceless Child: The Changing Social Value of Children.* New York: Basic Books, 1985.

INDEX

Black Metropolis (Chicago), 129–30, 172. *See also* Chicago

Black Metropolis (Drake and Cayton), 39, 129, 172, 204n19, 219n59, 220n85

blacks: adoption and foster care, 3–4, 21–23, 74–75, 118, 141, 207n26, 215n13; black culture, 7, 172; civic activity, 167, 171–76; domesticity, 4, 49, 66, 99, 156–59; education, 40, 88–89, 93–95, 120–21, 165–66, 171, 173–75; employment, 70–71, 74, 87–90, 115–20, 127, 219n59; family relationships, 63, 87, 91–98, 117–18, 139–40, 153–54, 176, 186; gender roles, 66, 92–93, 114–22; housing, 38, 129–36, 139–40, 143–45, 148–56, 225n34; parenthood, 86–96, 120–21; poverty, 89–90, 148, 152, 223n57; race consciousness and pride, 93–95, 119–20, 171–72, 174, 176, 219n66, 220n85; women's paid work, 102, 115–22, 223n58, 223n61

Blevins, Jack and Edith (applicants), 55, 59–60

Block by Block (Seligman), 224n14, 228n1

Blue-Collar Marriage (Komarovsky), 107

Blum, John Morton, 210n31

Boarding Homes Act of 1919 (Illinois), 17

Bodnar, John, 82; "Immigration, Kinship, and the Rise of Working-Class Realism in Industrial America," 218n45

Bond, Earl and Gladys (applicants), 53, 94, 161–62

Booth, Albert (applicant), 45, 73

Bowling Alone (Putnam), 228n20

Brace, Charles Loring, 205n9

Branch, George and Mary (applicants), 36, 141–42

breadwinner male role, 10, 69–83, 86–92, 95–96, 98, 116–18, 122. *See also* gender roles

Brenner, Ruth F., 208n34

Brieland, Donald, 208n34

Briggs, Laura, 14, 207n26; *Somebody's Children*, 207n30

Bronzeville (Chicago), 144, 150, 171–72. *See also* Chicago

Brooks family (applicants), 135

Brown, Louis and Eleanor (applicants), 58, 119

Brown v. Board of Education (1954), 165

Bungalow Belt (Chicago), 140, 142. *See also* Chicago

Burgess, Earnest, 43–44

Butler, Duane and Fannie (applicants), 153

Campbell, D'Ann, 210n31, 210n41

Campbell, Steve and Ella (applicants), 138–39

Carby, Hazel, 228n1

Carter, Arthur and Norma (applicants), 54, 111

Carver, George Washington, 94

Cash, William and Anna (applicants), 52, 54, 81–82, 148–51

Cavan, Ruth, 34

Cayton, Horace, 129–30, 171–72, 196, 223n61; *Black Metropolis* (with Drake), 39, 129, 172, 204n19, 219n59, 220n85

Chafe, William Henry, 203n3

Chicago: black community, 7, 38–39, 41–42, 129–30, 140–45, 171–72; housing, 128, 131–33, 140–44, 151–52, 202, 224n12; politics, 7, 41, 130, 171, 174, 210n25; race, 40–42, 128–33, 150–52, 201, 224n12; social and economic conditions, 34–35, 44, 78

Chicago Defender (newspaper), 39, 174, 196, 230n43

Chicago Institute for Psychoanalysis, 205n18

Chicago Tribune, 196

Chicago Urban League, 173–74, 196, 229n38

childhood, 1–4, 37, 84, 163–65, 213n45; juvenile delinquency, 13, 43–44, 159, 164, 169

Child Welfare League of America Bulletin, 195

Chinoy, Ely, 79

"Chosen Baby, The" (Wasson), 208n35

Chudacoff, Howard P., 218n45

civic activity: as adoption criteria, 165–66; church and union, 34, 70, 172–73, 178, 230n53; class and race,

Graham, Nancy (applicant), 61–62
"Gray Market in Child Adoption,
The" (University of Chicago Round
Table), 19
Great Arizona Orphan Abduction, The
(Gordon), 205n9
Great Depression, 4, 9, 18, 34–37, 41,
120–21, 163–64, 183
Great Migration, 9, 33–34, 37–42, 46–47,
129, 193
Green, Adam, 127, 182
Gregory, Muriel (applicant), 119
Griswold, Robert L., 74, 217n39;
Fatherhood in America, 215n5
Grossman, James, 39

Hahn, Keith (applicant), 146–47
Hall, Shirley (applicant), 52
Hampton, Arnold (applicant), 82
Handel, Gerald, 107
Hanks, Kenneth and Edna (applicants),
54, 154–55
Hansberry, Lorraine, 127–28
Harley, Sharon, 121
Harris, Ervin and Della (applicants), 92
Harrison, Barbara, 232n3
Hartmann, Susan M., 210n31; *The Home
Front and Beyond*, 210n41
Hawkes, Billy and Rita (applicants), 63
Helen Lampe, 232n3
Henry, Earnest and Lucille (applicants),
42, 55, 178
Herd, Pamela, 179
Herman, Ellen, 23, 204n3, 205n9; *Kinship
by Design*, 205n13, 207n30, 215n6;
"The Paradoxical Rationalization of
Modern Adoption," 205n13; "Telling,"
208n35
Herrington, Raymond (applicant), 46
heteronormative nuclear family, 23. *See
also* family
Hicks, Tom and Opal (applicants), 118–19
Higginbotham, Evelyn Brooks, 228n1
Hill, Earnest and Hattie (applicants), 119,
143–44, 161
Hirsch, Arnold R., 5, 129–30; *Making the
Second Ghetto*, 223n3, 224n12; "Massive
Resistance in the Urban North," 223n3

Hirsch, Susan E., 210n31
"Historical Comparison of Catholic and
Jewish Adoption Practices in Chicago,
A" (Pfeffer), 205n12
Holmes, Andrew and Jane (applicants), 61
Holt, Thomas, 196
Holt family (applicants), 101
Home Front and Beyond, The
(Hartmann), 210n41
Home of Another Kind, A (Cmiel), 205n13
Homeward Bound (May), 203n3, 210n31,
214n78, 220n2, 223n3
homosexuality, 6, 23, 48
Honey, Maureen, 43; *Creating Rosie the
Riveter*, 210n31
Honeymooners, The (1955), 1
Hoover, J. Edgar, 43
Houghton, Dorothy Deemer, 229n28
Household Accounts (Benson), 222n33,
231n61
housing: adoption criteria, 134–35,
190–91, 225n38; diversity of use, 128,
145–48, 155–56, 184–85; emotional
importance, 122–23, 128, 135–36, 145,
159; family and domestic ideals, 5,
10, 127–28, 134–47, 159–60; financial
resource, 118, 145–48, 152, 154; home
ownership, 129, 136–40, 143, 146, 148–
52, 169, 224n13; integration, 41, 127–34,
156–60, 224n13; postwar Chicago, 34,
39, 41, 127–60, 201–2; race, 34, 129–34,
148–56, 162, 223n3, 224n13; research
sample, 201–2, 232n1; social mobility,
69, 87, 139. *See also* neighborhoods;
suburbanization
Howe, Louise (applicant), 80
Howe, Norman and Louise (applicants),
54, 62, 80
HPKCC (Hyde Park-Kenwood
Community Conference), 156–60,
196, 227n71; "Are You Getting Good
Neighbors?," 158–59
Huck's Raft (Mintz), 204n3
Hulbert, Ann, 228n10
Humphreys, Sidney (applicant), 94
Hunter, Tera, 223n58
Hurley, James and Helen (applicants), 44,
77, 169

ICH&A (Illinois Children's Home and Aid Society): adoption process and practices, 27, 128, 190–94, 207n31; case records, 8, 189–90, 194–96, 198–202, 206n23; diversity, 3, 22, 207n26; history, 17–18, 189, 205n12; Negro Adoption Project, 22, 207n26, 215n13; pre-adoptive foster care program, 3, 22, 25, 92, 193; staff professionalization, 20–21, 50, 205n18, 208n34

Illinois Writers' Project / "Negro in Illinois" Papers (Chicago Public Library), 196

"Immigration, Kinship, and the Rise of Working-Class Realism in Industrial America" (Bodnar), 218n45

"Impact of Psychodynamic Theory on Social Casework, The" (Field), 205n18, 207n25

income: adoption criteria, 22, 26, 30, 60, 71–72, 75, 215n13; economic stability, 102, 104, 111–12, 143, 146, 148–52, 169; family, 75–76, 78–79, 102, 109–10; race and class, 75, 88–90, 152, 203n5, 218n59; research sample, 200–201, 218n59; social mobility, 70, 81–82, 86–88, 186, 206n23, 216n14. *See also* gender roles

infertility, 4, 6, 24–25, 48, 59–62, 100–101, 220n11

"Inventing Family Values" (Lassiter), 231n5

"I Want a Girl, Just Like the Girl That Married Harry James" (Westbrook), 210n31

Jackson, Kenneth, 128–29, 223n3
Jackson, Mahalia, 172
Jackson, Vincent (applicant), 93
Jacobs family (applicants), 60–61, 101, 169
Jenkins family (applicants), 139
Jennings, Herman and Julia (applicants), 80
Jim Crow South, 38, 40, 93
jobs: class, 6, 34, 40–41, 75–76, 83, 216n14; family and quality of life, 6, 74, 76–87, 90–91, 95, 178; gender roles, 70–72, 74, 98–107, 111–22, 184, 223n58, 223n61; race, 40, 74–75, 87–92, 171,

174–75, 219n59, 223n57; social mobility, 70, 75, 81–82, 85–86, 93, 146, 206n23, 216n14; working conditions, 78–80, 85, 118, 223n58

Johnson, Jerome and Harriet (applicants), 117–18

Jones, Jacqueline, 115
Jones, Morris and Christine (applicants), 142, 169

"Jurisprudence of Good Parenting, The" (Gill), 205n13

juvenile delinquency. *See* childhood

Katz, Michael B., 231n7
Kefauver, Estes, 13
Kellogg, Susan, 203n3, 211n3
Kelly, Edward, 41, 130
Kennelly, Martin, 41
Kern, Dora (applicant), 83, 145–46
Kinship by Design (Herman), 205n13, 207n30, 215n6
Kline, Draza, 50
Komarovsky, Mirra, 63, 107–8, 111–12; *Blue-Collar Marriage*, 107
Kozol, Wendy, 43
Kruse, Kevin Michael, 223n3

Ladd-Taylor, Molly, 213n36
Ladies Home Journal, 43, 48
Lampe, Helen, 232n3
Landry, Bert, 115–16
Lane, Cora (applicant), 161
LaRossa, Ralph, 93–94, 215n12
Lassiter, Matthew D.: "Inventing Family Values," 231n5; *The Silent Majority*, 223n3
Laumann, Peter and Wilma (applicants), 77–78
Lawrence, Ronald and Irene (applicants), 33, 51, 63, 139–40
League of Women Voters, 169–70, 175, 185, 229n30
Leave it to Beaver, 1, 48
Levenstein, Lisa, 230, 232n7; *A Movement without Marches*, 223n57
Levitt, Joseph (applicant), 78
Lewis, Sam and Marilyn (applicants), 83, 143

Life, 3, 43, 48, 70
Lingeman, Richard R., 210n31
Local Community Fact Book: Chicago Metropolitan Area, 1960 (Kitagawa and Tauber), 232n1
Local Community Fact Book for Chicago, 1950 (Hauser et al.), 232n1
Local Community Fact Book of Chicago (Wirth et al.), 232n1
Look, 48

Making Marriage Modern (Simmons), 211n8
Making the Second Ghetto (A. R. Hirsch), 223n3, 224n12
Malone, John (applicant), 35
Man in the Grey Flannel Suit, The (1956), 48
Mapping the Stacks (University of Chicago), 204n19
marriage: adoption, 31, 51–52, 163, 191, 196; companionate, 51, 211n3, 211n8; divorce, 36, 58–59, 184, 203n3; domestic ideology, 33–34; gender dynamics, 70, 98–99, 117, 207n23; social and family networks, 62–65; social pressure, 48–50, 52–53, 57–59, 66, 220n2; World War II, 33, 44–47, 108, 203n2, 210n41
Martin, Roland (applicant), 37, 85–86
"Massive Resistance in the Urban North" (A. R. Hirsch), 223n3
Matthews, Warren and Grace (applicants), 56–57, 169
Maxwell, Martin and Kathleen (applicants), 81–82
May, Elaine Tyler, 58, 210n41; *Barren in the Promised Land*, 221n26; *Homeward Bound*, 203n3, 210n31, 214n78, 220n2, 223n3
McCall's, 3, 48
McElroy, Edith Wasson, 229n28
McGreevy, John T., 231n53
McKay, Claude and May Della, 41–42
Melosh, Barbara, 102, 205n13; *Strangers and Kin*, 204n3, 207n30, 215n6
men: breadwinner role, 10, 69–83, 86–92, 95–96, 98, 116–18, 122; class, 75–79, 81;

domestic masculinity, 10, 111, 116–17, 152; parenthood and family role, 71–78, 81–85, 91–93, 95–96, 215n5, 215n12, 217n20, 217n39; race, 66, 92–93, 114–15
Men in the Middle (Gilbert), 215n12
Meyer, Madonna Harrington, 179
Meyerowitz, Joanne, 98–99
Miller, Archie and Rosie (applicants), 148, 150–51
Mills, C. Wright, 80–81
Mintz, Steven, 211n3; *Huck's Raft*, 204n3
Mitchell, Leroy and Bernice (applicants), 60
Mom (Plant), 213n36
Montgomery, Joyce (applicant), 65
More Perfect Unions (R. Davis), 231n5
Moskowitz, Eva, 98
Motherhood in Black and White (Feldstein), 203n7, 213n36
"Mothers . . . Our Only Hope" (Hoover), 43
Mott, Calvin and Eva (applicants), 77
Movement without Marches, A, (Levenstein), 223n57
Moynihan, Daniel Patrick, 231n7
Murray, Sylvie, 168; *The Progressive Housewife*, 229n30
My Blue Heaven (Nicolaides), 223n3

NAACP, 174
Negro Adoption Project (ICH&A), 22, 207n26, 215n13
"Negro Family, The" (U.S. Department of Labor), 231n7
Negro Family in the United States, The (Frazier), 38
neighborhoods: adoption criteria, 140; civic activity, 3, 142, 160, 171–73, 228n20; family ideals, 122–23, 140–45; race and class, 141–42, 226n43, 228n1. *See also* Black Belt (Chicago); suburbanization
Nelson, Leon and Lola (applicants), 40, 88–89, 172–73
Nicolaides, Becky M., 5, 223n3
No Direction Home (Zaretsky), 231n5
Norton, Daisy (applicant), 168–69

Oh, Arissa, 207n30
O'Niel, Karen Elson, 196
Organization Man, The (Whyte), 167
Origins of the Urban Crisis, The (Sugrue), 219n59, 223n3, 224n14, 231n7
orphans, 16–17, 205n9, 205n13

Pappas, Samuel (applicant), 56, 79
"Paradoxical Rationalization of Modern Adoption, The" (Herman), 205n13
parenthood: ambitions for children, 55, 83–86, 93–95, 112–14; benefits and fulfillment, 5–6, 51–57, 60, 62–65, 98, 229n29; care of children, 35, 76–77, 82–87, 91–93, 102, 108, 191; childrearing advice, 84, 164, 228n10; class and race, 83–84, 116–17, 121; domesticity, 5, 10, 26, 50–59, 98, 221n26; momism (overmothering), 55–56, 92, 212–13n36; role of father, 73–77, 215n5, 215n12, 217n20; social networks, 64–65; social workers, 99–103, 196; unwed mothers, 13–14, 18–19, 23, 25, 38, 185, 192. *See also* infertility
Parish Boundaries (McGreevy), 231n53
Parker, Nathaniel and Myrtle (applicants), 121, 178
Paxton, Alton (applicant), 178–79
Payne, Richard and Elizabeth (applicants), 36–37
Pearson, Robert and Evelyn (applicants), 35–36, 78
Penny Serenade (1941), 1
Petigny, Alan, 5
Pfeffer, Paula E., 205n12
Phillips, Hubert and Bonnie (applicants), 108–9
Phyllis Schlafly and Grassroots Conservatism (Critchlow), 231n5
Pierce, Patrick and Rosa (applicants), 147–48
Pike, Frank and Ruth (applicant), 51–52, 61
placing-out. *See* adoption and foster care
Plant, Rebecca Jo, 213n36
"Policing the Black Woman's Body in an Urban Context" (Carby), 228n1

Potter, Sarah, 225n38
poverty, 34–35, 38–42, 109–11, 114–15, 127–30, 147–48, 215, 231n7
Progressive Housewife, The (Murray), 229n30
pronatalism, 3–4, 8, 13, 18, 97, 183
Pruitt, Harry (applicant), 53, 82
psychodynamic psychology, 20, 50, 71, 95, 100–101, 208n34
PTA (Parent Teacher Association), 65, 173, 177
Public Vows (Cott), 210n41
Putnam, Robert D., 228n20

race: adoption, 74–75, 99–100, 118; civic activity, 161–62, 165, 167, 171–76, 180–81; domesticity, 49–50, 66, 159–60; education, 40–41, 70, 84–85, 88–89, 93, 165–66, 173; employment, 70–71, 74–75, 87–90, 102, 115–16; family relationships, 40–42, 63, 74–75, 86–87, 90–93, 98, 115–22; gender roles, 70–71, 87–96, 103, 115–22; housing, 127, 129–34, 136–39, 141–45, 148–56, 223n3, 224n14; race consciousness and pride, 71, 93–95, 171–72, 196–97, 215n13, 219n66, 220n85, 228n1; research methodology, 189, 198–202, 206n23; social mobility, 40, 87–90
"Race and 'Value'" (Solinger), 207n26
Rainwater, Lee, 107, 177
Raising America (Hulbert), 228n10
Raisin in the Sun, A (Hansberry), 127–28
Ranck, Katherine, 34
Reagan, Ronald, 6–7
Recording III (Harrison, Lampe, and Thomas), 232n3
Reed, Lester and Florence (applicants), 40, 53, 88, 117
research methodology, 7–8, 22, 26, 189–202, 206n23
Reynolds, Willie and Annie (applicants), 53
Rice, Gloria (applicant), 55–56
Richard J. Daley (Biles), 210n25, 226n43
Richard J. Daley Library Special Collections and Archives (University of Illinois at Chicago), 195